Shamanism in Siberia

The focus of this book is on the phenomenon of cursing in shamanic practice and everyday life in Tuva, a former Soviet republic in Siberia. Based on extensive anthropological fieldwork where the author interacted with a wide range of people involved in cursing practices, the book examines Tuvans' lived experience of cursing and shamanism, thereby providing deep insights into Tuvans' intimate and social worlds. It highlights especially the centrality of sound: how interactions between humans and non-humans are brought about through an array of sonic phenomena, such as musical sounds, sounds within words and non-linguistic vocalisations, and how such sonic phenomena are a key part of dramatic cursing events and wider shamanic performance and ritual, involving humans and spirits alike. Overall, the book reveals a great deal about occult practices and about social change in post-Soviet Tuva.

Mally Stelmaszyk is a research associate in social anthropology working on a European Reasearch Council-funded project 'Cosmological Visionaries' at the University of Manchester.

Routledge Contemporary Russia and Eastern Europe Series

94 The Sense of Mission in Russian Foreign Policy
Destined for Greatness!
Alicja Curanović

95 Soviet Films of the 1970s and Early 1980s
Conformity and Non-Conformity Amidst Stagnation Decay
Edited by Marina Rojavin and Tim Harte

96 Europe, Russia and the Liberal World Order
International Relations after the Cold War
Timofei Bordachev

97 Russia after 2020
Looking Ahead after Two Decades of Putin
J. L. Black

98 The Russian Minorities in the Former Soviet Republics
Secession, Integration, and Homeland
Anna Batta

99 Tatarstan's Autonomy within Putin's Russia
Minority Elites, Ethnic Mobilization and Sovereignty
Deniz Dinç

100 The State and Big Business in Russia
Understanding Kremlin–Business Relations in the Early Putin Era
Tina Jennings

101 Queering Russian Media and Culture
Edited by Galina Miazhevich

102 Shamanism in Siberia
Sound and Turbulence in Cursing Practices in Tuva
Mally Stelmaszyk

For more information about this series, please visit: www.routledge.com/Routledge
-Contemporary-Russia-and-Eastern-Europe-Series/book-series/SE0766

Shamanism in Siberia
Sound and Turbulence in Cursing Practices in Tuva

Mally Stelmaszyk

LONDON AND NEW YORK

First published 2022
by Routledge
4 Park Square, Milton Park, Abingdon, Oxon OX14 4RN

and by Routledge
605 Third Avenue, New York, NY 10158

Routledge is an imprint of the Taylor & Francis Group, an informa business

© 2022 Mally Stelmaszyk

The right of Mally Stelmaszyk to be identified as author of this work has been asserted in accordance with sections 77 and 78 of the Copyright, Designs and Patents Act 1988.

All rights reserved. No part of this book may be reprinted or reproduced or utilised in any form or by any electronic, mechanical, or other means, now known or hereafter invented, including photocopying and recording, or in any information storage or retrieval system, without permission in writing from the publishers.

Trademark notice: Product or corporate names may be trademarks or registered trademarks, and are used only for identification and explanation without intent to infringe.

British Library Cataloguing-in-Publication Data
A catalogue record for this book is available from the British Library

Library of Congress Cataloging-in-Publication Data
A catalog record has been requested for this book

ISBN: 978-1-032-15699-6 (hbk)
ISBN: 978-1-032-15702-3 (pbk)
ISBN: 978-1-003-24539-1 (ebk)

DOI: 10.4324/9781003245391

Typeset in Times New Roman
by Deanta Global Publishing Services, Chennai, India

For Woody

Contents

List of figures	viii
Transliteration and names	ix
Glossary	x
Distinctive usage list	xi
Preface	xiii

Introduction: Encountering Tuvan curse — 1

PART I
Curses and shamanic practice — 25

1   In the midst of cursing battles: Curses, proximity and sociocosmic drama — 27

2   The artisans of curses: Characteristics of shamanic practice in Tuva — 49

3   Cursed person(hood) — 70

PART II
Sound and turbulence — 91

4   My drum is thunder: Cursing rituals, turbulence and the
sound of drums — 93

5   Voiced into being: The power of sound and shamanic voice in the
cursing rituals — 113

6   Beyond curses: In the midst of turbulent Kyzyl — 130

Index — 149

Figures

0.1	A fragment of Kyzyl in late November, 2014	10
0.2	One of the streets in Kyzyl	10
1.1	A street advert encouraging people to contact a practitioner who can deflect curses	28
1.2	Members of the clan walking through the smoke in order to cleanse and increase their good fortune	37
2.1	The shaman assessing the amount of pollution and preparing for the cleansing practice	56
3.1	Ritual during which the client (the man on the left) is introduced to the spirit – his future mother	75
3.2	The shaman's drawing	83
4.1	Sound unit in the classical (12-tone) musical system	100
4.2	Sound unit in throat singing	100
4.3	Sound theory in classical 12-tone system and in throat singing	106
4.4	Ritual structure in liturgical and shamanic orders	106
6.1	Shamanic society	134

Transliteration and names

On transliteration: I have used the following system when transliterating Tuvan terms from the Tuvan' Cyrillic alphabet:

А (a) Б (b) В (v) Г (g) Д (d) Е (je) Ё (jo) Ж (zj) З (z) И (i) Й (j) К (k) Л (l) М (m) Н (n) Ң (ng) О (o) Ө (ö) П (p) Р (r) С (s) Т (t) У (u) Ү (ü) Ф (f) Х (h) Ц (ts) Ч (ch) Ш(sh) Ъ (") Ы (y) Ь (') Э (e) Ю (ju) Я (ja)

On names: Due to the general secrecy surrounding cursing practices, the identity of all of my interlocutors has been protected through the use of pseudonyms. However, the shaman Hovalygmaa is identified, as requested, by her real name in order to maintain the legacy of her and her family's work in the context of the practice and preservation of Tuvan shamanism.

Glossary

Aas kezzik	good fortune
Algysh	shamanic chant
Aryg	clean
Aryglaashkyn	cleansing ritual
Aza	evil
Buk	the spirit responsible for inflicting curses
Bürülbaazyn	seeing what cannot be seen, hearing what cannot be heard
Chetker	the spirit responsible for inflicting curses
Dünggür	drum
Düvülendir	whirls
Eeren	shamanic token
Eezi	masters of places or spirits of locality
Ezinneldir	swirl
Ham	shaman
Kargysh-chatka	curse
Khöömei	throat singing
Kyshter	energy
Sünezin	soul

Distinctive usage list

Sünezin
Bürülbaazyn
Süzükei
hirlig chüül
dükpürer
üreer
sülde
sülde-sünezini
kudu-sünezini
xülüreesh
ötküt
chüve
tölüngerge
tölünerzje
üн
dürzü
örütejleen
ürzjee
üsh-le
üzükte-le
khoomei
özeen
öjze cögleer
kööry
mönge
köörgulur
hörek
söök
Öcke
Öleng
Örsheel

xii   *Distinctive usage list*

Örütejleen
Tölge
Dört-le
höj-le
körgyzer

Preface

Do you believe in shamanic practice? Can you teach me how to curse someone? Have you seen any spirits? Are you cursed? These are the most common questions that some of my friends, students or colleagues would usually ask me when hearing about the topic of my research and my journey to Tuva. I hope I will not disappoint anyone by mentioning that in this book I am not going to provide any powerful recipes for curses or instructions on how to deflect them (not that I am, sadly, any kind of expert in it anyway). I do hope, however, that through this book I will encourage people to engage with some of the questions that make anthropological inquiry quite unique in comparison to other disciplines. These are the kind of questions that put us on the spot while challenging our well-established patterns of thinking, relating to one another or describing the world we live in. How do you know that you are awake and not dreaming? How can you prove to someone that you are a human and not a spirit? Where exactly does living end and death begin? Can the past precede the future? Perhaps, some of us might instantly consider the answers as obvious. I hope that the stories, experiences and knowledge of the Tuvan shamans and their clients presented in this book will prove otherwise. At the very least, they will create small pockets of curiosity and uncertainty.

The latter is particularly relevant in the Siberian context. I have always been drawn to Siberia ever since I was a child, an enchantment I have never been able to sufficiently explain (not that it is necessary to do so). There is a certain kind of appealing unpredictability about this part of the world, not to be conflated with chaos or randomness. Nothing is fully defined in Siberia, and things, ideas and even people often fluidly shape-shift between one another. Events and encounters occur, abruptly demanding flexibility and patience. At one moment you are having a light-hearted conversation with your friend (who is also a shaman) about making *buuzy* (Tuvan dumplings) when just seconds later you discover that you are being surrounded by spirits who are randomly describing bits of your future while also making jokes and having a smoke. Perhaps you have a well-planned day, when completely unexpectedly you receive a phone call from a neighbour: 'We are going to the South of Tuva, be ready in 10 minutes'. One hour later, you are all sitting in a car though not driving anywhere, yet no one is concerned or impatient. As simple or naïve as these examples might appear to some, Siberia xiv *Preface*

encourages us to look at 'the uncertain' in a different, more welcoming light, and to seek and appreciate the unexpected encounters we come across as we travel through this part of the world.

Uncertainty is also welcomed in Tuvan shamanic practice and tightly interweaves with the experiences of sound and voice. My encounter with Tuvan shamanic practice happened through meeting and becoming friends with Shaman Hovalygmaa. She is the key person who took me on an extraordinary journey through Kyzyl (the capital of Tuva) while discussing and teaching about the shaman's work, what it implies, why it matters and why I have to become a much more attentive listener. It is my hope that her voice can be, to some extent, heard through this book, that her knowledge can be brought to the wider audience and will continue to echo within and beyond academia, just as she requested. The discussions and explorations presented in what follows are also a form of conclusion to my first, long-term anthropological fieldwork that I conducted in Tuva between 2014 and 2015. Perhaps some of the experiences mentioned here and situated within the wider analyses of shamanic practice, curses, sound and turbulence might be of interest to those who are thinking of, or are just about to embark on, their first long-term ethnographic adventure.

This book would have not happened without a number of people who I had the pleasure to meet and work with in Kyzyl and without whom my doctoral research would have never been possible. In the first place, I would like to thank Hovalygmaa Kuular and her family for introducing and sharing with me their wisdom and knowledge about shamanic practice in Tuva, a unique experience for which I will remain forever grateful. Secondly, my gratitude goes to Valentina Süzükei for hours of discussions and teachings about Tuvan music and life in Kyzyl and for her extraordinary theoretical work on throat singing which deeply inspired my research. I would like to thank Sailyk for all her support in terms of documents, papers, visas and protection without which my trip to Tuva would have never been possible. I would also like to sincerely thank a number of my esteemed colleagues, in particular Dr Dimitri Tsintjilonis, Prof Richard Baxstrom, Dr Magnus Course, Dr Casey High and Dr Angus Bancroft for the intellectual support I continuously received while doing my research and completing this manuscript. I am very grateful that they never stopped challenging me while truly believing in my ideas. My gratitude equally goes to Sandra Piai without whose extraordinary linguistic skills and knowledge, as well as her sharp eye, I would not have been able to complete this book. I am equally grateful to Dr Olga Ulturgasheva for kindly providing me with additional time in order to complete the writing process. I would like to thank Barbara and Woody for numerous discussions and suggestions that greatly inspired this book. Finally, I would like to particularly thank Duncan for constant and diverse forms of support and overall patience without which this book would have never come to a successful conclusion. This book is part of a project that has received funding from the European Research Council (ERC) under the European Union's Horizon 2020 research and innovation programme (Grant agreement No. 856543).

Introduction

Encountering Tuvan curse

Ak burak – 'May you have a white road'.
A Tuvan saying used when embarking on a long journey.

The first encounter

In Tuvan shamanism, the cosmos is vertically organised in nine distinct worlds, the ninth being occupied by the god Kurbustu. It is the most sacred of all of the cosmological planes. When you travel from Europe to Kyzyl, the capital of Tuva, you cannot help but get the impression that you are steadily climbing (both literally and figuratively) towards that ninth, most sacred and most mysterious of all worlds. To reach Tuva after landing in Moscow, you have to first experience the noisy and seemingly chaotic block C of the Domodedovo airport, which serves most flights to Siberia. Then, after a 5-hour flight to Abakan, you embark on a bus journey through the vast terrains of Khakassia territory. Siberia welcomes you with Tuvan taxi drivers intent on encouraging you to pay them for a ride to Kyzyl, with its Soviet blocs of flats intermixed with 19th-century Russian wooden houses, with a new group of travelling companions whose faces tightly conceal their stories and dreams. Right up to the top of the Sayan mountains, the bus continues to climb a dangerously narrow path where car accidents take place on a weekly basis. Tuvans recognise these dangerous events as a curse called *aily halap* ('crash'). Unexpectedly, the bus reaches the top and there, out of the blue, a new world opens up before you. It is as if the curtain has just risen in the theatre, as from between two slopes a valley emerges with a long singularly straight road leading far up to the horizon, a vast steppe punctuated by spectacular hills. A different world, a different cosmology.

However, my first encounter with Tuva was rather different. I travelled to Kyzyl from Abakan in November in the middle of a severe winter, and in the middle of the night. Curled up by a frozen bus window and completely unaware of the dangers that the road kept in store, I looked at the stars in the sky and barely noticed the silhouettes of the hills and slopes we passed by. I arrived in Kyzyl shortly after midnight and was left at the local drop-off point, in the middle of the pitch-black road. After some anxious moments, my first Tuvan hosts finally found me and I was very warmly welcomed with food and conversation. They

DOI: 10.4324/9781003245391-1

2 *Introduction*

kept asking why someone this young, from Europe and with no prior Siberian experience, would travel to Kyzyl in the middle of November. A sensible question, indeed. In all honesty, I was not sure what to answer. All I could think of was – why not? Today, seven years later I fully understand their surprise and concerns. However, back in 2014 when I began my first anthropological fieldwork, I was mainly focused on getting as much fascinating data as possible with little consideration given to how much Tuva might actually wish to reveal to me and on what terms. When I woke the next day, I instantly saw a massive hill, a famous landmark in Kyzyl, with a phrase in Sanskrit inscribed on it – *om mani padme hum* – an ancient Buddhist mantra meaning 'Praise to the Jewel in the Lotus'. Who were the people I was about to encounter? Would I meet any 'real' shamans here?

My goal was to conduct research focusing on the proliferation of shamanic societies and schools for shamans in post-Soviet Tuva. Given my initial interests, I was often perceived by Kyzylians as one of the many visitors who arrive in the city chasing stories about local shamans and studying the tradition of *khöömei*, the Tuvan art of throat singing. As a result, I was continually directed to the libraries and academic literature regarding Tuvan and Siberian shamanism while my attempts at spontaneous interviews and discussions were rather dismissed with suspicion or annoyance. Rethinking my methodological strategies and wandering through the streets, I remained convinced that there was something somehow hidden from me, yet also very present in the everyday life of the city. Nonetheless, Kyzyl and its people, like the massive layers of ice and snow on the Yenisei river, remained silent and unmoved by my persistent attempts to get behind the sociocultural scenography (to call it what it felt like), which was carefully crafted for outsiders.

It was not until a few months later, in early spring, that I was accidentally introduced to the very subject of this book. I had just finished a meeting with the students of English philology at the state university. We had talked mostly about the Scottish referendum and Harry Potter. The students expressed their particular interests in the Scots and their 'fight' with the English, comparing the political tensions to hidden frictions between Tuvans and Russians. The person who invited me to the meeting was Shonchalgaj, the enthusiastic Head of the English Language Department. She was giving me a lift home, and we were discussing my reasons for undertaking research in Tuva. Driven by discreet rumours overheard earlier in the corridors of the university building, I asked Shonchalgaj if it was true that people in Tuva cursed each other. She gave me a very confused look. 'It will be very hard for you to find anything about curses, we are a clean nation you know. The shamans as well, we are clean (*aryg*)', she quickly replied. 'It is the Russians, the Uzbeks, and the Tajiks. We do not do such things'. She kept on assuring me while I looked at her, unconvinced. Eventually, Shonchalgaj pulled up the car and looked at me. 'Listen, I will tell you my story, but this is something we don't like to talk about in Kyzyl'. This was the first time I heard about *kargysh-chatka*, the Tuvan curse.

As we sat in the car parked outside the Tuvan Cultural Centre in the heart of Kyzyl, Shonchalgaj described how a few years earlier she was competing for the position of head at the aforementioned department. The choice had been narrowed down to her and another female lecturer. Shonchalgaj won, which seemed to trigger a lot of anger in her opponent. When Shonchalgaj came back from the summer holidays, she suddenly fell ill. The doctors struggled to find the cause of her condition; however, after a week, she felt fine again. A year passed and around exactly the same time Shonchalgaj suddenly fell into a coma. As before, a few days later she woke up feeling perfectly well. One more year passed, and this time she was told she was suffering from leukaemia, only to 'miraculously' improve within a week. Encouraged by her husband, Shonchalgaj met a representative of a local Buddhist temple, the family lama,[1] who gave her a string with sutras[2] to wear on her wrist as protection. She would always have it with her while travelling and always remembered to pass it on to her children and husband when they were undertaking any trips to remote places. Despite the lama's help, Shonchalgaj still felt weak at times and worried about her family. Eventually, she decided to contact a local shaman. The shaman, Hovalgymaa, agreed to come to Shonchalgaj's office early in the morning before anyone else came to work and could notice them. She instantly informed Shonchalgaj that she was suffering from a powerful curse inflicted by her rival from three years before. The shaman conducted a 'cleansing ritual' (*aryglaashkyn*) and provided Shonchalgaj with a personal token (*eeren*) that she was supposed to always carry with her for protection. While Shonchalgaj never had any problems again, her story unexpectedly opened curses to my ethnographic enquiry.

Kargysh-chatka

This book is about curses and shamans. It is about the way in which the proliferation of curses in Kyzyl today foregrounds the significance of shamanic practice and provides us with the opportunity to understand Tuvans' lives in the unpredictable and 'chaotic' context of the capital in a way that does justice to their fears and hopes. As we take a journey through a gallery of stories concerned with the instances of *kargysh-chatka* ('gossip, curse'),[3] infliction and deflection, curses emerge as distinct social mechanisms which, while intertwining with some of the economic and political ramifications of the end of the Soviet regime, also reveal dynamics and tensions embedded in a dangerous sociality of today, a sociality that involves spirits and humans alike. In this way, cursing in Tuva constitutes an instantiation of a wider sociocosmic political scene emergent from human and non-human turbulent interactions.

Due to its geographical location, Tuva reveals itself as a rather unusual place in comparison to other indigenous territories in Siberia. Given its remoteness and difficult access through steep mountains, the Tuvans were somehow left on the edge of the process of Sovietisation, which enabled them to partially resist outside influences (Humphrey & Sneath 1999). On the one hand, unlike other indigenous Siberian communities, they have managed to preserve their native language, numerous practices – such as throat singing – and certain rituals, as well as avoid the dispersion of the population. On the other hand, the process of Russification,

4   *Introduction*

which also dominated the life of other indigenous communities in Siberia, was never fully successful in Tuva. Instead, Tuvans have continued to balance elements of Sovietisation with Tuvan practices, and the problems characteristic of life in the post-Soviet realm. More than that, strong echoes of the Soviet regime, along with the challenges presented by the emergence of the free market economy and a number of new political arrangements, have created an atmosphere of deep anxiety and unpredictability characterised by continuous dependency on other, more influential or powerful, people and their decisions. Anthropologists have widely engaged with the questions of post-socialist transformation and its abrupt and pervasive ramifications while stressing the zones of epistemic and ontological ambivalence and uncertainty. Many scholars, including Buyandelgeriyn (2007), Pedersen (2011) and Swancutt (2012) have demonstrated the challenges faced by the indigenous communities in Siberia and Mongolia, where experiencing post-socialist realia has often been closely interlinked with an increased attention given to shamanic practice. Similar trends can be seen in Tuva, in particular in the context of curses.

Thirty years after the Soviet disintegration, Kyzyl constitutes a rich platform upon which diverse practices, including cursing and the deflection of curses, flourish while being described as 'magical business' (Rus. *magicheskije dela*). On the edge of this landscape, it is the shamans who deal with continually proliferating instances of *kargysh-chatka*, while operating in deep secrecy. Before the arrival of the Soviets, *kargysh-chatka* was suspected only in cases of theft and murder. During the Soviet times, persecution of shamans significantly hindered any practices associated with curses or any forms of shamanism. Siberian shamans were widely perceived as medical charlatans and religious deceivers (Balzer 2003). In Tuva, shamanic practice was extremely risky and undertaken on a significantly smaller scale. Very few shamans would agree to perform, offering only divination practices (normally conducted through the use of objects, such as stones or animal bones) and some healing rituals (performed, for example, through food offerings and feeding the fire). A rare occurrence constituted private feasts to which only selected friends were invited. During these secret ceremonies, spirits were provided with food offerings while delivering, through shamans, answers to some of the guests' questions. The use of shamanic instruments and techniques, such as drums and chanting, however, was strictly forbidden. The process of Sovietisation radically changed the lives of many Tuvans, providing a rich soil for the exacerbation of diverse challenges and tensions. Nevertheless, it was a period of time where things were more or less controlled by the state, whilst conflicts were subdued. People were provided with a job, a place to live and some food which imbued them with a sense of security offered by the state.

In the post-Soviet era things have dramatically changed resulting in a familiar post-Soviet scenario discussed in many other contexts in Siberia (see, for example, Grant 1995; Pedersen 2011; Ssorin-Chaikov 2003). Thus far dormant tensions have been abruptly revealed and intensified, resulting in the proliferation of cursing. Life suddenly became erratic, with escalating unemployment and poverty leading to increases in violence, crime and alcohol addiction. Thirty years later, as Tuvans often stress, life in Kyzyl still remains unpredictable and uncertain as people struggle with the continuous threat of losing jobs, suffering from diseases and being cursed. In flats, houses and offices, they engage in cursing and inflicting *kargysh-chatka* while seeking revenge, attempting to secure job positions, or channelling their anxieties and jealousy, on a regular basis. Sudden success, a new car, a potential quarrel with the wife's relatives or neighbours, as well as daily interactions in the working environment constantly generate the possibility of inflicting curses, leading to an almost omnipresent fear of curses in the city. Additionally, the possible presence of clan curses, characterised by their potency to last for over seven generations, leaves little to no chance that people in Kyzyl could live their life without being affected by curses. Although cursing can be associated with people's direct intentions (in the form of thoughts and words) to harm, it is only shamans who have the ability to inflict or deflect them (Chapter 1). This is due to the fact that curses, perceived as energies (*kyshter*), are delivered and removed by particular spirits with which only shamans have the expertise to negotiate successfully and safely. While inflicting a curse, the spirits trigger a condition of turbulence in which the victim remains until the curse is deflected. As people in Tuva are said to be constructed from multiple layers held together by their centre – 'soul' (*sünezin*), in the presence of a curse all of these layers begin to tremble (Chapter 3). This type of turbulence that victims experience while being cursed is the first one which comes to the orbit of attention while exploring Tuvan curses and shamanism. It is also the one which remains the most dangerous and unpredictable. At the heart of this book is the question of how shamans tend to confront this turbulence and thus deflect or inflict further curses.

My first encounter with Hovalygmaa, a powerful Tuvan shaman, took place in January 2015, in one of the rooms of the Tuvan Cultural Centre in Kyzyl. On that day, we came up with a friendly agreement by which I was welcome to shadow her at work in exchange for some English language classes. Some weeks later, I began to regularly visit different flats where Hovalygmaa conducted rituals, primarily involving curses. The very first client we visited together was a young language teacher who lived on the outskirts of Kyzyl. A few weeks earlier her husband had been seduced by an evil neighbour and the young woman was afflicted with sudden misfortune and had developed a penchant for drinking alcohol. Almost instantly, Hovalygmaa identified the presence of curses and both women agreed on a curse deflecting ritual. I was very excited to observe the event and, perhaps based on my secondary knowledge of shamanic practice, I anticipated a visually dramatic and physically engaging performance. The shaman commenced the ritual with a loud piercing howl while hiding in the corridor. Then, she entered the room and sat on a chair. She continued her performance by uttering different kinds of cries alternated with humming. A few minutes later, she began drumming and singing *algysh* (a shamanic chant) while still seated on the chair. Her voice would momentarily rise or fall and sometimes she would suddenly change the rhythm or intonation. Finally, Hovalygmaa stood up and walked around the client with a drum. Then, she took off her coat and both women vigorously engaged in a discussion about Tuvan cartoons and their damaging influence

6 *Introduction*

on children. The ritual was over. Contrary to my expectations, the shaman did not exhibit any conventional features of shamanic trance, such as speaking odd languages, rolling eyes or physically engaging her body (see also Hamayon 1993). The whole performance seemed to centre around producing sounds and singing while she remained still. I asked her whether the ritual had been successful. 'It worked well, the spirits liked how I sang', she replied.

In Tuvan shamanism, the efficacy of the ritual (including the ones concerned with either infliction or deflection of the curse) remains highly contingent on a proper articulation of sounds, which either please, irritate or manipulate the spirits – it is this articulation, the mastery of the sounds, that is seen as pertaining exclusively to shamans. There are two key elements which may affect the result of ritual proceedings. The first one concerns the sounds produced by the drum (Chapter 4). Given its particular power to create a kind of semi-controlled turbulence (qualitatively different from uncontrolled turbulence triggered by curses), the drum becomes a centre of the ritual event that unsettles and opens up a given ritual event, allowing the shaman to undertake negotiations with spirits within it. The second element concerns the shaman's voice (Chapter 5). Through producing diverse sounds, ranging from gasps and screams to chants, the shaman voices into being a given fragment of the cosmos and engages in the process of (de)forming it. In short, sounds uttered by the shaman, while operating within turbulence triggered by the sounds of the drum, produce new cosmic configurations, for example, curse deflection. In this way, I set out to illuminate how shamans through the creative use of sounds continuously confront and report on fragile and uneasy cosmic configurations characterised by the conflicts and tensions between humans as well as humans and spirits.

Therefore, this book is about curses and shamanic practice, but also the ways in which we can comprehend sound and voice. During the ritual, shamans and their clients become involved in a seemingly chaotic landscape filled with visions, smells, movements and sounds. Within this sensory scenery, as I will show, it is sound that becomes the most potent and transformative tool of all. The sounding power of drums and other shamanic instruments along with a transformative potency of the shamanic voice bring into being a distinct sonic ontology, in which relations, including the cursed one, are established and exchanged through sound. Moreover, the potent qualities of sound turn the shamans, the clients and spirits into what I refer to as *sonic beings*, whose presence and behaviour become actualised and validated in the ritual event through sound. In what follows, I'm going to explore the historical trajectory of local and regional processes and shifts which ultimately led to the proliferation of cursing practices in Tuva and intensified the importance of their deeply sounding character.

A brief history of Tuvan shamanic practice

The Tuvans, about whom this book is written (also known as *Tyvans, Tannu-Tuvans, Soyots* or *Uryankhays*), are descendants of the Turkic peoples who inhabited Siberia and vast areas of Asia at the beginning of the 1st century AD (Forsyth

Introduction 7

1992). The Tuvan language is a part of the Turkic group of the Altai language family which includes Turkic, Mongolic, Tungusic, Koreanic and Japonic languages (Menges 1968). The Republic of Tuva lies in the centre of Asia and shares its borders with Mongolia and a number of subdivisions of Russia: Buryatia, the Altai Republic, Khakassia and Krasnoyarsk Krai. It is composed of a group of high valleys at the head of the Yenisei River and is cut off on all sides from Siberia and North-west Mongolia by steep mountains. Within diverse spheres, including ethnic, religious, economic and political, Tuva has always stood at the confluence of different, at times conflicting, influences. The first historical references to the current geographical territory of Tuva go back to the 7th century BC and describe of Iranian-speaking Scythians inhabiting this area (Forsyth 1992). From the 2nd century BC up to early AD, the lands of modern Tuva were occupied by the Hunnic Empire. The first semi-nomadic forms of existence were developed during this period (Vainshtein 1981), while the second half of the first millennium AD marked the arrival of the ancient Turkic tribes on Tuvan territories. The north-eastern mountain taiga regions were then simultaneously inhabited by the Siberian Samoyeds and Kets tribes (Forsyth 1992). The 6th century brought the establishment of the principal features of nomadic pastoralism which involved the use of yurts as the chief form of dwelling, a specialised herding economy and distinctive types of clothing and food (Vainshtein 1981). In 1207, the territories of Tuva were conquered by the Mongol armies which led to integration with a number of Mongol tribes. By the 18th century, Tuvans were culturally Turkicised and became an ethnically integrated whole. The current population of Tuva resembles a mosaic of various ethnic origins – principally Turkic, Mongol, Samoyed and Ket.

In the 18th century, Tuva was taken over by the Manchu or Ch'ing Empire. Simultaneously, under the rule of Peter the Great, Russia started to express its interest in the mineral wealth of the Altai (Forsyth 1992). In 1911, after the collapse of the Manchu dynasty, Tuva, known as Uryankhai krai by the Russians at the time, became a Russian protectorate. In the aftermath of the Russian revolution in 1917 and after the Tuvan people's revolution in 1921, the Tuvans established the Tuvan People's Republic – Tannu-Tuva – with Kyzyl as its capital. The Russians maintained their political and mercantile interest in Tuva and retained it as a Soviet satellite. In 1944, much later than any other indigenous group, the Tuvans were finally incorporated into the Soviet Union. After the collapse of the USSR, Tuva remained a part of the Russian Federation in the form of a Republic. In 1993, the Tuvans adopted their own constitution, which declares their political status as a 'sovereign democratic state in the Russian Federation' with its own anthem and its own flag.

Also within the economic sphere, Tuva remains a unique area where three key economic systems of Central and Inner Asia meet (Humphrey 1981). While operating today on a much smaller scale, these are a reindeer-herding and hunting economy in the mountainous forest zones; a small-scale cattle and horse-herding and hunting economy in the taiga-steppe zone; and a complex steppe pastoralism with different kinds of herds in the dry upland steppes of the south and east

8   *Introduction*

(see also Vainshtein 1981). Before Sovietisation, Tuvan society was divided into clans, something which had particular implications for the economic system. Members of each clan were strictly exogamous, sharing particular economic relations arising from membership in a particular clan, for example, clan territories, and gathering to offer prayers to the spirit owners of the mountains for successful hunting and for the good health of the clan (Vainshtein 1981). Simultaneously, of high importance were patronymic groups, that is, groups of nuclear or extended families (Vainshtein 1981). The members of each patronymic group lived in dispersed *aal* communities – a number of households migrating together. Each *aal* had equal landholding rights and conducted communal tasks on the basis of working in turns and moving back and forth across the territory. The communal element was always an important aspect of the social and economic life of nomadic peoples, and the Tuvans retained their nomadic communities up until the 1950s (Vainshtein 1981). In the process of Sovietisation, the nomads' pasturing places were transformed into collective farm-settlements. The introduction of collective institutions of *sovkhoz* (state farm) and *kolkhoz* (collective farm) transformed the Tuvans' lands into large-scale agricultural enterprises with hundreds of members, controlled by the local government. Sovietisation included further permanent settlement of nomads, universal education and creation of urban centres, such as Chadaan, Turan and, built in 1921, the capital Kyzyl. This, in turn, has had a direct influence on the dynamics of cursing practices, a point which I develop in Chapter 1. Spatial shifts, generated by the move from the steppe to the city, resulted in shifts in social proximity, leading to the escalation of tensions and conflicts that had always been there, but only fully revealed themselves in the post-Soviet realm, resulting in a significant increase in the instances of cursing. The establishment of the urban setting and its further transformations under changing political systems have equally had direct implications for the shifts within the shamanic landscape and perceptions of shamanic work with different religious, social, business and personal agendas interweaving regularly (Chapter 6).

Prior to the Soviet Union, shamanic practice, as opposed to Buddhist ceremonies, was somewhat private and conducted only for the shaman's closest neighbours and relatives (see also Pimienova 2013). Shamans functioned on the outskirts of the community, subsisting on herding and hunting in the same manner as the other members of the group, whilst only using their skills on demand. During the Soviet period, one of the fundamental goals of the new regime was the renouncement of the so-called superstitions of tribal religion in favour of the 'scientific ideology' of Marxism–Leninism. As a result, during the 1920s, all shamanic practices in Siberia, which were immediately characterised as religion, were banned. In Tuva, however, the status of shamanism was rather unclear. Due to the relative lack of an obviously collective dimension in shamanic rituals, the Tuvan shamans were mostly outside the scope of interest of the Soviet authorities (Pimienova 2013). There was no organised milieu, such as a clergy, which made it difficult for the Soviets to persecute shamans and easier to eradicate Buddhist practitioners who always worked and trained collectively. In this way, shamanism in Tuva managed to maintain its form as a discreet practice, difficult to target

Introduction   9

for 'antireligious' policies. Until the 1990s, it avoided being the object of close attention from the authorities and survived the Soviet regime on the margins of society (Pimienova 2013).

After the collapse of the Soviet Union, the status of Tuvan shamanism shifted significantly, and, as among other indigenous communities, it quickly became a political tool in the attempts at re-establishing political and ethnic autonomy (Lindquist 2005; Pimenova 2013). Simultaneously, the extremely challenging living conditions in Kyzyl, which unfolded after the end of the Soviet Union, triggered a strong demand for shamanic assistance; this ultimately led to its concentration in the capital. In 1995, shamanism was recognised, along with Buddhism and Orthodox Christianity, as a traditional confession (Pimenova 2013), which resulted in the establishment of numerous schools and societies for shamans. This process, although successful in the international arena, failed within the context of everyday life, triggering uncertainty and doubt around the status of shamanic practice in the new economic and political system. Soon after the establishment of the societies, the shamans divided themselves into those affiliated with the organisations and the independents, the latter having operated in an almost underground kind of secrecy ever since. Within this diversified landscape, tensions between 'real' shamans and 'fake' shamans ensued creating yet another kind of turbulence which reaches far beyond the ritual arena (Chapter 6). Interestingly, for 'fake' shamans, the threat of curses has become a useful business tool, allowing 'charlatans' to lie to their clients while increasing monetary profits – a practice highly condemned by Kyzylians. Thus, the reputation of shamans and the efficiency of their work have been, to a certain extent, dependent on their ability to quickly and permanently remove curses, which closely intertwines with the way they perform, i.e. how they use the drum and their bodies, if they sing accurately and long enough, if they request any money in return and so on. Taken together, contemporary Tuvan shamanism constitutes a complex multivalent phenomenon intimately intertwined with diverse political and socioeconomic processes while remaining central to cursing practices.

Like its historical, economic and social features, Kyzyl is also remarkable for its blended overlays of architectural styles and spatial organisation. In a sense, walking through the streets of the city is almost like experiencing architectural and historical polyphony. Kyzyl emerges abruptly from behind a hill when a taxi or a bus takes a sharp turn to the west at the end of the main road (see Figure 0.1). In winter, the city, like any urban area in Tuva, is covered in dark clouds of soot. In summer, the streets are scoured by constant sandstorms and winds. The suburbs of the city consist mainly of small Russian-style wooden houses, whereas the city centre is distinguished by numerous grey blocks of flats, often accompanied by fields of metal garages and massive electricity pylons and cables hovering over the city. The heart of Kyzyl includes a tidy, modern shopping mall with a sign in English reading 'I love Tuva'. A university building, a cultural centre and numerous government establishments are also found in the vicinity of the main square. Nearby is a park boasting the Centre of Asia monument, a few hotels and a coffee shop catering mainly to tourists from Russia.

Figure 0.1 A fragment of Kyzyl in late November, 2014

Figure 0.2 One of the streets in Kyzyl

Most buildings and roads are marked with endless cracks and deep holes giving the impression that the city is being slowly consumed by the underlying steppe (see Figure 0.2). Younger generations tend to leave Kyzyl to seek education and employment in other Russian cities, such as Krasnoyarsk, Novosibirsk or Irkutsk. Those who decide to stay often stress the importance of family ties, as in Tuva

Introduction   11

it is mainly through kinship that some financial stability and general support is obtained. Everyday life in the city, as the majority of my Tuvan friends confirmed, is difficult in many respects and is often challenging for outsiders to comprehend. During my stay in Kyzyl, I lived in one of the blocks of flats situated in the very centre of the city, while sharing a two-bedroom apartment with a retired widow who kindly opened the doors of her household to me. Initially, I spent most of my days working at the local state university, where I provided English language lessons. After I had established more contacts, I began to regularly follow a local family of shamans, in particular, Shaman Hovalygmaa, who shared her extensive knowledge of shamanic practice and curses with me and introduced me to her wide network of clients (such as Shonchalgaj, whose story I recounted earlier). It is Hovalygmaa's experiences and our joint journey, in a both figurative and literal sense, through the world of Tuvan curses that constitute the ethnographic centre of this book.

I also spent a significant amount of my time at the Tuvan Cultural Centre, where I learnt, among other things, about Tuvan music traditions and theoretical approaches to Tuvan sound. Given the fact that most of the people I worked with, including the family of the shamans, lived within a close distance of my flat with the university and the Cultural Centre also being close by, my fieldwork revolved primarily around three main streets in Kyzyl where I spent my time investigating instances of cursing and learning about my friends' daily existence. As a result, material for this book was gathered during 12 months' intensive fieldwork from 2014 to 2015. During this time, I routinely interacted with a wide range of people (clients, shamans, family members, friends and neighbours) involved in curses in the contexts of private houses, shamanic organisations, independent shamanic businesses, the university, private enterprises and political spheres. Most of my interviewees whose stories, observations and knowledge I recount in this book (although it is difficult to generalise) came from diverse backgrounds and include local vendors, accountants, secretaries, policemen, sportsmen, journalists, musicians, political and government figures, petty criminals, teachers and lecturers as well as students from the state university. They are mostly of the generation born and brought up during or immediately after the collapse of the Soviet regime. Before becoming submerged, however, in the complex and mysterious world of cursing events and shamanic practice in Tuva, let us first turn to a discussion of some of the theoretical points on occult practices, shamanic systems and sound which foreground my further analysis.

Curses in Inner Asia

In Kyzyl, the increasing instances of *kargysh-chatka* deeply permeate the economic and political spheres, often being associated with direct expressions of jealousy and revenge. Cursing practices, as I have mentioned earlier, are also a part of the wider network of services offered by diverse 'spiritual' practitioners in Kyzyl, described as 'magical business' (Rus. *magicheskije dela*). In this way, curse infliction and deflection rituals may become career driving tools, especially

12 *Introduction*

for 'fake' shamans seeking a quick financial fortune. The dynamics of power and suspicion that people experience in Tuva bears many similarities with the context of witchcraft and occult economies in some countries in Africa. One of the main explorers of witchcraft practices in Cameroon, Geshiere (1997), equates it with subversive and accumulative forces which simultaneously guarantee a surge of wealth and power, but also enable the tackling of sociopolitical inequalities. In other words, occult economies portray witchcraft as a discourse of ambivalence, which allows the experiences of uncertain modernity, such as an abundance of wealth, sudden surge in profits, injustice, global production and power to be confronted. It becomes a starting point for critical understandings of modernity and its mysterious dynamics enveloped within the context of politics, globalisation and a changing economy. In a similar fashion, Comaroff and Comaroff (1999) show how occult practices constitute mystical means to attain material ends in the process of retooling culturally familiar technologies (1999: 284). In their analysis, witchcraft allows the extent of global, cultural and economic forces on the dynamics of local relations and the ways in which indigenous communities perceive markets and money to be measured (Comaroff and Comaroff 1993: xxciii–xxix). *Kargysh-chatka* echoes conceptualisations of occult practices elsewhere, in particular witchcraft, through frameworks like 'occult economies' where occultism is directly associated with the inexplicable or suspicious increase of wealth and power. However, curses in Tuva are much more than that. While instances of witchcraft in Siberian and Inner Asian contexts are engendered by similar postcolonial and global processes (as looked at by Geshiere and the Comaroffs), exploring them through the notions of 'occult economy' could come at the risk of oversimplifying and obscuring the more complex dynamics which are at play.

Anthropologists have been keen to look at shamanic practice and witchcraft in Siberia and Inner Asia through the questions of uncertainty and anxiety created by the clash between socialist and post-socialist worlds (see, for example, Buyandelgeriyn 2007, High 2007/2008; Swancutt 2012). Nonetheless, these works also highlight the importance of paying attention to the complexities of the social worlds emerging from the end of the Soviet regime rather than rushing towards well-established explanatory paradigms, which tend to turn shamanism into 'a symbolic projection of one type of content ("politics" or "economics") onto another type of content ("religion") in someone's ideological and/or existential interest' (Pedersen 2011: 35). In this book, in order to frame my challenge, I draw particularly from Empson (2011) and Pedersen (2011) and their studies of curses and shamanism in Mongolia. In an important analysis of *arson*, the curse of fire, Empson (2011) makes a crucial point by showing how these curses bear some similarities to paradigms of 'occult economies'; however, in the context of Mongolia they also tend to speak to the notions of personhood and reveal what it means to be a moral person. Thus, as Empson suggests, curses in the Inner Asian context do not fully conform to the explanatory paradigms aiming at a mere rationalisation of past events. Rather than being about 'modernity', they function within it while opening up new avenues to further consider the dynamics of inequality, animosity and communication in Inner Asia. Similar criticism comes

Introduction   13

from Pedersen (2011) in the context of *agsan* – the drunken rage of untrained Darhad shamans. The proliferation of *agsan*, as Pedersen points out, could not be simply explained by people in Ulaan-Uul as a direct consequence of the calamities brought about by the introduction of the new market economy. Thus, in a similar vein to Empson, Pedersen challenges perceptions of shamanic practice as a form of dealing with abrupt economic and political changes. As he argues, looking at shamanism as a way of making sense of the new situation is to dismiss wider dynamics, such as loss, ignorance, agency and predestination. Darhad shamanism and events of *agsan* associated with it are engendered by uncertainty. However, rather than reducing anxiety, they instead reinforce the sense of cosmological breakdown as experienced in Ulaan-Uul (Pedersen 2011: 39).

A similar kind of complexity takes place in Tuva. Proliferation of curses is a manifestation which evinces much more than a way of dealing with post-socialist transformations. Therefore, in my discussion about Tuvan curses and shamanic practice I move beyond the discourses that understand 'economics' as narrowly pertaining to wealth, power and the circulation of goods. By shifting the conversation from economic disruption to a kind of cultural dynamic that expresses problems associated with the post-Soviet repercussions, I come from the perspective of dramatic cursing events and their mechanics as they involve humans and spirits alike. In short, I show how curses in Kyzyl are distinct, social mechanisms within an 'occult economy' that constitutes a wider sociocosmic politics that emerges from human and non-human interactions. It is a kind of politics which helps to delineate how cursing phenomena 'bring people to the limits of their understanding of others in regard to themselves' (Siegel 2006: 10). Engaging with the mechanic of cursing, I further illuminate how Tuvan curses are perceived as fluctuating energies that pertain to the wider network of energies that can be exchanged, increased or tamed. I suggest that this plasticity attests to the wider characteristics of social and cosmic dynamics in Tuva as embedded in perpetual fluctuation and movement – a fluctuation and movement intrinsically related to people's lives in the cosmos and their understanding of it. At the same time, I have set out to illustrate something more than simply the dynamics of curses.

The core themes addressed by existing anthropological scholarship on curses and shamanism in Inner Asia hover around the questions of dangerous interactions and communication brought together under the notion of the ontology of bad speech that can be malicious gossip with curse-like effects called *hel am* (Højer 2004; Humphrey 2012; Swancutt 2012) or curse *haraal* (Delaplace 2014; High 2007/2008). The role of the spoken word is particularly instructive here. Within Inner Asian ethnography, Swancutt's *Fortune and the Cursed: The Sliding Scale of Time in Mongolian Divination* (2012) opened the way for the study of ontology of bad speech. While looking at the inventive capacities in shamanic rituals, where curses necessitate new ritual inventions, Swancutt explores the intrinsic connections between the spoken word and inflicted harm. She shows how Mongolian curse *hel am* is part of a sliding scale of speech acts which can cause different degrees of pain and harm (2012: Chapter 5). While *kargysh-chatka* carries some similarities to *hel am* and *haraal* (Chapter 1), the potent qualities of Tuvan curses

14   *Introduction*

lie not exclusively in words, i.e. the ontology of bad speech, but more in the ontology of sounds. In my analysis of Tuvan curses, I move, therefore, beyond the magical power of words and engage with the array of sounds produced during shamanic performances. In particular, I focus on the role of the shamanic drum and explore how sounds of the drum commence the process of negotiations with spirits while opening up and discomposing things and, thus, producing a platform for conducting cosmic (re)arrangements by the shaman. Extending the discussion on sounds produced by the drums, I evaluate the importance and role of sounds produced by the shaman's voice in the rituals. I argue that, as the sounds of the drum unsettle things, the sounds produced by the shaman's voice do the opposite by providing temporary forms of sociocosmic arrangements and patterning (such as curse infliction or deflection). In this way, curses become distinct sonic actions allowing Tuvans to maintain a certain degree of agency and control over their being (rather than merely acquire monetary and material profits), the control which is ultimately sought both by humans and spirits.[4]

Equally germane to the exploration of the potent qualities of sounds are the questions of manipulation and danger associated with everyday interactions. Højer (2004, 2019) discusses how malicious gossip constitutes a concrete mode of anticipating and engaging with others in Northern Mongolia, placing manipulation and uncertainty as central to everyday communication. The element of manipulation and ambivalent communication is also conveyed in the Tuvan case. Following Højer's point, my own exploration looks at the kinds of manipulation and dangerous interactions which are established and validated through sound. In other words, I explore an array of relationships which are defined and experienced through (un)controlled and often risky articulation of diverse sounds. The ethnographic inquiries of the interrelations between curses and shamanic practice presented in this book form, therefore, a critical component of sound studies. Sound emerges as a fitting point of departure to think about curses and shamanism, without reducing them analytically to socioeconomic breakdowns caused by the end of the colonial regime. Within this landscape, tapping into the themes of communication, inequality, agency and uncertainty, I espouse sounds as potent and transformative sonic actions rather than representative tools. Tracing trajectories of different relationships, which include shamans, spirits, victims, clients, families, neighbours and colleagues, I intend to show how these relationships are defined and experienced through an array of sonic phenomena, such as musical sounds, sounds within words and non-linguistic vocalisations. In this way, the wider economy of social relations is revealed, which is produced through ascribing predominant authority to sound rather than to words or objects.

Experiences of sounds and turbulence

Throughout this book I argue that sound is an important starting point to consider a kind of phenomenology of sound and voice which focuses on the sonic as it unfolds in its own forms and modalities. But what does it mean to say that sound has power? Sounds continually reverberate through both indoor and outdoor shamanic rituals that take place in Tuva. These are the sounds of shamanic instruments, their voices, their costumes, the sounds of the street, people's breathing and abrupt gasps as shamans scream or howl, the sounds of winds and silence as the shamans are about to commence their rituals. During one such shamanic ritual, the outdoor ceremonies dedicated to accumulating good fortune for one of the clans, I was particularly struck by a comment made by the head of the family. She turned to me during an interval between the shaman's chant and whispered, 'This is a really powerful shaman, we could see the spirits, they were so tall, dressed in golden gowns and watching us'. I asked her how she could see them. She replied that it was thanks to the shaman's great singing. 'A good shaman is the one that can show you something', she concluded. In this example, an important connection emerges between the participants in the ritual and the spirits that is both sensorial and cosmological. I shall now explore this point further.

To think sound, I turn to the anthropologist Steven Feld and his key concept of acoustemology, which he describes as 'knowing-with and knowing-through the audible' (Feld 2015: 12). Throughout his work, Feld (see, among others, 1982, 2001, 2012) considers what it means to think and experience the world through sound and what kind of knowledge these processes might generate. He also stresses the importance and personal preference for an ethnographic enquiry into sound:

> Let me put it this way, many people who ask me or who hear a presentation of mine where I am talking about this (acoustemology), say to me 'Why aren't you making this more legible? Why aren't you theorising this more?' And my response is always 'Well, I am theorising it, but I am theorising it from the ground, from the material. I am attracted to ethnography, as I always was, as a process of learning to think about larger things through the materiality and the forms and the practices of the everyday sphere and the ritual sphere'.
> (Rice & Feld 2021: 129)

Following Feld's consideration for an ethnographic approach, Steingo and Sykes (2019) call for three essential shifts in analytical frameworks. First, they propose moving away from perceiving technology as developed within a specific time and space and thus defined as a 'modern' Western practice. Instead, they suggest attending to 'the infinite series of objects and techniques through which culture is always already constituted' (2019: 11). Next, they call for a re-evaluation of the relationship between a listener and what is listened to, highlighting in this way how sounds have both sensorial and ontological propensities and dispositions. To this end, they stress the need for a broader exploration of sonic efficacies in the context of establishing and exchanging social relations. In order to contribute to their proposals, I wish to offer a kind of sensory ethnography in this book, where ethnographic sensitivity to the intricate linkages between sounds, curses and everyday life guide the anthropological study of shamanism as it takes shape in diverse social settings in Kyzyl and Tuva today. Tuvan shamans have the power to voice into being a particular kind of social configuration while establishing

16 *Introduction*

specific sensory experiences which, apart from hearing, also include tactile, olfactory, visual and proprioceptive senses, such as a sudden gust of wind, a partial image, an inexplicable cry or a particular smell shared by spirits. In this way, Tuvan cursing rituals not only pose important questions regarding the modes in which we recognise an Other in terms of similarities and differences (Descola 2013), but they also shed light on what other senses can reveal about sound while expanding our understanding of what constitutes communication.

Everyday life in Tuva is deeply permeated by the significance of sounds and music making, which are perceivable in the art of throat singing (*khöömei*), animistic relations with the environment, perceptions of time and space, hunting practices and wide ritual practices (Harrison 2004; Levin 2006; Süzükei 2010; Van Deusen 2004). Singing and producing music are not restricted to people exhibiting specific talents. Instead, they are considered an everyday skill which may be held by anyone (Levin & Süzükei 2017). In fact, the inspiration to perform and make sounds in Tuva is deeply connected with the surrounding environment. The importance of sound in the context of landscape is particularly clear in the study of the throat singing practice. Levin and Edgerton (1999) explore the mimetic faculty of sound in *khöömei* and argue that throat singers interact with the natural sound world through imitating the sounds of places and beings. Thus, throat singers construct specific images or sketches of the landscape (Levin 2006). In other interpretations (Hodgkinson 2005/2006), however, *khöömei* is considered an intimate reflection of the relationship between the singer and the environment.

Sounds in Tuva, then, do not pertain only to the sphere of artistic performance and representation. As mentioned earlier, Harrison (2004) analyses the agentive role of sound in hunting practices, in particular when Tuvan hunters seek to control their prey. The songs performed on such occasions include specific ideophones that are meant to trigger a desired mental state or behaviour in an animal. Van Deusen (2004) illuminates how music and sound making constitute key components of ritual practices. In her account, drumming, shamanic singing and words used by shamans during rituals are imbued with the power to communicate with spirits and provide healing. In Tuva, sound, as already discussed, also occupies a central position in shamanic rituals bringing together the sounds of shamanic instruments, in particular the drum, shamanic costume, shamanic chants and shamans' voices. In shamanic studies, within the ritual context, the potent qualities of sound, while acknowledged, tend to be overshadowed by broader analytical discussions concerned with performative, visual and structural elements of shamanic practice (Gow 1996; Humphrey & Onon 1996; Riboli & Torri 2016). Shamanic chants and their role are often looked at through the study of language and speech where the potency to affect change is given to words (Hoppal & Sipos 2010; Olsen 1996; Townsley 1993). Sounds themselves are, therefore, considered as sonic by-products of words or inherent elements of music.

As I have mentioned earlier in this introduction, in my exploration of Tuvan shamanism, I move beyond the well-established analytical gaze on shamanic music, words and utterances as powerful. Focusing on how sounds in Tuvan shamanic practice are imbued with a potency of their own, I stress how they cannot be merely considered as a by-product of the utterance of speech and fulfil mimetic or metaphorical roles. Instead, they are key in coming to terms with how a subject identifies his/her environment and experiences the relationships within it. Although I recognise that shamanic performances often combine the sensory tools (sound, smells) with linguistic forms (words and their meaning) in a complementary fashion, I am less invested in language as the fundamental field of the sonic. In my discussion, I am also less concerned with music as a distinct category and more focused on the potent qualities of human sounds and voice. More than that, I believe that in the Tuvan ethnographic context a rigid conceptual differentiation between music and sound may conceal rather more than it reveals (Chapter 5). My contribution aims to show instead that, in order to fully understand the potency of performance in shamanic rituals, we have to also pay attention to the whole pallet of sounds produced by shamans. Therefore, in line with the aforementioned recent theoretical propositions in sound studies, my analysis follows a 'conjunctural approach' to sound (Steingo & Sykes 2019: 7), which seeks to bring together different fields, such as musical, linguistic and the paralinguistic. I focus on an array of sonic phenomena, such as musical sounds, instrumental sounds, sounds within words and non-linguistic vocalisations.

In my analysis, I do not seek to isolate sound from other senses. Unquestionably, shamanic rituals involve a whole plethora of diverse sensory experiences, such as different smells, touch and visions. However, as Sykes encourages us, we must consider 'how different cultures have their own debates about relations between sound, speech, hearing listening, vision, writing, representation, objects' (2019: 221). Given the centrality of sound in a Tuvan onto-epistemic system, the example of curses allows for this kind of exploration. As I will show, cursing rituals, while connecting sounds with haptic, tactile, oral and olfactory experiences, create what Silverstein describes as a sensory totality (2019: 242). The ways in which these senses come together in and through sound reveal important aspects of wider auditory experiences and, in the long run, how communication can be defined and validated by Tuvans. By taking an ethnographic approach, cursing events in Tuva allow, therefore, the potent qualities of sound to be better understood while at the same time contributing to studies of the sonic which seek to disturb and redefine ways in which we understand listening, voice and silence. In particular, this is a chance to explore what it means for Tuvans, and perhaps other shamanic peoples as well, to listen and thus create and experience relations with one another, that is, with other beings, such as humans, spirits, the dead and the surrounding landscape. It is also an opportunity to take these experiences, as argued by Steingo and Sykes (2019), as conceptual problems on their own terms, that is, as concrete conceptual unsettlements of well-established frameworks rather than mere examples of the difference.

The idea of sound foreshadows another theme with which this book engages. That is the concept of turbulence. In Tuvan throat singing tradition, the production of sound entails a condition of turbulence (Rus. *turbulentnost'*). In the Tuvan language, my interviewees would express this idea as 'swirls' (*ezinneldir*) and 'whirls' (*düvülendir*). Turbulence (although a different kind) is also central to

18 *Introduction*

experiences of cursing. As I have mentioned earlier in this introduction, people who suffer from curse infliction are said to become turbulent, while their human personhood is abruptly pervaded by swirls and whirls. The condition of turbulence remains equally crucial to the efficacy of shamanic rituals dedicated to cursing and curse deflection when shamanic drums are used to produce a semi-controlled turbulence. Turbulence also constitutes one of the ideas with which my Tuvan friends describe diverse challenges of life in Kyzyl today. Thus, over the course of this book I show how turbulence extends through the drivers of personhood, ritual, shamanic instruments, singing practices and experiences of everyday life in Kyzyl. As the book unfolds, it becomes one of the key concepts permeating Tuvan imagery and revealing the characteristics of diverse aspects of life in Tuva, inside and outside the ritual settings.

As a way of conclusion, I wish to briefly engage with the question of *shamanism* and *shamanic practice*. Stressing a difference between these two terms is not coincidental. In the past, the conventional frames of anthropological explanations approached shamanic work as a system of psycho-social tensions (Shirokogoroff 1935), as the archaic origin of all religions (Eliade 1972), as compensation for social insecurities (Lewis 1971) or as a system of exchange between humans and 'nature' (Hamayon 1996). These approaches depict shamanism as an 'it', something that 'is' and therefore can be gathered under an overarching theory. Avoiding an 'it' and expanding the idea of the flow characteristic of curses, I refer to the studies that understand shamanic practice as fluid, ambiguous and fragmentary (Ashforth 2005; Bubandt 2014; Geshiere 1998). Therefore, the kind of shamanic practice that I describe in this book constitutes a form of creative endeavour embedded in the pragmatism of everyday life in Kyzyl, rather than a distinct religious, political or any other kind of ideology. Drawing inspiration from literature preoccupied with problematising 'shaman*ism*' as a noun and focusing on what shamans actually do, therefore alluding to the verb 'shaman-ise' (Atkinson 1992; Campbell 1989; Vitebsky 2003; Willerslev 2007), I want to emphasise the plasticity of shamanic practice and, thus, the ease with which it adapts and interweaves with changing circumstances, such as those related to post-socialist shifts, but also to the pressing issues of today, such as climate change (Chapter 6). While the implications of the Soviet dissolution do, to a different extent, echo throughout this book, I also hope the ethnography presented here will encourage readers to think beyond the post-socialist processes. I believe it is time to allow Siberia to join broader anthropological debates on questions, such as sound, curses and shamanism, without reducing their dynamics and characteristics to the well-established and widely discussed encounter between socialist and post-socialist realms (see Buyandelgeriyn 2008). The chapters that follow allow such a contribution to take place. Through the lens of the mechanics of cursing, each of them engages with the characteristics of Tuvan shamanic practice while touching on diverse issues, including the idea of cursed personhood, the role of drums, the organisation of ritual events, the conceptualisation of sounds and spirit encounters as well as technological changes and the environmental crises.

Introduction 19

The book is divided into two parts. Part I sets the scene by introducing the intricacies of Tuvan curses and shamanic practice. It focuses on the three parties involved in the process of cursing, that is, the shaman, the spirit and the victim. In what follows, Chapter 1 begins with an introduction to the phenomenon of cursing in Kyzyl today. It provides a gallery of cursing stories as described by the inhabitants of the capital. This leads to an exploration of the overall characteristics of Tuvan curses. The first part of the chapter focuses on the taxonomy of curses, discussing how cursing constitutes an intrinsic element of a wider network of fluctuating energies, which includes the attributes of misfortune and good luck. The second part of the chapter delineates the distinct topography of cursing in Kyzyl. Particular stress is placed upon the urbanised environment and the way its compactness and forced proximity contribute to the proliferation of curses. Along these lines, the chapter traces the flow of curses from pre-Soviet Tuva to post-Soviet Kyzyl, presenting the city as an enforced, bounded space of coalescent forces and people as opposed to the dispersed features of being in the steppe and taiga. To illustrate this, the chapter engages with kinship relationships as well as economic and political interactions that are deeply shaped by a nearly inexhaustible penchant for cursing. Given the centrality of shamanic practice to the phenomenon of cursing, Chapter 2 moves on to discuss the distinctiveness of shamanic practice in Tuva in the wider Siberian context. Through introducing the life story of the great Tuvan shaman Hovalygmaa, it explores certain features of contemporary Tuvan shamanic practice, including the role of sound and the importance of divination rituals while rejecting classical trance-like experiences. In this way, the chapter gives a unique insight into shamanising perceived by Tuvans as a pragmatic form of housekeeping, which is contingent on a skill described as 'seeing the invisible and hearing the silent' (*bürülbaazyn*). Weaving through the conversations with Hovalygmaa, the chapter opens a surprising window onto the differences between shamans, their personalities and the hierarchies among them. Chapter 3 pursues the experiences of curse affliction as essential to the understanding of the complexity of occult phenomena and shamanic practice in Kyzyl today. It commences with the exploration of what it means to be a human person in comparison to other kinds of persons in Tuvan ontology, such as spirits and animals. The chapter follows Hovalygmaa as she visits the victims of curse infliction. Looking at different case studies, it discusses how cursing creates turbulence and transforms people into turbulent entities. Through analysing images of the curse victims drawn by shamans during the rituals, the chapter concludes by exploring the idea of what it means to have a cursed personhood.

Having discussed the tripartite relationship between shamans, clients and curses as well as having introduced the notion of turbulence, Part II of the book extends the discussion on turbulence and moves towards the potent qualities of sounds in shamanic rituals, in particular the ones which involve curse infliction and deflection. Chapter 4 thus develops previous reflections and analytically explores how shamans, cursed victims and turbulence come together in the ritual context. The chapter illuminates how turbulence is integral not only to experiences of cursing, but also to cosmic dynamics, language and, crucially, sound. In

20   *Introduction*

particular, the chapter focuses on the role of the shamanic drum as central to the rituals of curse deflection and infliction. Engaging with different ritual orders, the chapter presents how the structure of sound production in the Tuvan tradition of throat singing is homologous to the way drums and musical sounds operate in shamanic rituals. It also delineates how the sounds of the drum unsettle things during the rituals while producing the experiences of semi-controlled turbulence indispensable to the success of the ritual proceedings. Chapter 5 focuses on a dramatic story of a death curse and continues the discussion of sound and its significance in shamanic rituals. Exploring the importance of the shaman's voice, it contrasts the unsettling qualities of musical sounds with the transformative power of sounds produced in the utterance of speech. Stressing the potency of sound rather than words, the chapter explores how through modulating their voices, shamans facilitate momentary encounters between spirits and humans. These experiences not only attest to the efficacy of the ritual but also confirm the authenticity of the shaman's skills. The chapter concludes by exploring how sounds remain key factors in defining, experiencing and validating diverse relationships, including humans and spirits. The focus of Chapter 6, the concluding chapter, expands on the themes of curses and shamanism by concentrating on wider sociocultural processes and shifts occurring in Kyzyl today. In short, it highlights how people experience and describe life in Kyzyl in ways that resonate with the accounts of persons who have been cursed, suggesting that day-to-day life in the capital could be compared to living a curse. By emphasising the role of turbulence and uncertainty associated with cursing, the chapter focuses on different representations of daily challenges, such as the dynamics between individual shamans and collective shamanic societies, different forms of affliction (alcoholism, HIV, depression), use of technology (internet, social media) and the environmental crises.

During the 12 months that I spent in Tuva, I learnt that Kyzyl constitutes a captivating ethnographic context in which to investigate the mechanics of cursing and the way curses are interwoven with shamanic practice. It provides a challenging opportunity to think about shamanism and cursing as well as Tuvan life in the context of apparent change and dis/continuity problematising the way anthropologists tend to rely on a link between post-colonial realms and 'modernity', a link often treated as intrinsic. More than that, Tuvan shamanic practice is distinctive in that it brings shamanism and cursing together in a way that sound and voice can also be comprehended. Thus, in what follows, Tuvan shamans will welcome us into a turbulent world of spirits, dead relatives, envious neighbours, revenge and conflict while compelling everyone to think about sounds as powerful and unsettling.

Notes

1 A Buddhist monk.
2 Buddhist scripture containing religious teachings.
3 Although, in some respects, cursing may be seen as similar to sorcery or witchcraft, Tuvans rarely refer to curses in those terms. Thus, in this book, when talking about

Introduction   21

occult phenomena, such as curse, I refer to the Tuvan expression *kargysh-chatka*, which translates as 'gossip, curse'.

4 In this sense, the kind of witchcraft that I discuss in this book has more of an instrumental rather than discursive character.

Bibliography

Atkinson, M. J. 1992. Shamanism Today. *Annual Review of Anthropology* no. 21: 307–330.

Ashforth, A. 2005. *Witchcraft. Violence, and Democracy in South Africa*. Chicago: The University of Chicago Press.

Balzer, M. M. 2003. Sacred Genders in Siberia. In G. Harvey (ed.), *Shamanism: A Reader*, 242–261. London: Routledge.

Bubandt, N. 2014. *The Empty Seashell. Witchcraft and Doubt on an Indonesian Island*. Ithaca and London: Cornell University Press.

Buyandelgeriyn, M. 2007. Dealing with Uncertainty: Shamans, Marginal Capitalism, and Remaking of History in Postsocialist Mongolia. *American Ethnologist* no. 34 (1): 127–147.

Buyandelgeriyn, M. 2008. Post-Post-Transition Theories: Walking on Multiple Paths. *Annual Review of Anthropology* no. 37: 235–250.

Campbell, A. 1989. *To Square with Genesis: Causal Statements and Shamanic Ideas in Wayãpí*. Edinburgh: Polygon.

Comaroff, J. & Comaroff, L. J. 1993. Introduction. In J. Comaroff & J. Comaroff (eds), *Modernity and its Malcontents: Ritual and Power in Postcolonial Africa*. Chicago: University of Chicago Press.

Comaroff, J. & Comaroff, L. J. 1999. Occult Economies and the Violence of Abstraction: Notes from the South African Postcolony. *American Ethnologist* no. 26 (2): 279–303.

Delaplace, G. 2014. Establishing Mutual Misunderstanding: a Buryat Shamanic Ritual in Ulaanbaatar. *Journal of the Royal Anthropological Institute* no. 20: 617–634.

Descola, P. 2013. *Beyond Nature and Culture*. Chicago: University of Chicago Press.

Eliade, M. 1972. *Shamanism: Archaic Techniques of Ecstasy*. London: Routledge & K.Paul.

Empson, M. R. 2011. *Harnessing Fortune. Personhood, Memory and Place in Mongolia*. Oxford: Oxford University Press.

Feld, S. 1982. *Sound and Sentiment: Birds, Weeping, Poetics, and Song in Kaluli Expression*. Third and Thirtieth Anniversary Edition, with a New Introduction. Durham and London: Duke University Press.

Feld, S. 2001. *Bosavi: Rainforest Music from Papua New Guinea*. Book and 3CDs. Washington, DC: Smithsonian Folkways.

Feld, S. 2012. *Jazz Cosmopolitanism in Accra: Five Musical Years in Ghana*. Durham and London: Duke University Press.

Feld, S. 2015. Acoustemology. In D. Novak and M. Sakakeeny (eds), *Keywords in Sound*, 12–21. London: Duke University Press.

Forsyth, J. 1992. *A History of the Peoples of Siberia*. Cambridge: Cambridge University Press.

Geshiere, P. 1997. *The Modernity of Witchcraft*. Charlottesville and London: University Press of Virginia.

Geshiere, P. 1998. Globalization and the Power of Indeterminate Meaning: Witchcraft and Spirit Cults in Africa and East Asia. *Development and Change* no. 29 (4): 811–837.

22 *Introduction*

Gow, P. 1996. River People: Shamanism and History in Western Amazonia. In C. Humphrey & N. Thomas (eds), *Shamanism, History, and the State*, 90–114. Ann Arbor: University of Michigan Press.

Grant, B. (1995). *In the Soviet House of Culture: A Century of Perestroikas*. Princeton, N.J.: Princeton University Press.

Hamayon, N. R. 1993. Are "Trance", "Ecstasy" and Similar Concepts Appropriate in the Study of Shamanism? *Shaman* no. 1 (1–2): 17–39.

Hamayon, N. R. 1996. Shamanism in Siberia: From Partnership in Supernature to Counter-power in Society. In C. Humphrey & N. Thomas (eds), *Shamanism, History, and the State*, 76–89. Ann Arbor: University of Michigan Press.

Harrison, D. 2004. South Siberian Sound Symbolism. In E. Vajda (ed.), *Languages and Prehistory of Central Siberia*, 199–214. Amsterdam: John Benjamins.

High, M. 2007/2008. Wealth and Envy in the Mongolian Gold Mines. *The Cambridge Journal of Anthropology* no. 27 (3): 1–18.

Højer, L. 2004. The Anti-Social Contract. Enmity and Suspicion in Northern Mongolia. *The Cambridge Journal of Anthropology* no. 24 (3): 41–63.

Højer, L. 2019. *The Anti-social Contract: Injurious Talk and Dangerous Exchanges in Northern Mongolia*. New York: Berghahn Books.

Hodgkinson, T. 2005/2006. Musicians, Carvers, Shamans. *The Cambridge Journal of Anthropology* no. 25 (3): 1–16.

Hoppal, N. & Sipos, J. 2010. *Shaman Songs*. Budapest: International Society for Shamanic Research.

Humphrey, C. 1981. Introduction. In S. Vainshtein (ed.), *Nomads of South Siberia*, 1–36. Cambridge: Cambridge University Press.

Humphrey, C. 2012. Hospitality and Tone: Holding Patterns for Strangers in Rural Mongolia. *Journal of the Royal Anthropological Institute* no. 18 (1): 63–75.

Humphrey, C. & Onon, U. 1996. *Shamans and Elders*. Oxford: Clarendon Press.

Humphrey, C. & Sneath, D. 1999. *The End of Nomadism?: Society, State and the Environment in Inner Asia*. Cambridge: Duke University Press.

Levin, T. 2006. *Where Rivers and Mountains Sing*. Indianapolis: Indiana University.

Levin, T. & Süzükei, V. 2017. Timbre-Centred Listening in the Soundscape of Tuva. In E. I. Dolan and A. Rehding (eds), *The Oxford Handbook of Timbre*. Oxford: Oxford University Press.

Levin, T. & Edgerton, E. M. 1999. The Throat Singers of Tuva. *Scientific American* no.281 (3): 80–87.

Lewis, I. M. 1971. *Ecstatic Religion*. Charmondsworth: Penguin Press.

Lindquist, G. 2005. Healers, Leaders and Entrepreneurs: Shamanic Revival in Southern Siberia. Culture and Religion. *An interdisciplinary Journal* no. 6 (2): 263–285.

Menges, K. 1968. *The Turkic Languages and Peoples: An Introduction to Turkic Studies*. Wiesbaden: Harrassowitz.

Olsen, A. D. 1996. *Music of the Warao of Venezuela: song people of the Rain Forest*. Gainesville: University Press of Florida.

Pedersen, A. M. 2011. *Not Quite Shamans*. Ithaca; London: Cornell University Press.

Pimienova, K. 2013. The "Vertical of Shamanic Power": The Use of Political Discourse in post-Soviet Shamanism. *Laboratorium* no. 5 (1): 118–140.

Riboli, D. & Torri, D. (eds), 2016. *Shamanism and Violence: Power, Repression and Suffering in Indigenous Religious Conflicts*. London: Routledge.

Rice, T. & Feld, S. 2021. Questioning Acoustemology: An Interview with Steven Feld. *Sound Studies* no. 7 (1): 119–132.

Introduction 23

Süzükei, V. 2010. *Problema konceptualnogo edinstva teorii i praktiki. [The Problematic Unity of Theory and Practice]*. Kyzyl: OAO.

Siegel, J. 2006. *Naming the Witch*. Stanford: Stanford University Press.

Shirokogoroff, S. 1935. *Psychomental Complex of the Tungus*. London: Kegan Paul.

Silverstein, S. 2019. Disorienting Sounds: A Sensory Ethnography of Syrian Dance Music. In G. Steingo & J. Sykes (eds), *Remapping Sound Studies*, 241–260. Durham, N.C.: Duke University Press.

Steingo, G. & Sykes, J. (eds), 2019. *Remapping Sound Studies*. Durham, N.C.: Duke University Press.

Ssorin-Chaikov, N. 2003. *The Social Life of the State in Subarctic Siberia*. Stanford: Stanford University Press.

Swancutt, K. 2012. *Fortune and the Cursed. The Sliding Scale of Time in Mongolian Divination*. The United States of America: Berghahn Books.

Sykes, J. 2019. Sound Studies, Difference, and Global Concept History. In G. Steingo & J. Sykes (eds), *Remapping Sound Studies*, 203–221. Durham, N.C.: Duke University Press.

Townsley, G. 1993. Song Paths: The Ways and Means of Yaminahua Shamanic Knowledge. *L'Homme* 33: 449–68.

Vainshtein, S. 1981. *Nomads of South Siberia*. Cambridge: Cambridge University Press.

Vitebsky, P. 2003. From Cosmology to Environmentalism: Shamanism as Local Knowledge in a Global Setting. In G. Harvey (ed), *Shamanism: A Reader*, 276–298. London: Routledge.

Van Deusen, K. 2004. *Singing Story, Healing Drum. Shamans and Storytellers of Turkic Siberia*. Montreal: McGill Queen's University Press.

Willerslev, R. 2007. *Soul Hunters: Hunting, Animism and Personhood Among the Siberian Yukaghiris*. Berkley, Los Angeles, London: University of California Press.

Part I
Curses and shamanic practice

1 In the midst of cursing battles

Curses, proximity and sociocosmic drama

'You know, the beauty of our city lies in the fact that you walk around and everything seems normal to you. Yet, unbeknown to you, it is behind these walls, in whispers, in curses and negotiations with spirits that our lives unfold', Ajlana said suddenly to me during one of our long walks around the city centre. She was a newly appointed secretary at the Tuvan State University, and we were discussing the challenges Ajlana was about to face at work, in particular with her tough-minded boss. I asked my friend if she could do anything in order to ease the job transition and soften her superior. In reply, Ajlana pointed to her cell phone and whispered: 'We could call a shaman'. I knew she had in mind a curse infliction request. Indeed, whilst highly ambiguous and rarely discussed, cursing practices are a constant and well-established element of everyday life in Kyzyl. Nevertheless, for a significant amount of time, my interlocutors either pretended they did not hear any curse-related questions or kept on angrily waving their hands towards the Sayan mountains, stressing it was a 'dirty thing' (*hirlig chüül*) coming from 'there' (*mynaar*), most of the time implying the Russians. Despite my interviewees' assertions, 'magical business' as one of my friends referred to it, seemed to be blossoming in Kyzyl. The local markets, which sold everything from meat, cheese, fish and clothes to jewellery and mobile phones, flourished with women called 'gypsies' by Kyzylians. Every day, dressed in long, dark skirts and covering their heads with colourful scarves, these women, the majority of them immigrants from Uzbekistan and Tajikistan, eagerly stopped people and offered different 'magical' practices, including curse detection and infliction rituals. A variety of posters displayed on the fences and walls of the buildings around the city encouraged future clients to call if they had queries about their love life, health, business or curses (see Figure 1.1). Television programmes alternated with colourful adverts where fortune tellers praised the efficiency of their magical services. Nonetheless, my Tuvan friends' resilience and apparent obliviousness to these practices were astonishing. Any questions about cursing were consistently met with laughter and assertions that it was the doings of the Uzbeks, the Tajiks or the Russians. Gathering information from discreet conversations at Ajlana's workplace, the content of which she occasionally shared with me, I knew there was something else happening in flats, offices and government buildings. It was

DOI: 10.4324/9781003245391-3

28 *In the midst of cursing battles*

Figure 1.1 A street advert encouraging people to contact a practitioner who can deflect curses

something that would not be talked about openly and yet it seemed to remain an integral element of peoples' everyday interactions.

Despite the fact that the Soviet regime ended over 30 years ago, everyday life in Kyzyl continues to feel as if permeated by the vapours of the Soviet era. It is a place where many events occur behind closed doors, as if in secrecy, where decisions and choices are imbricated in the complex nexus of connections and ties contingent on the wider factors and figures that remain unknown to Tuvans. Everyday life in the capital seems to be characterised by perpetual ambiguity and unpredictability. This, in turn, has particular implications for conceptualisations of the practice of cursing among Tuvans. Curses are often described as a concrete way (Rus. *sposob*) through which a certain degree of control in the otherwise uncertain environment can be exercised. While doing fieldwork in Kyzyl, I was regularly involved in the confusing labyrinth of connections and decisions when trying to obtain diverse permissions, establish contacts with people or, simply, find a place to live. Rarely did things progress according to any obvious rationale and even less frequently could I rely on distinct legal tools, such as contracts or formal agreements. In one case, I felt particularly concerned about the future of my research and initially sought to exercise legal rights I believed I had as a foreign citizen. Much to my surprise, I quickly found out that if I wanted to continue my work, I had to forget official disputes and quietly give in to local politics. However, I still lived with the conviction I had an option to simply abandon the fieldwork at any given time. Indeed, it was not until then that I truly experienced the instrumental character of curses and the ways in which cursing reflected the wider characteristics of social interactions. While remaining deeply disturbed, I shared some concerns with one of my Kyzylian friends, Sajan, as well as Hovalygmaa. After I had described the problem to them, Sajan gave me a slightly condescending smile and concluded: 'Now you have felt on your own

In the midst of cursing battles   29

skin, what it means to live here. We often feel hopeless. You curse so that you have some control over your own life'. The shaman's reaction was much more pragmatic. I had not even finished the story when her face froze and she sprang to her feet: 'What do you want to do? Do you want me to curse this person? What is their name? Should I break a leg, or perhaps make them fall into coma?' Indeed, she was not joking. When I refused to undertake any actions, the shaman seemed upset and confused. 'I do not understand, if someone hurts you, you have to send it back'. She gave me an angry look.

Within the ethnographic context of Kyzyl, the proliferation of cursing indisputably intertwines with political and economic shifts triggered by the disintegration of the Soviet regime. The abrupt change from one economic system to another has generated more uncertainty and risks while introducing what Humphrey (1999) defined as new 'post-Soviet sensibilities' (1999: 8). People have become more sensitive to their privacy and remain concerned about being spied on, judged or envied by others. Thus, they resort to cursing in order to secure their jobs, to have a stable financial income or to take revenge on their neighbours, colleagues and ex-partners, which can be driven by jealousy but also by anger, fear or hopelessness. As such, rather than through a general discourse of increasing material ends by magical means (as I have discussed in the Introduction in relation to 'occult economies'), *kargysh-chatka* can be conceptualised as a practical social action perceived as an instrument of basic control in the uncertain socioeconomic and political landscapes. The instrumental use of curses is, however, one of the many elements which come together in the cursing event, the one which has been also widely subjected to anthropological inquiry. While recognising its importance, in this chapter, I would like to look slightly beyond the mere functional implications of *kargysh-chatka* and understand what it reveals about the wider patterns of living in Kyzyl. What it is like to bargain with spirits when a marriage fails or a love-affair ensues? What possible curses can one expect when facing conflicts with colleagues at work? How dangerous gossiping with the next-door neighbour might be?

Engagement with the mechanics of cursing allows to explore how the idea of control that my interlocutors describe pertains not only to humans but also to spirits revealing a sociocosmic dimension of curses. As I will show, on the one hand, people face fears concerned with a job security and marriage while spirits, on the other hand, tackle their own concerns with isolation and social instability. Moreover, social tensions which trigger the urge to deploy cursing practices in Tuva are not necessarily rooted directly in the economic transformations from state to capitalistic economies. Conversely, while proliferating within the urban arena, I suggest that they are intimately associated with shifts in the mechanics of sociality generated by changes in spatial proximity. In other words, the closer people are in both physical and emotional interactions, the less sociable and the more dramatic their relations become (including the relations with spirits). This, in turn, becomes visible when compared and contrasted with pre-Soviet and post-Soviet patterns of being in the sphere of family as well as economic and political realms in Tuva. I suggest that the proliferation of curses does not introduce new

30 *In the midst of cursing battles*

obstacles. Rather, it manifests an intensification of fears and uncertainties which have always been there, although remained dormant and less obvious in pre-Soviet and Soviet times. In other words, the escalation of cursing practices has unveiled these challenges while increasing sociocosmic exposure to more risk. However, before engaging further with this point, let me open the discussion by delineating the key characteristics of Tuvan curses and the basic mechanics that the process of cursing involves.

Introducing Tuvan curse

In Tuva, when someone is under the influence of a curse, people say that they 'run down the roads in swirls' (*oruk ezinneldir mangnaar*). Their behaviour is meant to resemble the erratic, unpredictable gusts of the wind. Curses are described as particular immaterial energies (*kyshter*) which can enter the victims through their head with great speed while triggering whirls (*ezinneldir*) and swirls (*duvulendir*). This process is also described in the Russian language as turbulence (Rus. *turbulentnost'*). Even though curses can be traced to one singular moment, they constitute an omnipresent, continuous threat that permeates people's interactions on a daily basis and flourishes among families and friends, in working environments as well as in the sphere of formal politics. Tuvans recognise two main types of curses; *chatka* ('curse') and *kargysh* ('gossip'). Both terms – *kargysh* and *chatka* – are used interchangeably with reference to cursing in general, and often, especially in shamanic chants, as one expression *kargysh-chatka*. Differences between the two are very subtle and, in fact, it is only the shamans who can easily provide a clear differentiation between them. *Chatka* occurs when a person intends to harm another person; however, in order to do so, one must turn for help to a strong shaman (*shydaldyg ham*). Inflicting *chatka* is meant to mainly result in a broken leg, a stroke, a prolonged disease and, in the worst case, death. *Kargysh* may, rarely, occur without shamanic help, simply by muttering ill words (*ass-dyldy-bile*) or thinking bad thoughts (*bodal-sagyzjy-bile*) about the victim. Among the other types of curses recognised by Tuvans the most difficult one to deflect is the clan curse (*doora nugul*).[1] *Doora nugul* can affect descendants in both female and male lines. It lasts for at least seven generations and is inherited through blood ties. The implications of this curse can be truly traumatising for the victims and their families, as illustrated in the case of one of my Tuvan friends, Sofia, who was suffering from a clan curse inflicted upon her kin nearly a 100 years earlier. At a time when food was scarce, one of Sofia's female ancestors tried to steal meat from another yurt and a host of the yurt cursed the woman. Since that day, every female descendant in Sofia's clan was meant to suffer from an unfulfilled and lonely love life. Indeed, Sofia never got married and men would always leave her abruptly after a few months into a relationship. She was a single mother and struggled in maintaining friendships with other women, who considered her as a possible threat to their marriages. The same thing happened to Sofia's mother as well as to her cousins and some other older female relatives. Sofia had a daughter and, at the time of our conversation, she was in the process of organising a clan ritual, which would break the curse and secure her child's future love life and happiness.

As in the case of Sofia, clan curses in Tuva are usually associated with a variety of particularly persistent problems ranging from obstacles in relationships to poverty or general perpetual turmoil in life. Interestingly, it is very common to ascribe clan curses to all forms of disabilities that children are born with, such as autism, bodily deformations or deafness. The possibility of suffering from curses is also often contingent on the previous lives of the victim. In this way, the potency of curse is intimately intertwined with the karmic system, which determines one's susceptibility to curses by the deeds (one had) executed in a previous life. In short, the more intentional harm someone caused in their past lives, the higher chance they have of suffering from curses in the next life. For instance, people who suddenly fall ill and subsequently die are described as those who in their previous life had intended to kill by lying, gossiping or wishing death upon another person. In a similar manner, the aforementioned disabilities, if not accounted for by a clan curse, are often considered as a result of attempting to curse or harm someone in a previous life.

The mechanics of cursing

In Inner Asian cosmologies, the agency of inflicting misfortune which involves cursing is often attributed to aggrieved ancestors (Humphrey 1996), neglected spirits (Pedersen 2011) or human–human interactions (Højer 2004, 2019; Swancutt 2012). In Tuva, the machinery of curse is contingent on a complex matrix of relationships, which includes humans, spirits and shamans. Curses explicitly acquire their initial potency from the bad intentions of humans. However, the mechanics of cursing require at least three actors for a curse to be successfully inflicted. This triadic relationship involves the victim, the one who casts the curse and the spirit who inflicts the curse on behalf of the aggressor. In short, people have no immediate agency in casting curses, and curse as energy has to be carried out by one of the spirits. It is thus the spirit that enters the victim's body, and it is the spirit who continuously manipulates how the curse affects the victim. In most cases, this procedure requires the simultaneous presence of the shaman, as the clients turn to them in order to summon the spirits as well as to ensure particular results of curse, i.e. death, broken limbs and addictions. Moreover, spirits, although acting on behalf of humans and responding to shamans' requests, often have their own agendas associated with cursing, a point to which I shall return later in this chapter. Occasionally, it is possible for the gods to inflict curses if they become aggravated by the actions of the humans. Inflicting these curses does not require the presence of a shaman and constitutes the phenomenon that is rather challenging to deflect.

The spirits responsible for inflicting curses come from the group of *aza* ('evil') spirits. People refer to them as *Chetker* and *Buktar* (sing. *Buk*). *Chetker* spirits are said to come from the 'country' (*oran*) where the yellow river flows and where *aza* spirits sit in circles in front of their yurts and smoke pipes. *Buk* lives among

32 *In the midst of cursing battles*

people, lingers in the streets or wanders around the steppe. Both spirits have particular physiques. *Chetker* is described as having only half of a face as well as a decomposing or rotten body whilst *Buk* wanders in dirty, shredded clothes. *Chetker* and *Buktar* usually work for the shaman or along with him/her in the process of inflicting curse. Sometimes, the spirits operate without the shaman's calling. This happens when they carry out and execute curses inflicted on humans as a result of their deeds performed in previous lives. Sometimes, the spirits spontaneously, without the shaman's calling, decide to respond to someone's angry gossiping (*kargysh*). This type of curse infliction bears some similarities to Mongolian curses *hel am* ('malicious gossip') where specific forms of speech acts are responsible for different degrees of pain and harm. Such dangerous gossip performed without the shaman's assistance in Tuva might have, however, tragic consequences. Many times, I was told stories about spirits meandering through the streets, hiding in gardens, and I was warned to be vigilant of what I say and think in their presence. This is how one of the shamans described this process to me:

> Once you start wishing someone unwell, spirits will come to you and do what you think or say. This is their role here; this is what they feed off. But after they always return for their price: an offering, some food or tea with milk. Sometimes, if the curse is bad, they can return and break your finger. If they do not receive their price they will send horrible curse as a punishment.

On rare occasions, when people decide to take the risk and inflict curses without shamanic help and protection, they usually demonstrate their intentions through spitting, throwing sand or vodka while muttering with specific intonation and rhythm harmful words (I shall come back to this point in Chapter 5). The shamans prefer to use vodka, black tea and, in cases of death curse, mutton blood. The use of all these substances is associated with the conviction that liquids, especially spit and blood, can easily convey information and thus quickly summon the spirits responsible for inflicting curses upon the victim. When spirits enter the body of the client they are said to nest in the stomach, intestines or chest. Sometimes, rather than entering the body, they begin to live with the victim, observe them and follow them in their everyday routines. In these instances, they can take on different animal forms, such as dogs, serpents or mice. On other occasions, they can transform into a beautiful woman or take on the physique of deceased relatives and linger around the room while watching their victims.

Once a curse enters the victim's physical body with help from spirits, it begins to 'disturb' (*üreer*) their emotions, interactions with other people and health. Simultaneously, the physical body begins to pollute and curse materialises in a form of 'mud' (*hir*) visible to the shamans. People suffering from curses may drastically change their behaviour and forget their usual routines and habits. While functioning out of character, they are stubborn and unpredictable in their decisions while often displaying fears of being observed and gossiped about. At the same time, they might suffer from unexpected medical conditions, become particularly aggressive and prone to crime or addictions. It is common to initially search for remedies to physical problems in hospitals, for instance, as in the cases of sudden illnesses. Very often, however, people turn simultaneously to shamans and Buddhist lamas in order to address all possible sources of affliction. In general, understanding the onset of sudden unusual symptoms, especially behaviour-related, from a perspective of a 'psychological' or psychiatric problem triggers anxiety and fear. Nonetheless, it gradually gains some recognition among people who decide to pursue psychological studies, primarily outside Tuva. Otherwise, sudden changes in behaviour are rather kept secret, perhaps still bearing stigma from Soviet times, when individuals suffering from, for instance, shamanic illness were taken by Russians to psychiatric hospitals. Shamans remain very vigilant when diagnosing the causes of given suffering. They clearly differentiate if the problem was triggered by curse or other factors and, therefore, whether it requires assistance from a shaman or other practitioners, such as medical doctors or a psychiatrist.

Sociocosmic drama

As discussed earlier, cursing constitutes a mechanism which involves humans and spirits alike and, as such, it often presents, what I refer to in this book as, a distinct *sociocosmic drama*. The crucial reason why the spirits are eager to engage in inflicting curses is that, similar to people, they are said to face numerous challenging conditions and problems, such as neglect, anger and even alcoholism (see also Pedersen 2011, Swancutt 2008). The usual places of residence of spirits are described as economically tormented and destroyed, thus mirroring, to a certain extent, the turbulent characteristics of everyday life in Kyzyl. The spirits feel poor, angry and lonely, and casting curses allows them to become closer to the spaces where humans live, which seem to them rich and economically stable. Being in, on or around a human is, as one of the shamans put it, like residing in a five-star hotel with all the associated luxury. In short, even though in the instances of cursing, spirits usually act on behalf of humans, they concurrently perceive the possibility to curse as a desirable instrument, allowing them to improve their otherwise challenging existence. The process of curse deflection, which heavily relies on sending the spirits back to where they came from, is therefore very dramatic. The spirits tend to cry and howl, and they often beg the shaman to stop while casting accusations of cruelty. It is common for the spirits to adopt the physical appearance of a deceased relative and, in this disguise, accuse the shaman of keeping the deceased away from their family. In the shamans' descriptions, these emotionally dense negotiations, which become an integral part of the rituals, can be gruelling and tormenting for both the shaman and the spirit. This dramaturgy develops further when people undertake actions in order to mislead the spirits and protect themselves from undetected cursing. The methods employed are based on a combination of trickery and amulets. After each curse deflection ritual, the shaman provides the client with a special *eeren* ('token'), which sometimes is inhabited by one of the protective spirits. The *eeren*, however, has to be blessed

34   *In the midst of cursing battles*

yearly with juniper; otherwise it may lose its protective energy. There are further methods by which *aza* spirits can be tricked. Wearing a hat the other way around or wearing clothes inside out while travelling is the best way of misleading *Chetker* and *Buk*. Moreover, there are particular methods of protecting children, which also apply to foreigners who decide to closely interact with the shamans. These strategies include placing soot on the nose while walking at night or carrying protective *eeren*, such as a bear's palm. Very often, children are called horrible names (*'öjze cögleer'*), for example, 'you shit boy' (*myjak ool*), 'glutton boy' (*hymtak ool*) or 'blue stomach boy' (*kok hyryn ool*) as these names are meant to disinterest *Chetker* and *Buk*. Once the curse obtains its potency it is impossible to avoid it without resorting to help from a shaman. Other methods, such as escaping curses through changing a family name (Swancutt 2008), prove to be unsuccessful. As a result, it is very common to visit the chosen shaman to conduct what can be described as 'curse check ups' and regular cleansing rituals in order to remove any evidence associated with being cursed (such as dirt), even if people do not experience any unexpected sufferings or harm. The most common time of the year to conduct a cleansing ritual (*aryglaashkyn*) is before *shagaa* ('Tuvan New Year'), which takes place in February.

Tuvan cursing reveals itself as a distinct sociocosmic drama contingent not only on the conflicts between humans but also on tensions and challenges that directly concern the spirits. On the one hand, people in Kyzyl are to a significant extent dependent on *Chekter-Buktar* spirits in the process of inflicting curses and constantly try to trick them. On the other hand, spirits strive to live around people and interfere in their lives while protesting and lamenting when being sent away by the shamans. In this way, the phenomenon of cursing is associated with the unfolding of wider sociocosmic dramaturgy that constitutes an imminent aspect of the Tuvan sociality, with all its dangers, trickery and intrigue.

Life without coincidence

Curses are part of the wider concept of (mis)fortune in Tuva. Neither bad fortune (*haj*) nor good luck (*kezjik, aas kezjik*) is accidental. Rather, they are continually controlled, navigated and accounted for. As one of the shamans put it: 'In our world there are no coincidences, everything has to be explained. Do you see how difficult our life is?' The system of explanations associated with a variety of sufferings and harm as well as fortune is a rich and complex structure and the potency of cursing constitutes one of its essential pillars. According to the Tuvan ontology of misfortune there is always an explanation as to why certain things occur. Unexpected and harmful events can be attributed to violation of taboos, such as polluting water, spitting in the fire, leaving rubbish or neglecting places occupied by *eezi* (masters of place) spirits. It can be further triggered by an event pertaining to the victim's *chol* (one of the terms for Tuvan 'destiny') or be associated with the Buddhist karmic system. In the majority of cases I have explored, however, misfortune has been linked with curses. Among the types of misfortune contingent on the potency of cursing, Tuvans recognise *doora* ('a thing that lies across the road'), *haj-bachyt* ('an abrupt event') and *halap* ('natural disaster'). *Doora* can reveal itself in the form of a tree on a path, an illness, being passed over for promotion or a broken car. When speaking about *haj-bachyt*, Tuvans refer to a tragic event which leads to an abrupt death. In these instances, they often say *haj-bachyt tovaryn*, which can be translated as 'something has swept a person from the road'. Finally, Tuvans recognise natural disasters, which can be instigated as a result of cursing, such as *hal-halap* ('wind disasters'), *sug-halap* ('water disasters') and *hurt-halap* ('fire disasters'). Interestingly, the continuing increase in car accidents has been categorised as a separate type of misfortune caused by curses called *aily-halap* ('crash'). During the diagnosis process, the shamans carefully assess which of the incidents is associated with curse or, for instance, with one's destiny (*chol*). If the shamans have honest intentions, then they will undertake ritual actions only if harm was triggered through external factors rather than someone's fate or deeds performed in previous lives. In latter cases, suffering is expected to be endured without any shamanic intervention. If the shamans are greedy and seek new business opportunities, then they may attempt to lie to their victims in order to secure recurring visits and continuous payment. Regardless of the proposed solutions, it is impossible to leave the shaman without knowing what the cause of any given incident or harm was. In a similar manner, good fortune is not accidental but must be controlled and navigated. It can be either acquired from previous lives or can be gradually improved through good deeds and a variety of rituals aiming at increasing one's luck in the current life and securing its growth in the next lives. Sometimes, however, one's sudden success, for example, a promotion, might be attributed to curses intentionally inflicted upon a rival.

This deterministic conceptualisation of (mis)fortune, in which causality is associated with concrete forces, does not pertain exclusively to Tuva. It bears strong similarities to, for example, Evans-Prichard's (1937) classical study of witchcraft among the Azande, which espouses the explanatory function of occult practices. Evans-Prichard explores how witchcraft functions as a direct and obvious explanation to and of diverse abrupt and mysterious events while rendering the world comprehensible. However, there is a lot more to Tuvan curse than simply its explanatory character which forecloses the possibility of coincidence. While I acknowledge that curses can be understood as imbued with a concrete function (explanatory or instrumental, such as exercising control), at the same time I have sought out to problematise something else in my analysis. Equally germane to my discussion is how curses can produce an economy of exchange and accumulation of energies that are represented in the form of (in)visible substances, and what this can further reveal about the sociocosmic interactions in Kyzyl. Moving from the functional paradigms towards the mechanics of occult phenomena, within the wider context of Siberian and Inner Asian studies, the notions of good and bad luck are approached as 'a fluctuating state of being' (Humphrey & Ujeed 2012: 153) that can be controlled, anticipated, produced, negotiated, as well as destroyed (see, for example, Broz & Willerslev 2012; Empson 2012; Hamayon 2012). Similarly in Tuva, bad and good fortune along with curses, which are intertwined with these, do not constitute afflictions that

36 *In the midst of cursing battles*

can be acquired or lost accidentally. Conversely, rather than 'finite possessions' (Humphrey & Ujeed 2012: 153), they are a part of the wider matrix of fluctuating energies that can be shared, increased and acted upon in multifarious ways. In order to illustrate these fluid characteristics further, I shall turn to a short ethnographic vignette from the shamanic ritual dedicated to increasing the fortune of one of the Tuvan clans.

Spring is the time of the year in Tuva when the shamans' schedules become very busy. It is the season when different clans gather in order to conduct annual rituals, which usually take place outside of the town. This yearly traverse of going out and coming back to the city is associated with re-establishing and maintaining connections with the spirits that do not inhabit urban spaces and yet remain integral to the Tuvan non-rural sociality through their ability to distribute good fortune and alleviate suffering. Each clan usually has its own *ovaa*, that is, a pile of stones where the spirit of the mountain or a hill resides, as well as a sacred spring (*arzjaan*) and a tree (*baj-yjash*) that are inhabited by the masters of place who take care of a chosen clan. The rituals taking place near these sacred spots are conducted every year for three consecutive years and, then, renewed after another seven years. The Tuvans are said to be born with a given amount of fortune (*kezzik*) and pollution or dirt (*nugul*) carried from previous lives which can be further increased as well as decay during the course of one's life. Each of the rituals is meant to cleanse the clan members, deflect curses and increase their good fortune. In the first week of May, I was on my way to the ritual dedicated to the master of place (*eezi*) living near the sacred tree that was chosen by the shamans for the Mongush clan. The ritual conducted in the previous year was particularly successful. The clan had asked for one of their members, a woman in her late 40s, to become pregnant. A few weeks after the ritual, the woman found she was expecting and eventually gave birth to a healthy boy. Encouraged by this successful outcome, a year later the clan gathered again hoping to obtain more good fortune, this time especially within the financial sphere. After the food offerings, the clan members hung strips of material (*chalama*) and small colourful sheets of fabric on the tree branches where they drew or wrote what they wished for. Then, everyone gathered a short distance from the tree and the shaman, as if in a small amphitheatre. We waited in silence as the shaman spoke to the spirit of the tree and then sprinkled us with tea and milk, consumed earlier by the spirit. People were trying to catch as much of the liquid as possible and applied it on their faces and arms. Next, the shaman walked around the tree drumming and shouting *kudaj kudaj kudaj, ass kezzik kudaj* ('please give us good fortune, please give us'). The clan members walked behind the shaman, each time repeating her words and putting their hands together as if trying to catch the streams of invisible fortune coming from the spirit of the tree while simultaneously touching the branches and leaves. We were instructed by the shaman to touch the tree with full hands and then to make big circles around our bodies in order to obtain as much energy as possible. Finally, everyone walked three times through the smoke from the nearby fire after the shaman extinguished it with tea and milk and, in this way, fed the spirit of the tree again and concluded the ritual (see Figure 1.2).

Figure 1.2 Members of the clan walking through the smoke in order to cleanse and increase their good fortune

This short vignette illustrates how the notion of (mis)fortune in Tuva represents a particular economy of exchange and (re)accumulation of energies that are reflected in the form of (in)visible substances. The practices of establishing the physical connection with different objects as vessels of energy, like trees, as well as applying tea with milk and smoke onto the body, constitute particular techniques of harvesting good energy and cleansing the person, including alleviating suffering triggered by curse. In a similar way, as mentioned earlier, curse infliction is associated with distributing different liquids, such as saliva, blood or black tea. The notion of (mis)fortune, including curses, rather than being externalised through zoomorphic or anthropomorphic representations (Humphrey & Ujeed 2012), becomes a process of distribution of energy, materialised through 'merging with elemental and formless things' (2012: 514) as well as objects which have the capacity to accumulate energy.[2]

Thus, the flow of (mis)fortune, rather than being accidental and unpredictable, becomes an integral element of a wider network of fluctuating energies that underpin human and non-human interactions. Within this system, distribution of fortune, as well as harm, is, on the one hand, about physical contact with different objects perceived as vessels of energies, both defined and shapeless. On the other hand, it is about peoples' capacities; for example, the shamans' roles and skills in the process of curse infliction and deflection as well as people's tendencies to think and pronounce in specific ways words in order to curse their enemies. The conceptualisation of interactions between humans and spirits as embedded in flowing energies points to a wider feature of being, entrenched in

38 *In the midst of cursing battles*

perpetual fluctuation contingent on the notions of coming together and spreading apart – what I shall call, coalescence and dispersion. This, as I propose, bears some implications for the sudden increase in cursing phenomena in the wake of Soviet disintegration. Given the fluid characteristics of curses as energies, which have to be navigated, increased or tamed, they prove to operate well within these dynamics of dispersion and coalescence. Their abrupt proliferation in the 1990s, therefore, reaches beyond the spread of capitalism and accumulation of wealth while unearthing trajectories of social and cosmic relations as they intensify or weaken in different spatial configurations. In short, as I will suggest in the next section, the increased cursing events can be conditioned by a kind of 'tyranny of intimacy' (Sennett 1994: 338), that is, an excessive closeness combined with too vigorous sociability triggered by changes in physical proximity that were initially related to a move from the steppe to the city.

Cursing battles: relations of social and spatial proximity

In order to understand this process, it is essential to look at the fabric of life in Tuva through a historical lens. As outlined in the Introduction, given its complex location, Tuva has remained for many years in relative isolation, resisting, to some extent, influences from the outside. In terms of the local economy, before the Soviet regime, Tuva constituted a distinct combination of different pastoral practices characteristic of Central and North Asia (Humphrey 1981: 1). Small-scale, subsistence agriculture dominated farming in the region, resulting in no strong differentiation between rich and poor herdsmen. Subsequently, the nomads of Inner Asia did not frequently settle down as, for instance, farmers. Everyday life was based on the cycle of nomad dispersion and concentration. The organisational aspect of economic life in Tuva reflected the units of economic production and consumption, but this organisation was not defined by structures of domination (Humphrey 1981: 18). At the beginning of the 20th century, Tuva was characterised by geographical isolation, distance from the industrial and cultural centres of neighbouring states and a relatively small population. There was no mechanised transport or efficient means of communication. These elements made the transition from pre-Soviet to sedentarised forms of living severe. This, in turn, had particular implications for the dynamics of sociability stemming from an abrupt and excessive closeness and revealing diverse tensions. Nevertheless, during Soviet times, as often stressed by my interlocutors, conflicts were kept at bay or quiet and everyone tried to refrain from any practices that involved shamans or spirits. More than that, people were provided with some stability and security offered by the state. After the abrupt end of the Soviet Union, everything changed and so far dormant tensions have been finally fully revealed and increased. The importance of physical proximity among Tuvans was explained to me by one of my friends Arzaana. We met with Arzaana during the outdoor ritual organised by her clan. While discussing the historical trajectory of local and regional processes and shifts which ultimately led to the proliferation of cursing practices in Kyzyl today, she suggested that Tuvans suffered, in particular, from the inability to interact with each other in small and congested spaces. She explained how, for generations, Tuvans had been taught about survival rather than about ways of dealing with other people. She said in conclusion to our discussion:

> We always used to live in small groups, scattered all over. An average Tuvan knows well how to count their animals, not how to openly address their emotions. People had been trained for centuries how to think about themselves and they are unable to interact with others in crowded and static places like cities.

While inspired by Arzaana's comments, I suggest that the proliferation of curses in post-Soviet Kyzyl has been, to a great extent, entrenched in the process of moving from wide spaces imbued with scarce and diffused interactions into the city, perceived by people as a small, congested urban structure. As discussed earlier on the example of the clan ritual, Tuvans describe the dynamics of social interactions as a nexus of different fluctuating energies. Given this, shifts in spatial proximity radically changed the parameters for the flow of these energies, from widespread or dispersed in the steppe to coalescent and congested within the urban arena of the city. Revealed in this way, tensions, while generally subdued during the Soviet period, escalated in the wake of the Soviet dissolution. In other words, enforcement of close distance and the corresponding intensification of social interactions, combined with the consequent changes in the dynamics of socioeconomic and political relationships led to an eruption of previously dormant or less obvious emotions and pressures. This, in turn, created the societal environment of what Sennett describes as tyranny of intimacy where 'the closer people come, the less sociable, the more painful, the more fratricidal their relations' (1994: 338), widening the spectrum of possibilities for social frictions and conflicts and thus curses. This form of dangerous communication intensified not as a result of an absence of social ties (Harrison 1995), but instead as a response to an increased sociability and intimacy intertwined with a lack of security and control over one's life. In order to illustrate this process, in what follows I am going to discuss some of the shifts in social dynamics within the sphere of family as well as within economic and political realms in both pre-Soviet and post-Soviet times, and illuminate how the latter can be generated and contoured by the phenomenon of cursing.

Tuvan family

In pre-Soviet Tuva, the kinship system (i.e. relations governed by the rules of marriage and descent) was strongly patrilineal. Nonetheless, the larger units, such as clans and lineages, lost many of their functions to the administrative institutions set up by the Manchus in the early 18th century (Vainshtein 1981). The essential productive group in Tuva was *aal*. Many *aals* were composed of closely related families, mainly family of the parents and those of their married sons and brothers.[3] In this way, they constituted a form of an 'extended family' in the nomadic environment. *Aal* was classless and considered as the most efficient way

40　*In the midst of cursing battles*

of using the pastures. It was also a requirement of the nomadic pastoral way of life in these regions. Large units were mostly attributed to non-economic military factors, primarily the need to unite for defence (Vainshtein 1981). Of crucial importance were also patronymic groups of related families, the heads of which shared a common ancestor through the male line. Each family had its own constituting name and, apart from blood relations, they were linked by economy and diverse practices (such as cult rituals gathering the whole group near *ovaa*). Mutual aid existed between the families. Unlike today, which was often pointed out to me by my female interlocutors, single mothers were never ostracised and women unhappy in their marriages were allowed to leave their husbands without any further repercussions from their families. The families could travel together or split; however, they would always remain in perpetual contact and try to stay close during migration.

The importance of physical closeness still deeply pervades family relations today. As one of my Tuvan friends put it, living with your family is the most important thing as it always keeps people together. Indeed, I became very familiar with the importance of 'togetherness' when I moved in with my landlady, Galina. Galina was a retired widow whose husband was brutally killed two years earlier. She lived in one of the blocks close to the city centre. When I arrived, she informed me that we would tell everyone I was her Russian relative in order to stop people from dangerous gossip. Galina spent every single day either with her neighbours or with her daughters who lived in the opposite block. She was rarely alone, and my occasional craving for privacy particularly irritated her. Moreover, Galina did not like my lengthy daily trips and constant habit of disappearing for a full day. In general, she found my overall independence deeply troubling. Eventually, a friend of mine explained that Galina was treating me as her daughter and my lack of subordination was appalling to her. As I learned, parents and grandparents were fully responsible for making any decisions concerning their younger relatives. For example, in the case of marriage, they would assess the potential future husband. Every choice made by the newlyweds had to be taken with the parents. In the case of divorce, it was the parents of the daughter who would take care of any children and set the conditions. As Galina revealed to me one evening, the worst curse was to have a foreigner as a son-in-law, as the family could not trace his background and thus predict what to expect from him. In other words, he could not be investigated and this was a threat the family could not afford. Taken together, within the unit of a family there was no sense of individuality in relation to decision making. Moreover, not being able to live surrounded by the family members was associated with great misfortune, including possible curses. In a particularly difficult situation were single mothers.

During my stay in Tuva, I became friends with Sajan, the only child of a divorced mother. Sajan was a Korean language teacher who loved fast cars and used to say that cars are like good horses. While emotionally comparing Kyzyl to his own Paris, he also vividly described numerous challenges he had to face as the only child in a city which thrived on familial ties. He was often ostracised in the community and his relatives would refuse to help him based on his mother's single parenthood;

> You need family and relatives to get a job – police, government, stable, secure jobs. Education is of secondary value. You can go and eat with your family, there is one meal a day you can cross out. Life in Kyzyl is difficult – a lot of gossip and backstabbing, being on your own is very hard.

In Sajan's stories, Kyzylians tend to focus on and stay entangled in their own family relations looking out for their relatives. Perhaps this image echoes, to some extent, the notion of amoral familism, based on generations of the nuclear family and lineage solidarity, common in pastoral and agricultural communities (see Gilmore 1982; Silverman 1968). Indeed, family units in Tuva bear some features of a social system lacking in moral sanctions outside those of the immediate family (Silverman 1968: 2). Nonetheless, this does not imply that family relations, immediate and extended, are always characterised by warmth and safety. In Kyzyl today, dynamics within families, which often include neighbours, have become more complex following the move from yurts separated by distance to densely packed blocks of flats where gossip and rumours easily operate. As people live closer to each other, their lives have become more transparent and gossiping has turned into a common form of scrutiny and entertainment. In the wake of Soviet disintegration and disappearance of the state support, spatial proximity has led to an increase in conflicts associated primarily with marriage and wealth as well as securing relatives' careers. In this way, family ties, rather than being about stability, have become infused with the threat that often comes from close by (see also Geshiere 2013). Unlike in pre-Soviet and Soviet times, cursing has begun to play a key role in the navigation of escalating conflicts, which concern affines (kin acquired through marital ties) as well as blood relatives.

One good example offers increasing divorces and love affairs, the consequences of which rumble through the streets and flats of the city. Gathering from the stories told by the elders, in pre-Soviet times, unhappy marriage would rarely trigger conflicts and result in revenge or ostracism from the community. In post-Soviet Kyzyl, however, divorce and love affairs are very common and both of these processes are intimately associated with a series of curse inflictions and deflections. The expected results often involve forcing an ex-spouse to become an alcoholic or a criminal. Interestingly, these requests are made not only by the divorcee or the parties involved but often include the whole families. This was vividly illustrated in a story described to me by the mother of one of my friends during a curse deflection ritual we participated in. The story concerned the woman's nephew, who got involved with an 'inappropriate' girl. Her behaviour was perceived as scandalous given her flair for drinking and arguing. The old lady attempted to reason with her nephew to no avail. The boy changed his phone number and ran away. One day, he appeared with a girl who was already pregnant. There was no other option but for the girl to be accepted

42   *In the midst of cursing battles*

as a part of the family through marriage. With time, the new husband started to spend all of his money on gambling, began to drink and lost all his social benefits. As it turned out, both the bride's and the groom's families could not accept the union and reverted to curses during the wedding. The bride's family was muttering curses, naming people and spitting so that the groom's family, including the groom himself, would suffer. The relatives of the groom asked the shaman to counter-curse. This had to remain a secret in order to stop the bride's family from re-cursing. I did not find out how the story of the newlyweds ended. However, as I have learned from the shaman, these forms of interactions between two families are a common occurrence in Kyzyl today when one of the families is unhappy with the future son or daughter-in-law. Moreover, curses are often enacted as a form of revenge for unhappy marriages, lack of interest from the husband's side or his absence and drinking. It is also common to use curse in love affairs as a form of revenge. Within this context, curses are equally popular outside kinship ties, when a woman, usually a neighbour or a colleague from work, intends to seduce someone's husband. Interestingly, single parenthood, even though considered as normal occurrence in pre-Soviet times, is perceived today as a direct consequence of cursing practices. A single mother is often described as suspicious and thought to be either mentally unstable, an alcoholic or troubling and stubborn which most likely occurred due to cursing. Conversely, before Soviet times, as I have mentioned earlier, single or divorced mothers had usually been taken care of by their kin with no stigma or curse accusations attached.

Even though cursing usually pervades relations of affinity, in some cases it is common to employ occult practices for or against one's own blood relatives. This is usually related to issues of education and a successful career. Relatives (mostly elder women) prefer to visit shamans and ask them to inflict curses so that their children and other relatives can receive promotion, enter university, obtain relevant papers or pass exams. In other cases, if a blood relative decides to go against the elder relative's view, the rest of the family might resort to cursing. This was a case of one of my interlocutors, Ania, who decided to go against the decision of her grandparents and moved away from Tuva. She became a successful businesswoman in Moscow. Sometime later, Ania found herself entangled in strange legal procedures and suddenly lost her job. When she confronted the shaman, she found out that her parents and grandparents had decided to curse her for not acquiescing to their decision. To a certain extent, cursing within the family sphere is gendered in Kyzyl. For example, it is primarily women who take an active role in the process of curse infliction related to love affairs as well as securing a relative's career. Men, on the other hand, are more involved in envy-based curses, with individuals invoking curse because of jealousy concerning, for example, property, a relative's wealth and general success. Although fear of being cursed by an ex-spouse or angry relative is prevalent among Kyzylians, it is within the economic and political spheres that curses are expected to acquire their full potential and constitute an integral element of everyday interactions.

Economic relations

In pre-Soviet Tuva, economic relations were concentrated around the household and *aal*. The household was mainly concerned with property and consumption, whereas *aal* was the basic productive unit (Vainshtein 1981). Each small family had their own livestock and animal and agricultural produce, which was consumed mainly within the family group. Pastures and certain buildings were, however, communal and a number of tasks were performed collectively, such as the pasturing of cattle, migratory removal and the watering of ploughland. Relations were egalitarian and based on reciprocity and mutual help. In the summer, when the pastures were richer, an *aal* usually joined with one or two other *aals* to form a more inclusive summer *aal*. Individual *aals* within such a community, however, were always distinct, each being defined by the existence of a common pen for the combined flocks of sheep and goats of the member households (Vainshtein 1981). Summer communities were fluid and dependent on the local conditions, reflecting again the dynamics of dispersion and movement.

In the process of Sovietisation, the nomads' pasturing places were transformed into collective farm-settlements. The introduction of collective institutions of *sovkhoz* ('state farm') and *kolkhoz* ('collective farm') transformed Tuvan lands into large-scale agricultural enterprises with hundreds of anonymous members, controlled by the local government (see Humphrey & Sneath 1999). Despite subverting Tuvan ways of living, these farms continued to provide their workers with employment and food. After the collapse of the Soviet Union, the government retreated from funding the collective farms in Tuva and, as in many other parts of Siberia, a free market economy was introduced. A sudden lack of state subsidies in the 1990s resulted in chaos, poverty and unemployment. Tuvans were left disoriented and confused about how to survive. The beginning of the 21st century has brought some stability; nevertheless, there is still a limited possibility of supporting a family and relatives through employment and regular income in Kyzyl.

With the introduction of commerce, the concepts of equality and reciprocity have changed. Economic ties are based now on private property with little to no financial and job security, which makes any employment fragile and any future unpredictable. As a result, fear and envy are the driving forces that venture into the sphere of economic relations. The prevailing uncertainty and despair eventuate in the story of one of my friends Katija, who held a position within the police force. Being funded by the state, the position offered her significant financial security and career prospects. At the same time, it also came with hidden dangers associated with curses. At one point, Katija became very sick and ended up having to take long-term sick leave. Concerned about her health, she turned to a shaman only to find out she was being cursed by one of her colleagues who was planning to take over her position at work. The main plot of Katija's story was repeated to me in different contexts and scenarios many times after. This type of cursing battle based on mutual fear and a need for success is a very common practice in Kyzyl today. In short, any job is accompanied by a constant concern that someone with a lower rank is trying to take over the position.

44   *In the midst of cursing battles*

Alternatively, a promotion may be blocked by a person with a higher degree of power. The only effective way of either developing a career or maintaining one is to engage in cursing. This procedure follows a particular pattern. Person A, who has a higher rank, will ask for person B to be cursed so that A can keep his/her job. Simultaneously, A will ask for a protection ritual in order to avoid potential curses from B. B does exactly the same thing only in a reversed manner. B requests curses that will remove A from their post so that B can get promoted. Simultaneously, protection rituals are conducted in order to save B from the curses afflicted by A. These cursing battles may continue endlessly, as A and B live in a constant fear that their opponent has just requested a more powerful curse.

In summary, people in Kyzyl no longer work with a small number of members from their own or nearby *aal*, and neither are they provided with minimal guaranteed income and work (as offered by the state economy in the Soviet area). Economic exchange happens with strangers, a few streets away from home and on a constant rather than periodic basis. From dispersed hills and pastures people have moved into a cramped matrix of streets and buildings where life has become pervaded by uncertainty and competition. The energies of (mis)fortune are no longer flowing between humans and distant places where spirits reside. They all coalesce within one bounded space of the city, which is exemplified by intensified instances of cursing, often reverted to as an instrument of basic survival and protection. Similar dynamics appear within the context of public affairs. The economic relations closely overlap with the sphere of formal politics and administration as these domains offer the most lucrative and financially stable positions, including, policemen, lawyers and government deputies. As such, they are also highly susceptible to cursing practices.

Political and administrative relations

The administrative and political system of pre-Soviet Tuva was an extension of the hierarchical Manchu state, the head of which resided in Mongolia. Tuva was divided into five *khoshun*, ruled over directly by hereditary princes, each of them having a certain number of households (Humphrey 1981). There were four *khoshun* under Mongolian rule and another seven under the rule of the Manchu administration. Each *khoshun* was divided into sections called *summon*, each of which had elected officials, and these were divided further into the smallest administrative units *arban* (Humphrey 1981). The system was a military-fiscal one, with selected officials being responsible for the mobilisation of a certain number of soldiers and the extraction of a stated tax in furs from the individual households under him (Humphrey 1981: 23–24). By the 20th century both *khoshun* and *summon* had agreed territorial boundaries. Most importantly though, this system had no destructive power or influence on economic organisation or the summer communities engaging in reciprocity and exchange (Humphrey 1981: 30). In short, political and administrative relations were almost detached from the everyday happenings in *aal*.

When Tuva officially became a part of the Soviet Union in 1944 it was rapidly and fully assimilated to the economic and administrative system imposed by the Soviet regime. The administrative and political situation in post-Soviet Kyzyl has, however, substantially changed. After the collapse of the Soviet Union, Tuva has remained a part of the Russian Federation in the form of the Autonomous Republic of Tuva. In 1993, Tuvans adopted their own constitution, which declares their political status as a 'sovereign democratic state in the Russian Federation' with its own anthem and its own flag. The centre of Kyzyl is mostly organised around government buildings, the national museum and the university. If one takes a stroll through Kyzylian streets, it is easy to count at least 16 different governmental and administrative institutions present in the heart of the city, such as High Court, City Hall, the Ministry of Internal Affairs, Federal Security Service, Federal Tax Office, the Ministry of the Tuvan Republic and the Ministry of Social Care and Employment. Working in and for one of these institutions provides the best positions and comes with a high level of job and financial security. As opposed to pre-Soviet and Soviet times, these political and administrative networks are neither detached from the everyday life of the family or household nor contingent on decisions made by the state. On the contrary, they are present, both figuratively and literally, in that many families reside in close proximity to the heart of the city and the institutions headquartered there. Moreover, often one or more of the family members work for these institutions or know someone who does. Given the financial and other benefits, it is the environment pervaded by the highest levels of envy. As a result, its internal dynamics remain secretive. The clients who visit shamans remain highly discreet about their jobs. It is very common for them to meet the shamans in the middle of the night, when they can remain unnoticed.

On a few occasions, I had a unique opportunity to participate in one of the curse deflection rituals ordered by a high member of the local government. I was taken to their home in a lavish car, but my questions remained unanswered. I was struck by the luxury of their house and its drastic contrast with the other places I visited in Kyzyl. The hosts – a mother and two sisters – were deeply concerned by my presence. However, they ended up inviting me to their clan ritual during which the high-profile status of these women was unnoticeable. Within the sphere of formal politics, cursing battles, following the same pattern as in the context of economic ties, constitute a common method of acquiring and losing power. The difference lies in the immediacy and desperation of finding a strong shaman willing to engage in the mechanics of cursing for the purpose of advancing someone's political career. Indeed, there are only a limited number of highly regarded shamans in Kyzyl who are willing to produce strong curses or apply strong protection in the context of politics. The choice of who the shaman is going to help is made on the 'first to arrive' basis. The shaman cannot curse and counter-curse while working for both of the clients simultaneously. Interestingly, in her analysis of curses among the Buryats, Swancutt (2012) emphasises that local government officials would rarely be suspected of cursing. This is due to their status, secure financial means and numerous privileges which ascribe them with model

46   *In the midst of cursing battles*

behaviour. Conversely, in Kyzyl and Tuva in general, it is particularly the government milieu where curses would be highly suspected. For example, the best way to secure a successful campaign is to request *kargysh-chatka* that can be inflicted on political opponents. Similarly, the possibility of maintaining power requires the mechanism of cursing battles. As Hovalygmaa told me, she finds the most difficult and exhausting time to be precisely that of election time. Bridging the spheres of formal politics and kinship, she only supports her relatives with counter-curses. Nonetheless, she often abandons Kyzyl during local government and council elections and lives in the taiga so that people will leave her alone. Indeed, it is a shared assumption among Tuvans that winning elections or securing a post can be achieved through curses.

Within the ethnographic context of Kyzyl, the phenomenon of cursing is embedded in a complex nexus of social as well as cosmological interactions, producing a unique platform of sociocosmic politics involving humans and spirits alike. The proliferation of cursing indisputably intertwines with political and economic shifts triggered by the disintegration of the Soviet regime. However, exploring the spread of cursing practices solely as a direct response to these transformations may obscure more complex dynamics at play. Interactions punctured by curses open the avenues to consider networks of relationships and communication deeply pervaded by danger, trickery and uncertainty that go well beyond the simple economy of wealth and power. In Tuva, curses become constitutive not only of human conflicts, but also human and non-human interactions and, in this way, remain intrinsic to wider sociocosmic dynamics. In other words, cursing practices provide an analytical platform that allows one to trace and investigate these dynamics as intensified and more obvious, rather than directly triggered by the collapse of the Soviet regime. Given the perception of curses as a part of the wider network of fluctuating energies embedded in the dynamics of dispersion and coalescence, their proliferation (starting from the nineties) is also contingent on excessive closeness and sociability stemming from the shift in spatial proximity. The instances of cursing battles heavily present in relations of intimacy, work environment and politics point to the mutlivocal characteristics of Tuvan curses embedded in wider historical and cosmological traits. A central position within this dynamic landscape of cursing occupies shamans; curses enacted without a shaman, while possible, are extremely rare. Mapping out the intricacies of Tuvan shamanic practice, let us then explore what it means to become a powerful shaman.

Notes

1 In the past, the Tuvans referred to clans as *söök* ('bone') (Vainshtein 1981: 238). These were patrilineal groups in which the heads of the families shared a common ancestor through the male line; however, they did not usually entail economic relations arising from the membership of the clan. With time, clans started to be confused with *arban* and *summon*, the administrative territorial units introduced during the Manchu empire (Humphrey 1981: 24). Consequently, patriclans gradually disappeared during the Manchu period (mid-18th to 20th century) as functioning units of society. Apart

In the midst of cursing battles 47

from patriclans, patronymic groups were also of high importance, in which the heads of the family shared not only blood relationships, but also economic ties (Vainshtein 1981: 240–214). Moreover, *aals*, the main productive groups, were, in fact, often constituted from small kinship groups. During the Soviet regime, *aals* and patronymic groups disappeared and were replaced with collective forms of production known as *sovkhoz* and *kolkhoz*. Today, patrilineal kinship retains its importance within the sphere of ideology and the realm of spirits, that is, in the context of interactions with spirits performed through rituals dedicated to curse deflection/infliction as well as ceremonies worshipping the spirits of places (*eezi*).

2 It is common for women who want to get pregnant to wear the underwear of particularly fertile women, or for men to touch a successful wrestler in order to obtain some of their energy and success.

3 As Vainshtein suggests, *aal* was formerly constituted in principle by agnates. However, it is reasonable to suppose that *aal* could be constituted also from a mixture of agnates, cognates and non-kin (1981: 30).

Bibliography

Broz, L. & Willerslev, R. 2012. When Good Luck is Bad Fortune. Between Too Little and Too Much Hunting Success in Siberia. *Inner Asia* no. 56 (2): 73–89.

Empson, M. R. 2012. The Dangers of Excess. Accumulating and Dispersing Fortune in Mongolia. *Social Analysis* no. 56 (1): 117–132.

Evans-Pritchard, E. E. 1937. *The Azande: History and Political Institutions*. Oxford: Clarendon Press.

Geshiere, P. 2013. *Witchcraft, Intimacy and Trust*. Chicago: The University of Chicago Press.

Gilmore, D. D. 1982. Anthropology of the Mediterranean area. *Annual Review of Anthropology* no.11: 175–205.

Hamayon, N. R. 2012. The Three Duties of Good Fortune. 'Luck' as a Relational Process among Hunting Peoples of the Siberian Forest in Pre-Soviet Times. *Inner Asia* no. 56 (1): 99–116.

Harrison, S. 1995. Transformations of Identity in Sepik Warfare. In M. Strathern (ed.), *Shifting Contexts. Transformations in Anthropological Knowledge*, 81–98. London and New York: Routledge.

Højer, L. 2004. The Anti-Social Contract. Enmity and Suspicion in Northern Mongolia. *The Cambridge Journal of Anthropology* no. 24 (3): 41–63.

Højer, L. 2019. *The Anti-social Contract: Injurious Talk and Dangerous Exchanges in Northern Mongolia*. New York: Berghahn Books.

Humphrey, C. 1981. Introduction. In S. Vainshtein (ed.), *Nomads of South Siberia*, 1–36. Cambridge: Cambridge University Press.

Humphrey, C. 1999. Shamans in the City. *Anthropology Today* no.15 (3): 3–10.

Humphrey, C. & Onon, U. 1996. *Shamans and Elders: Experience, Knowledge and Power Among the Daur Mongols*. Oxford: Clarendon Press.

Humphrey, C. & Sneath, D. 1999. *The End of Nomadism?: Society, State and the Environment in Inner Asia*. Cambridge: Duke University Press.

Humphrey, C. & Ujeed, H. 2012. Fortune in the Wind. An Impersonal Subjectivity. *Social Analysis* no. 56 (2): 152–167.

Pedersen, A. M. 2011. *Not Quite Shamans*. Ithaca; London: Cornell University Press.

Sennett, R. 1994. *Flesh and Stone: The Body and the City in Western Civilization*. New York; London: W.W. Norton.

48 *In the midst of cursing battles*

Silverman, F. S. 1968. Agricultural Organization, Social Structure, and Values in Italy: Amoral Familism Reconsidered. *American Anthropologist* no. 70 (1): 1–20.

Swancutt, K. 2008. The Undead Genealogy: Omnipresence, Spirit Perspectives, and a Case of Mongolian Vampirism. *Journal of the Royal Anthropological Institute* no. 14 (4): 843–864.

Swancutt, K. 2012. *Fortune and the Cursed. The Sliding Scale of Time in Mongolian Divination*. The United States of America: Berghahn Books.

Vainshtein, S. 1981. *Nomads of South Siberia*. Cambridge: Cambridge University Press.

2 The artisans of curses

Characteristics of shamanic practice in Tuva

It was early December when Valentina, one of my closest friends and, an ethno-musicologist from the Tuvan Cultural Centre, decided to help me arrange a meeting with shamans in Kyzyl whom I could interview. The process of approaching shamans without being tricked and treated as another naïve tourist was rather tedious and, at times, highly frustrating. However, one day Valentina shared with me an encouraging story about a mysterious family of four shamans who used to organise little feasts for the spirits in their house during Soviet times, when the use of the drums was forbidden. Valentina was invited to one of those unusual dinners and suggested I should accompany her and introduce myself to the Kuular family, as they might be willing to help me with my research. Hovalygmaa, Olchejma, Lodoj and Damba were four shamans born into a family of six.[1] They came from a long line of powerful Tuvan shamans, and the history and origins of their shamanic powers were part of a legend passed on from one generation to another. I had a chance to hear this story before I met the woman who not only welcomed me to the world of Tuvan shamanism, but also became a dear friend.

The legend describes Samdan, who was Hovalygmaa's great-great-grand-mother, one day suddenly left her husband and children and moved to the taiga (boreal forest). She felt she was losing her mind and wandered among different *aals*. In one *aal* she met a shaman who revealed that Samdan was suffering from a 'shamanic illness' (*albystap aaraash*). The shaman decided to 'open the road' (*oruk azzydaar*) for Samdan and help her learn how to shamanise. Samdan followed her calling and became a shaman. She gave birth to 11 children. Seven of them were born with pure blood and white bones, which was meant to indicate that they had shamanic powers. Never before had so many shamans been born from one mother. When the seven siblings were young, their father took them to the taiga and left them to be brought up by wolves. He asked the wolves to teach the children how to live in peace, how to have good thoughts and help one another. When the siblings reached adulthood, they started travelling around *aals* and fulfilling their fate by helping people as shamans. They never quarrelled and became known as *Chedi-hamnar* ('The Seven Shamans'). From then onwards, among their descendants there would be at least four shamans born to each mother. Their helping spirits have always presented themselves as wolves.

DOI: 10.4324/9781003245391-4

50   *The artisans of curses*

I was very intrigued by the legend, and a week later Valentina arranged a meeting with Hovalygmaa. A short woman in a fashionable blue dress entered the room, wearing heavy make-up and two braids. She studied me carefully, and we had a brief conversation about her work. Afterwards, she gave me her phone number. 'Can you teach me some English'? she asked. As I later found out, she was very eager to learn new languages and felt she should continuously expand her scholarly knowledge. 'Yes, of course', I replied instantly. 'Ok, then you will teach me English and, in exchange, I will answer all your questions'. This was a bargain that took me on an unusual journey into a complex world of shamanic practice in Tuva.

As discussed in Chapter 1, humans cannot inflict curses by themselves and cursing constitutes a tripartite mechanism, involving the victim, the spirits and the aggressor. The spirits do not inflict curses without a price, and wishing harm upon another human leads to the inflictor's suffering too, exemplified in broken limbs or an unexpected illness. Given this, in order to secure infliction of a curse that will result in particularly desired effects, such as physical harm, job loss or sudden misfortune, and in order to ensure that the spirits will not claim further sacrifices from the inflictor, people turn to shamans. It is only they who can summon and negotiate concrete outcomes with the spirits. Moreover, it is only the shamans who can remove curses and provide protection from further harm. Negotiations with spirits are expected to involve active and, at times, dramatic engagements; a form of creative performances with a variety of manipulative strategies ranging from subtle pleas to threats and trickery. These practices trigger fear among laymen and are expected to be fully mastered only by shamans. Shamans, therefore, remain central figures in the process of (un)folding sociocosmic interactions, which entails humans and non-humans alike and which is exemplified in curses. In order to understand better the phenomenon of cursing in Kyzyl it is important to explore what shamanic practice in Tuva implies. However, rather than approaching it from the stance of a comprehensive theory, it is important to look at what shamans actually do rather than what shamanism *is* or *is not* about.

After the collapse of the Soviet Union, the status of Tuvan shamanism shifted significantly from a peripheral practice (in pre-Soviet times) and a forbidden practice (during the Soviet times) to a central network of support in all sorts of matters ranging from quick divination to assistance in legal actions (see also Zorbas 2013, 2021). The extremely challenging living conditions in Kyzyl, which unfolded after the demise of the Soviet Union, triggered a strong demand for shamanic work; this ultimately led to its concentration in the capital. At the same time, as among other indigenous communities shamanism quickly became a political tool in the attempts to re-establish political and ethnic autonomy (Balzer 2002, 2005; Lindquist 2005; Vitebsky 2003). Shortly after the end of the Soviet Union, shamanism, along with Russian Orthodoxy and Buddhism, was declared a 'traditional confession' by the Republic of Tuva. This process was officially initiated by a group of Kyzylian intellectuals and was considered a key argument in their quest for the international recognition of local cultural heritage. This new status of shamans led to the further institutionalisation of shamanic practice in the form of

The artisans of curses 51

shamanic societies, and quickly transformed shamanism not only into a religious category but also into an intellectual virtue and a vibrant subject of academic and political debate (Pimienova 2013; Stepanoff 2004).

Over time, shamanic societies have become a stable source of income in a difficult economic environment and have begun to constitute an easily accessible reflection of the 'exotic' past, cherished by tourists but resented by Tuvans. Today, nearly 30 years after the end of the Soviet Union, shamanic practice in Kyzyl represents a scene of complex tensions with a few remaining shamanic societies, a discreet network of individual shamans and a rich group of all sorts of practitioners offering a variety of practices, including divination, curse infliction and job security rituals. The efficacy of the shamans' work in the capital is deeply permeated by suspicion and doubt (I discuss this point further in Chapter 6). The intensified distrust towards shamans in the post-Soviet context has been present in other parts of Inner Asia. Buyandelgeriyn (2007) and Pedersen (2011) point to how shamanic practice, while seemingly expected to fulfil explanatory functions in response to the post-Soviet turmoil, instead intensifies and reproduces the feelings of uncertainty and doubt triggered by a changing sociopolitcal and economic landscapes. Similar process conveys, to a certain extent, in Tuva. What makes, however, the Tuvan shamanic scene particularly unique is the multivalent and often highly controversial character of shamanic practice. It is a remarkable phenomenon for its blended overlays of shamanic skills offered by highly controversial shamanic societies, individual shamans and adepts of neoshamanism, with shamanism itself considered as an official confession. This, combined with historical endurance and a high concentration of shamans in the capital, situates Tuvan shamanic practice in a distinct position within the wider Siberian and Inner Asian contexts. I shall unpack this complexified landscape by turning first, in this chapter, to a discussion of shamanic practice as presented and experienced by Shaman Hovalygmaa in order to begin to attend subsequently to questions of turbulence and sound as pertinent to Tuvan curses.

Living with spirits

In Kyzyl, there is a strong division between real (*shyn*) and fake (*shyn eves*) shamans. Information about those shamans considered as authentic[2] is carefully kept away from strangers and shared through the means of *sarafanowoje radio*, that is, 'Chinese Whispers'. In short, news about reliable practitioners is discreetly spread in the corridors at different work places, between neighbours or between family and friends. Pieces of information are carefully given away, always in a lowered tone of voice and preferably in an isolated spot or through short, partially encrypted text messages. Trusted shamans work and live as if in the background of the city and do not particularly enjoy socialising. So was Shaman Hovalygmaa through whose stories the intricacies of Tuvan cosmology centred on cursing practices will be now unfolded.

During one of our first English lessons, Hovalygmaa decided we should visit her home. After a long journey to the outskirts of the city, we finally arrived at

52   *The artisans of curses*

a small wooden house hidden behind a blue fence. As we sat for a while in the small garden Hovalygmaa lit a cigarette. 'Look, this is the spirit of this garden, she is walking around us, right there is her *ovaa*[3]', she pointed to a small pile of stones. 'Then, there is a fire spirit, he sits on a stove in there', she pointed again towards a small cabin opposite the main house. We passed by a small corridor where Hovalygmaa's father greeted me with a deep bow. Then, he sat down and continued to watch the news on a big TV screen as we quietly moved to the kitchen. I chose the first chair available, but Hovalygmaa corrected me instantly truly bewildered by my obvious ignorance: 'The spirits are sitting at the table; you are in their spot right now'. I moved away quickly while trying to, to no avail, notice any signs of the spirits' presence. After tea with salt and milk followed by some biscuits we went to Hovalygmaa's room, which she shared with her sister. At the top of each bed sat a massive drum in a military bag. On the walls hung different *eerens* (tokens and instruments used in the rituals). Hovalygmaa started to describe different elements of the room: 'This is a hat that I always wear when removing curses, these are my protecting *eerens* and these are for the battles with spirits'. She pointed to a small orange piece of material. 'Do you know what that is? It is a dragon. What can he do? I can kill you with it right now', she smiled. The rest of the room was covered with cosmetics, books and jewellery. We opened the English course book and began revising the alphabet. Hovalygmaa laughed and made comments about the irritating, in her view, sounds in the English language. I could not help but think that here I was, surrounded by a number of powerful *eerens* and hats used for cursing, with this terrifying orange dragon observing me, while spirits were feasting in the kitchen and walking through the garden. And all of this, as Hovalygmaa's father was watching television and the shaman and I were practising how to say 'how are you' in English. I looked at my friend and she only smiled at me possibly reading my confused thoughts.

In Tuva, the realms of humans and non-humans are perpetually entangled and often impossible to discern from one another. As such, they produce the form of a horizontal landscape, rather than a vertical and multilayered cosmology characteristic of the shamanic structuring of the cosmos. For Tuvans, interactions with spirits are not conceptualised through clear-cut differentiations between the realm of spirits and the realm of mundane, everyday life. Instead, spirits are expected to wander around streets and gardens as well as live with people in their houses. They also inhabit the landscape as spirits of locality or masters of places (*ezzi*). All spirits are said to have their own personalities, desires and needs while actively participating in diverse processes, ranging from travelling and cooking to partaking in the development of personhood. Relationships with spirits are described as a part of everyday habits, complicating the ideas about 'the supernatural' and 'the mundane' worlds as discrete and isolated. For example, people always greet and feed masters of places at *ovaa* when travelling or when passing a tree (*bay yjash*) or a spring (*arzaan*) where spirits reside. It is also common to leave food for spirits in flats and houses. However, these practices, although implying recognition of spirits and a form of respect, are neither considered symbolic nor ascribed exclusively to the domain of 'the sacred' as opposed to 'the profane'. Instead, they are simply part of the fabric of everyday life.

The spontaneous encounters with spirits can be further achieved by, for instance, performing songs and music while travelling through the steppe. People might also momentarily confront spirits during the rituals or notice shadows of spirits following them in their daily tasks. These ongoing interactions are usually articulated in the context of wider relationships with the surrounding landscape. This, in turn, is often defined by Tuvans through the idiom of 'feeling the place' (*eskeril horrur*) or 'living' it (*amydyraar*) by means of smell (*chyt*), sight (*kööry*) and sound (*daash*). Spontaneous communication with spirits is sometimes described as 'having a third eye' (*ysh ataj*), but most commonly it is referred to as *bürülbaazyn*, which my interlocutors would translate into Russian as 'the invisible' (Rus. *newidimoje*). The word *bürülbaazyn* indicates that a given person can see and hear things which usually cannot be seen or heard.[4] *Bürülbaazyn* constitutes a distinct technique of knowing which pertains to laymen and shamans alike; however, most likely due to a stigma surrounding the realm of spirits instigated during Soviet times, today it remains cultivated only by the latter and is deeply feared by the former. Conceptualisations of shamanic practice as contingent on a distinct skill which pertains to shamans and laypeople is not exclusive to Tuva and prevails in other ethnographic contexts in Siberia, for example, in relation to an artistic performance (Lavrillier 2012) or hunting practices (Willerslev 2007). Lavrillier (2012: 115) describes *onnir*, a spirit charge omnipresent in the background of everyday life among Evenki. *Onnir* illuminates a specific capacity that every human is bound to have in themselves and exercises or 'plays' with through singing, drawing or shamanising in order to perform ritual actions. The difference between a shaman and a layman lies in the degree with which *onnir* is exercised. Similarly, while challenging depictions of 'shamanism' as a system of beliefs, Willerslev (2007: 120) refers to the transformation of perspectives in hunting between the predator and prey. He argues that it is an activity or a technique that both hunters and shamans can master. Like with *onnir*, what differentiates the shaman and the hunter is the degree or intensity with which they execute this technique. In Tuvan shamanism, the ability to practise and, thus, master *bürülbaazyn* is inherited through blood, whereas the ability to communicate with spirits and gain access beyond the 'empirical' realm is something that might spontaneously happen to anyone towards whom spirits are particularly inclined. Shamans have the capacity to control spirits as well as actively engage and negotiate with them, whereas non-shamans remain rather static receptors of particular visions. The older generations of Tuvans often argue that the arrival of the Soviets, followed by the rapid development of technology, somehow muted Tuvans' 'abilities' to interact with spirits and to intuitively know things (see also Chapter 6). Moreover, some people fear the spontaneous encounters with spirits and consider them as a potential sign of misfortune. As a result, many Tuvans prefer to have their 'third eye' shut or undergo cleansing rituals in order to transfer their skills to shamans. Very often these abilities are described in terms of a burden that people do not want to carry as well as a possible threat of being sent to a psychiatric hospital.

54   *The artisans of curses*

Given this, in Kyzyl today it is mainly the shamans who cultivate and master the skill of *bürülbaazyn*.

The concept of *bürülbaazyn* also has particular implications for how knowledge can be produced, including knowledge acquired and distributed by the shamans during the rituals. Once the shaman sees a cursed person, the image they have received offers access to a complex cosmological setting, multifarious and dynamic, rather than a flat, one-dimensional representation of the world (Espirito Santo 2012). Thus seeing and hearing 'beyond' may be perceived as being similar to what Ingold (2011) refers to as wayfaring, that is, integrating knowledge through continuously moving from one place to another rather than through the point-to-point data collection. In this way, shamanic practice represents 'an ensemble of techniques for knowing rather than a system of facts known' (Townsley 1993: 452). Knowledge obtained through the means of *bürülbaazyn* evades any formal codifications, such as in the form of a text. It is, for example, very common for shamans to forget the content of the chants they sing and, perhaps conveniently, claim that information they often receive from the spirits evaporates soon after the ritual. Thus, knowledge generated by shamans during the rituals is intrinsically ephemeral in a sense that it can disappear or escape and, as such, it is a form of knowledge in motion.

These diverse ways of interacting with spirits pertaining to laymen and shamans alike have particular implications for the ways cosmology in Tuva is conceptualised and described. When asked directly, shamans in Tuva have a clear, intellectualised construct of a cosmological system, confluent with classic descriptions of shamanic cosmologies (Eliade 1972). The Tuvan cosmos is said to be split into nine cosmic subzones (*tos orannar*) organised further into three cosmic zones of the upper world (*deer oran*), the middle world (*ortaa oran*) and the underworld (*aldyn oran*). The upper worlds are populated by the dwellers of the Sky and the god *Kurbustu*. The middle world is the one where the blood is flowing and where humans live. It is governed by the god *Cher – Hajrakan*. Finally, in the underworld resides the god *Erlik Han* and the goddess *Alash Kadyn*, who are described as a powerful tsar and tsarina rather than deities. Nevertheless, both shamans and laypeople refer to the places where spirits live or come from using the word *oran* or, in Russian, *strana*, which both translate as 'country' rather than 'world'. Moreover, when talking about non-humans, Tuvans resort to the aforementioned adjectives of (in)visibility or talk about things that are 'eternal' (*mönge*) or 'everyday' (*hyn-byry*), rather than differentiate between 'the supernatural' and 'the human' worlds. Given this, interactions between humans and non-humans are arranged within a distinct landscape composed of diverse 'domains' (Pedersen & Willerslev 2010: 265) pertaining to non-humans and humans, rather than organised in an abstract structure of a multilayered and vertical cosmology composed of discrete and separate worlds. However, this is not to argue that the Tuvan world constitutes a homogenous whole or a totalising structure where different elements come together to produce one overarching whole. In a similar manner, the relationships between Tuvan spirits and humans are continuously fragile, heterogeneous and permeated by fractions and turbulences prevailing in, for example, the phenomenon of curse. Given this, shamans constitute central personas in the process of (un)folding the sociocosmic politics deeply pervaded by conflicts, breaks and gaps. In short, it is they, to echo Pedersen & Willerslev (2010: 314), who engage in a variety of 'holistic practices' balancing the domains of humans and spirits while confronting and provisionally (re)arranging the world the way people imagine it fits. A lack of clear-cut differentiation between the world of humans and the world of the supernatural, as artificial as it may appear, bears particular implications for the perceptions of shamanic practice in Tuva. Given the integrity of spirits to the production of everyday life, shamanic practice in the Tuvan ethnographic context is considered a mundane activity; the one which was often described to me in the Russian language as 'housekeeping' (Rus. *uborka doma*).[5]

Shamanic practice as housekeeping

Hovalygmaa and I spent a lot of time during our interviews in her garden on the outskirts of Kyzyl, where she shared her shamanic wisdom while smoking cigarettes. During one of these interviews, we were talking about the implications of being a shaman in the city when I asked her what shamanising meant to her. She looked at me and said firmly, in Russian, 'shamanism is like housekeeping' (*shamanism eto prosto kak uborka doma*). In short, shamans are perceived as active participants in the fabric of everyday happenings, the executors of particular kinds of social actions rather than practitioners performing in distant spiritual plateaus. At the beginning of my research, I struggled to establish how my Tuvan friends understood the connection between shamanic practice, Buddhism and influences from the Orthodox Church. Given the political attempts at transforming shamanising in Tuva into a 'traditional confession' as well as considering the significant role of Tuvan shamans in the processes of 'cultural revivalism' right after the collapse of the Soviet Union, I was expecting to find clear-cut definitions of what shamanic practice meant to people in Kyzyl today. The concept of shamanism as a religion, however, was often met with consternation and surprise among my interviewees. Religious context was primarily associated with Buddhism, which was perceived as an ideology as well as a form of moral philosophy. Shamans, on the other hand, were described as craftsmen, dealing with everyday problems and meandering in the mundanity of people's lives. Whilst Buddhist monks were associated with prayers and teachings, descriptions of shamanic practice included, among others, references to fear, something that resides in blood, that has existed in Tuva for centuries, that has to be lived and could provide knowledge from the ancestors. How does this relate to Hovalygmaa's comment about housekeeping? Given the fact that curses are meant to accumulate in people in the form of dirt (*hir*), they are often associated with pollution, which requires regular cleansing and constitutes an intrinsic element of an annual routine performed by Tuvans, especially towards the end of the year. During this time, shamans are invited to conduct particular cleansing rituals (*aryglaashkyn*) which are understood as a form of cleaning exercise (see Figure 2.1). These practices are described as a set of mundane tasks and are often followed by throwing away old furniture and

56 The artisans of curses

Figure 2.1 The shaman assessing the amount of pollution and preparing for the cleansing practice

clothes. The shamans are also known and feared for being able to see through people, hear their thoughts as well as recognise the spirits that live in and on the victims of curses. Crucially though, these 'occurrences' are not considered as specific extraordinary visions, but normal observations, which can be compared, for example, to reading a diary or a bus timetable (see also Sneath 2009). Such understanding of shamanic practice generates among Tuvans regular comparisons to housekeeping. How then does one become a shaman in Tuva? In the next section, while unfolding further my experiences with Hovalygmaa, I turn to different aspects of becoming and being a shaman, such as initiation and training as well as the social life of shamans in Kyzyl today.

Becoming a shaman

When I began to get to know Hovalygmaa she was very reluctant to talk about how she became a shaman (*ham*). Even though she considered her calling a 'gift' (*belek*) from spirits, she often referred to it as a burden and, given the historical context, a dangerous occupation. Her fears about the future of shamanic practice in Tuva often precipitated through our conversations. Perhaps, driven by the concerns about how much of what Tuvan shamans experience will be remembered, Hovalygmaa eventually agreed to discuss her own path to becoming a shaman.

Tuvan shamans can be male or female cognatic descendants of shamans, although it is impossible to predict which descendant will become the shaman (Stepanoff 2015). Ability to shamanise prevails usually from an early stage when children begin to see spirits playing, wandering or talking to them. Interestingly,

The artisans of curses 57

the shamanic skill is also recognised by having a piercing stare or, for example, when children show no fear of the shaman and find the sounds of the drum and shamanic instruments particularly entertaining and joyful (see also Chapter 5). Numerous features of shamanic practice in Tuva, such as initiation, education and inheritance of shamanic powers, echo the elements of shamanic practices described in the canonical studies of shamanism in other cultural contexts of the world (Eliade 1972). Shamanic initiation begins with a sudden loss of mind, coma or tormenting disease triggered by a vision of a spirit. The process of initiation, which involves physical changes in the shaman's body, is what most explicitly separates shamans from people who can spontaneously 'see more' (*köörgulur*). Shamans in Tuva can have various bodily features that differ from those of non-shamans. My friend suffered from the rare heart condition, which made her heart 20 percent bigger than the heart of an average human. This was directly associated with the process of initiation, during which the spirits prepare the shamans and their bodies to handle the advanced levels of engagement and negotiations with spirits and gods. According to Hovalygmaa, in this way the spirits equip shamans to gain access to things that otherwise drive people mad, which, to some extent, resonates with definitions of mental illness as an excess of uncontrolled spiritual ability generating chaos in a place of information (Espirito Santo 2012: 264).

Tuvan shamans often undergo the education process in dreams when their soul splits and travels between different realms while studying with spirits and deities. Education is then completed by following and learning from a more experienced shaman. Shamans in Tuva often stress that you become a 'real' (*jozulug*) shaman only once you are able to pass a final test in which you overcome your own ego. Although shamanic calling is mandatory, future shamans often attempt to change it. Hovalygmaa tried to 'escape' her fate by converting to different religions. She was first baptised, then became a Muslim. Despite all her efforts, the spirits would continue to torment her making her sick for many months until she finally gave in to her calling. She was about to become a very powerful shaman, and the spirits were very persistent in forcing her to follow her fate.

The strength and abilities of the shamans depend on whether they are classified as earth, sky, white or black shamans, a distinction that is contingent on the origins of shamans' *sünezin* ('soul') as well as the training they receive from the spirits. Earth shamans (*deer-danger ham*) are supposed to be fast like lightening. Their strength always comes to them immediately. When they conduct rituals they can do things, as Hovalygmaa put it, 'right there, right now'. The summoned spirits arrive in front of them swiftly. It is easier for them to live an everyday 'earthy' life than for the sky shamans. They 'fit better', as they experience emotions in a similar way to laypeople. For example, they can 'be in love' and 'get on' with other people, as well as be warmer, more empathetic and enjoy sexual intimacies more fully than sky shamans. Conversely, sky shamans (*deer kurbustu*) work in stages. They are much slower. If an earth shaman were to decide to invite a sky shaman for a duel, the latter would lose, as their power would come too late. Sky shamans are colder and more withdrawn from the social interactions of everyday

58 *The artisans of curses*

life. However, they are described as the experts in bestowing good fortune on people. Only a sky shaman can help *sünezin* during the trip among the realms after death and negotiate the length of the next life with the spirits and gods.

Despite her gratefulness for becoming a shaman, Hovalygmaa often spoke of shamanising as a form of a social struggle. 'Shamans are lonely, you serve the community, you rarely have anything for yourself', she explained. 'Also, what if Soviet times happen again? We do not want to be reborn then as shamans'. During my stay in Kyzyl, I was particularly intrigued by the social life of the shaman. Even though they were considered people of the highest authority, they were also widely feared, which limited their opportunities for social interactions. I was particularly struck by my friend's uneasiness when I asked her to come with me to a nearby coffee shop. Hovalygmaa and I usually met in her house or in one of the rooms of the Cultural Centre. She did not enjoy being seen in public and always insisted on having our meetings in rather discreet places. 'Shamans do not go for coffees. We do our work and spend the rest of the time at home', she noted once. However, one particular day we struggled to find free space and I managed to convince my friend to take a walk through the streets. As we were passing by the shops along the main street, I noticed her increasing lack of confidence and a sort of anxiety. People who recognised her were crossing over and Hovalygmaa urged me to find a free coffee shop. Once we got inside, the owner gave us a suspicious look. We sat in a corner and tried to talk. Suddenly, Hovalygmaa stood up after 15 minutes and asked to leave. After this incident, I realised the extent to which the unexpected presence of a shaman may trigger uneasiness for both the shaman and the client. It is common for people to talk about shamans anxiously as those who deal with mysterious powers, whose actions can be ambiguous and whose path should not be crossed. Shamans are also very familiar with a lot of intimate stories and possess knowledge of secrets and struggles of many people. Encountering them in the streets therefore often can make former and current clients uncomfortable.

Indeed, even though shamanic practice is commonly associated with cure and the establishment of order, shamans are deeply ambiguous personas, both feared and admired. Very often I was warned against shamans and their ambiguous skills, their tendencies to make jokes as well as to trick people and 'steal' their energies or inflict particular maladies on them. This intrinsic ambiguity of shamanic practice has particular implications for the understanding of the mechanics of cursing as well as the wider dynamics within Tuvan cosmology, and dovetails with the conceptualisations of life as perpetually fragmented, fragile and unstable. To this end, in what follows, I explore how cursing, described often in anthropological studies as 'dark shamanism' (Whitehead & Wright 2004), in the ethnographic context of Tuva remains an intrinsic element of the overall sociocosmological ideas, rather than constituting an obvious ethical choice or moral descriptor.

Shamanic practice: an intrinsic ambiguity

Shamanic practices are very often conceptualised through their diverse healing functions as a vital service to the community. Nonetheless, the shamans' work

The artisans of curses 59

goes well beyond the positive, therapeutic and socially integrative dimensions, and the shamans have a dual capacity to both kill and cure. In the ethnographic context of Tuva, shamanising thrives on an ambivalence that pertains to both shamans and spirits alike. However, the curing and killing abilities remain in a complementary rather than an antagonistic realignment. In other words, the same set of practices that can heal the client is also employed in order to inflict curses. In many ethnographic settings, the skills to cure and kill are differentiated and looked at through a prism of strict dichotomies, such as darkness and lightness (see, for example, Strathern & Stewart 2016; Wright 2004), or defined as horizontal versus vertical shamanic practice (Hugh-Jones 1996). Power to inflict harm might be associated with shamans' inability to exercise self-control and master emotions and aggressive desires (Hugh-Jones 1996). It can also stem from an excess of agency resulting from being overtaken by the perspectives of spirits and animals, that is, a transformational process which is associated with witchcraft (High 2012). However, the capacity to kill is used only in exceptional circumstances given the assumption that any harm done will be reciprocated. The Tuvan shamanic practice brings into the orbit of attention the complexity with which shamanic skills are employed, while also showing how some of the clear-cut classifications of shamanic powers (such as black and white shamanism) might occlude what actually takes place during the rituals. This becomes clearer when we look at some of the important ethnographic confluences between Siberian and Amerindian shamanism. As Fausto (2004) suggests, what prevails in Western thinking is a desire for moral standards, based on the assumption that there must be 'good and bad, both a light and a dark side and a clear-cut frontier in order to demarcate a basic contrast of ethic' (2004: 172). He argues that there are no such dichotomies in South American shamanism, and neither are there in Siberian shamanic practice. Indeed, similar arguments prevail in both classic and more recent studies of Siberian shamanism. The meaning of the categories of 'blackness' and 'whiteness' as associated with harming and curing powers, respectively, is discussed thoroughly by Eliade (1972: 186). While describing the characteristics of Altai shamans, he argues that classifying shamanic practices within the categories of black and white shamans is, in fact, merely a practical organisation of different powers deprived of any discrete associations with harming or curing abilities. Echoing Eliade, in her ethnographic accounts, Swancutt (2008: 851) mentions how the Buryats make a basic distinction between black shamans, who invoke the spirits of deceased black shamans or the sky shamans, and white shamans, who invoke the Buddhist deities or the spirits of deceased white shamans without ascribing the particular harming skills to any of the categories. Similarly, Kara and Kunkovacs (2014) illuminate how in the Altai region the Telengit people turn to black shamans in order to be cured from serious, and especially mental, diseases rather than directly associating black shamanising with 'black magic', in other words, harm. In Tuva, the integration of the ambiguity of shamanic skills remains essential to the understandings of the efficacy of shamanic practice overall and spiritual and cosmological ideas in general. Given this, shamanic practice is about acting upon the world through cure, but also through the ability to curse,

60   *The artisans of curses*

disturb and kill. To echo Atkinson (1992), Tuvan shamans' work is, therefore, about both establishing and disrupting order, that is, 'their assertions of control through rhetoric of order are as significant as their flirtations witch chaos and anarchy' (1996: 319). This complexity is vivid in a classification of shamanic skills. In what follows, I will show how the abilities to inflict and deflect curses are not directly associated with any discrete categories of shamans, for instance, 'black' (*kara*) or 'white' (*ak*), and these categories do not impose, at the same time, any immediate ethical considerations. Instead, Tuvan taxonomy of shamans illuminates how the ideas of 'black', 'white' and 'evil' (*aza*) can bear first and foremost ontic rather than mere moral implications (Pocock 1983).[6]

As mentioned earlier, shamans in Tuva can be described as earth or sky. In addition to these, they can be also classified as black and white, leading to different combinations between the four groups. In this way, Hovalygmaa is a black and sky shaman, her brother Lodoj belongs to black and earth shamans whilst her sister, Olchejma, is a white and sky shaman. In essence, cursing is not associated in particular with any of these categories. There are some distinctions, however, in the way laypeople and shamans describe the differences between black and white shamans. Among Kyzylians, black shamans are associated with the whole machinery of cursing, which involves not only the infliction of curses but also deflection and protection. White shamans are often meant to be the ones who are working with the dead, who are concerned with astrology and good fortune. The distinction between whiteness and blackness tends to be associated further with Buddhist lamas and shamans, presenting the former as from the 'white pole' (Rus. *belyj poljus*) and the latter from 'the dark pole' (Rus. *chjornyj poljus*). The category of 'blackness' is often used to explain or conceal what is not known, what is mysterious and thus causing fear or what should not be revealed. Conversely, the shamans offer a very clear definition of the roles of black and white shamans. In short, black shamans (*kara hamnar*) are the ones who are expected to be experts in detecting, inflicting and deflecting curses. Moreover, black shamans have exclusive powers to conduct negotiations with *Erlik*, the spirits of the underworld who often need to be tamed and encouraged to provide help and protection for people. Black shamans always suffer and sweat when singing *algysh*, the shamanic chants, which last at least 20 minutes and are accompanied by regular drumming. They also sing their *algysh* in deep strong tones and their faces look older and worn out at the end of the ritual. Their shamanic coats are heavy and challenging to wear in the heat. Finally, it is harder for black shamans to give people good luck (*aac-kezzik*). In Tuvan cosmology, there are nine 'layers' of good luck that shamans can provide. The basic ones include family, a place to live, good health and food. Another three are concerned with careers, money and general prosperity. The final two are, as described by Hovalygmaa, the 'extra credits' that can be taken onto the next life. Black shamans can provide only seven of these layers. All nine of them can only be offered by white shamans (*ak hamnar*). White shamans can also cast and inflict curses; however, their expertise lies in conducting the death rituals of 7 and 49 days, assisting *sünezin* in their trips between different realms and negotiating the length of the following lives.[7] Finally, only a white shaman can guarantee that *sünezin* will be reborn as a human in the next life. Unlike black shamans, white shamans have lighter coats and their voices are softer. While conducting rituals, they appear to be less tired and drum effortlessly. Thus, although black and white shamans do have particular characteristics, their powers are not easily differentiated according to the abilities to curse and cure. Similar ambiguity prevails among the spirits, who can simultaneously carry curses and harm people as well as provide help and assistance in particular contexts.

The pantheon of deities and spirits in Tuva includes gods who are not expected to interfere with people's existence. It simultaneously involves spirits and masters of places who are constantly entangled in people's everyday lives. As discussed in Chapter 1, there are particular groups of spirits who are responsible for spreading curses on behalf of the shamans and at the request of an inflictor. These spirits, along with others, belong to the group of *aza* spirits, which can be translated as 'evil'; nonetheless, this does not necessarily imply merely harmful intentions and skills. In order to fully grasp the characteristics of Tuvan spirits, it is essential to illuminate the ways in which their actions are being described. Indeed, their doings are never defined as causing suffering due to harmful desires. Rather, spirits' actions occur as a result of them having a concrete 'job' (*azjyl*) to 'disturb' (*üreer*) people. Subsequently, shamans constantly stress the fact that all spirits require respect and should be acknowledged. *Aza* spirits, although expected to provide disturbance, assist shamans and people in particular circumstances. For example, small *Erlik* spirits, who are supposed to create fear in people and prevent them from uncovering secrets, are simultaneously an essential support for the shaman in death rituals. In rare cases of exhumation, *Erlik* are called in order to calm down the 'thoughts and emotions of the deceased' (*sagysh satpaa*), which might be still lingering around the body. *Chetker* spirits responsible for cursing are, concurrently, playing the crucial role of protectors in death rituals. They are the guardians of the household of the deceased and ensure that the living relatives are protected from the *sünezin* of the dead who will try to claim more lives.

The pantheon of *aza* spirits includes further *Dinger* spirits. *Dinger* offer happiness, wealth and love to people; however, they always demand something in return. People who interact with *Dinger* are described later as millionaires in worn out clothes who wander lost and confused and can be seen especially in small villages. They are said to always smell bad, wear only one shoe and never cut their nails. This happens because the clients of *Dinger* often become suddenly rich; however, there is a price to pay for their luck. If *Dinger* spirits offer love instead of money, then people are expected to lose their mind, as this allows the spirits to feed off their energy and happiness. There are also *Albys* and *Shulbus* spirits, who are working with 'what is negative in people' (Rus. *shto plohoje v ljudiah*) and become particularly active in the third part of the day when the red 'bloody' (*hanna*) sun is setting behind the mountains. It is a very dangerous part of the day as, in Tuva, nights 'open everything up' (Rus. *vsjo otkryvajut*). People can be then confronted with *Albys* while accidently keeping their mouths wide open at that particular moment of the day. Ambiguity as a feature prevails not only among *aza* spirits. As discussed earlier in this chapter, the Tuvan landscape is heavily

62 *The artisans of curses*

populated by spirit masters and spirits of locality. Even though they are expected to share good fortune and wealth with humans, they often are described by the shamans as moody and capricious and enjoy joking and tricking people. Their changes in attitude can affect people spending time or living nearby and cause harm or misfortune. According to Hovalygmaa, each spirit of locality can claim three human lives in order to surround themselves with spirit children.

Thus, as I hope to have shown here, abilities to either curse or harm are not associated with the categories of black or white shamanising. Furthermore, ambiguity is deeply embedded not only in shamanic practice but also in the characteristics of spirits. Instead of becoming a form of moral descriptors pointing to what people should or should not do, concepts such as 'black' and 'white' have, to echo Pocock's (1983) discussion on the use of the word 'evil', more of ontic implications, differentiating what things are and what they are not. In this way, rather than being merely understood within the framework of ethics, cursing and ambiguity become essential to the overall understanding of spiritual and cosmological ideas in Tuva as well as to the characteristics of sociocosmic interactions.

Having explored some of the complexities of the shamanic landscape, both political and cosmic let us look more closely towards some of the unique features of shamanism in Tuva, including the absence of what is often described in shamanic studies as trance and the importance of sound. Whilst focusing on diverse stages of shamanic practice in the presence of curses, I am going to show how Tuvan shamanic practice constitutes an 'art to exert' (Hamayon 1993: 79), an art which involves seduction, negotiation and trickery achieved through the mastery of sounds and voice. In this way, in the remaining chapters of this book, I present Tuvan shamans as active artisans of curses who become discrete *sonic beings*, rather than 'passive receptacles for spirits' (Atkinson 1992: 317).

The artisans of curses

Sulchuk was a short woman in her early 30s, working for the local government. Like many Kyzylians, she was struggling with job security as well as promotion opportunities. We met for the first time in Hovalygmaa's office, situated in a wooden shed right next to the shaman's house. Inside, there was a large sofa designated for the visitors, a stove and the shaman's chair. Sulchuk, like all clients, called Hovalygmaa's cell phone when she arrived at the gate. She was wearing a white, summery coat, high-heeled shoes and smiled enthusiastically. Hovalygmaa sat on her chair and, as usual, crossed her legs, lit a cigarette and closed her eyes, asking Sulchuk to begin her story. The woman was deeply concerned about her financial future and expressed concerns about her inability to climb the ranks at her job. The shaman opened her eyes and pointed to Sulchuk's stomach saying she could see a lot of mud (*hir*) and that the woman was suffering from a powerful curse. She suggested that Sulchuk should request a cleansing ritual and that they should meet again in a few days. Sulchuk agreed and the shaman dictated a list of items she had to prepare for the ritual. The woman thanked the shaman and offered to pay 300 roubles (approximately 3 pounds) for her advice. A few days later, the shaman and I arrived at Sulchuk's flat, situated in the city centre. Hovalygmaa asked me to carry the drum to the second floor of one of the numerous grey blocks of flats in the street. Sulchuk welcomed us in her kitchen where we found some food on the table. Her daughter played in the room next to us and showed little or no interest in our presence. When the shaman had finished eating, we moved to the living room where I made myself comfortable on the sofa, one of the only two pieces of furniture in the room. The shaman took Sulchuk's fingers and put on them five different threads. Next, she cut the threads and asked Sulchuk to carefully throw them away using special brass claws and wearing a hat turned upside down in order to mislead the spirits. Then, both women took a piece of red material which they cut into strips. 'The spirit is cold and needs to be dressed up', the shaman explained to us. The material was burnt afterwards, and the ashes were thrown away from the balcony. Next, the shaman sat on a chair and began drumming and singing. We stayed in silence as Sulchuk put her hands close to her face as if praying. Halfway through the ritual, the shaman paused and revealed that Sulchuk was, in fact, suffering from five different curses that were inflicted on her by the same woman, an envious colleague. She also informed us that there was a spirit with us in the room, which had been lingering in the flat for days and looking nastily at Sulchuk's daughter. Before Hovalygmaa recommenced drumming and singing, she asked us to concentrate on our wishes. Then, she resumed singing while still sitting on the chair. The shaman's voice was ranging from loud howls to gentle humming, and after another ten minutes she collapsed exhausted onto the sofa. Much to my surprise, the shaman did not seem to lose consciousness, fall on the floor or make any gestures that would suggest changes in her physical and psychic state and thus indicate she was in trance. Instead, Hovalygmaa simply concluded the ritual by telling Sulchuk how to protect herself and avoid further curses. She also confirmed that the spirits inflicting curses on behalf of Sulchuk's colleague were particularly nasty and did not want to leave. Sulchuk listened carefully and finally bowed deeply and offered the shaman 3000 roubles (approximately 30 pounds). After we left, I asked the shaman about what had happened during the ritual and why she did not look as if she was travelling to different realms and being in trance. The shaman gave me a clearly irritated look: 'We do not roll on the ground like crazy, this is the show for the tourists', she scolded me delicately. What does it mean then, when Tuvan shamans claim they never fall into trance during the rituals?

In Tuva, the quality of being a shaman is something that is hidden within the body with particular powers being ascribed to the shaman's voice. Unlike other ethnographic contexts in Siberia and Inner Asia (Humphrey 2007; Pedersen 2006; Ellis 2015), among Tuvan shamans significantly less attention is given to the role of shamanic costume and diverse tools (with the exception of a drum) as a way to establish contact with spirits or obtaining information. Instead, shamans claim that most of the time they can work without wearing a costume and their divinatory techniques do not necessarily require any instruments, such as cards, fabric threads, stones or bones. An array of procedures, such as those present in Sulchuk's ritual (putting the fabric on the client's fingers, burning the material),

64   *The artisans of curses*

are often considered as complementary rather than mandatory. During a preliminary divinatory meeting, which constitutes the first step in the shaman's work, Tuvan shamans rarely use any classic divination mechanisms, such as readings of cast objects or esoteric texts in order to reveal the causes of cursing. Instead, a client is visible to the shaman in such a way that the shaman can often instantly recognise curses by the presence of pollution or spirits gathered around or in the client's body. Given this, it is the clients themselves, rather than particular objects such as cards or stones, who resemble what Sneath calls 'metonymic fields' (2009). Instead of seeking information by means of material objects during initial divination the shamans are immediately presented with the sought knowledge in the form of visions. The process of obtaining further details regarding the client's condition and offering solutions always takes place during the ritual and remains strictly associated with effectuating power of sounds.[8] During the rituals, however, shamans never claim to be 'possessed' by the spirits and spirits do not try to speak to people whilst using the shamans' bodies. Moreover, rather than undertaking journeys to diverse realms, the shamans invite spirits to the place of the ritual in order to negotiate with them. Negotiations are then conducted by means of diverse sounds that are produced through drums, the shaman's voice and shamanic instruments. This is sometimes accompanied by numerous complementary activities, such as burning different materials used for curse deflections (threads, fabric), sprinkling tea and milk and using smoke from burnt juniper. Through uttering diverse sounds, singing and drumming the shaman invites additional spirits to arrive or reveal themselves at the scene. This gives the shaman the opportunity to establish further sources of harm as, for example, in the case when the shaman noticed a spirit angrily watching Sulchuk's daughter. It is also the main way through which shamans can undertake negotiations with spirits and inflict or deflect curses. The effectuating power of sounds that shamans employ in the rituals transforms them, then, into distinct sonic beings who report on and confront spirits while being submerged into the landscape of musical sounds, sounds within words and semi-linguistics expressions, such as gasps and screams. Thus, sounds in the ethnographic context of Tuva become a central vehicle of the shaman's power (Townsley 1993: 449) and a key technique of shamanic practice. This, however, does not fully explain why Tuvan shamans do not 'fall into trance'.

In classic approaches to shamanic practice, techniques of shamanising have been described in terms of possession, as incarnation of spirits or as ecstatic and mystic journeys to the Under and the Upperworld (see, among others, de Heusch 1981; Eliade 1972). Establishing communication with non-humans has been comprehended as contingent on falling into trance, which includes trips to other worlds interwoven with the ability to invite spirits in order to establish contact with the clients through the shaman's body (Humphrey & Onon 1996) while adopting or submitting to the spirit's perspective (Willerslev 2007; Holbraad & Willerslev 2007). These processes are often exemplified in radical alternations in the states of consciousness. By contrast, as I have mentioned earlier, shamans in Tuva never talk about travelling to the places where spirits reside. Moreover, the clients do not interact with spirits directly through the mediumistic body of the shaman. Instead, if the shaman's work is particularly efficient (which depends on the efficacy with which the shaman produces sounds), the clients might physically experience the spirits' presence in the form of a cold wind, distant murmur or a fragmented image or an abrupt touch (I discuss this process thoroughly in Chapter 5). In addition, shamans do not lose consciousness or exhibit the typical features of falling into trance, such as speaking odd languages, falling on the ground or rolling their eyes. Nevertheless, they retain their role as mediators between humans and non-humans and have access to the realms which lay beyond the perception of laymen. How can we then analytically grasp what occurs during the ritual without dismissing the shamans' rejections of trance as an intrinsic method of shamanising?

The use of the terms 'mediumship' and 'trance' triggers specific descriptive and analytical problems, often echoed in the comments made by my interlocutors when confronted about diverse techniques of shamanising. Unquestionably, the shamans in Tuva do mediate between clients and spirits whilst engaging in interactions that exceed the cognitive experiences of non-shamans. As discussed by Hamayon, however, the word 'trance' is often absent from indigenous languages due to its Latin roots: *transire* means 'to die, to go beyond, to pass from one state to another' (1993: 21). Following on from that, Hamayon challenges the applicability of terms, such as 'trance' and 'ecstasy', in her analysis of shamanism. Instead, she argues that rather than with a system of representation in which every gesture and movement that shamans perform points to a concrete psychic or physical state, the shaman's behaviour during the rituals is commonly associated with active forms of producing relationships with spirits. Moreover, as stated in other works (Lewis 1971; Tsintjilonis 2006), there are a variety of afflictions which include trance, yet do not involve any alternations in the physical or mental states of the person affected. These points do apply to the Tuvan context. There is no word for trance, spirit possession or mediumship in the Tuvan language, and Tuvans often object to such interpretations, taking some of them even as a slight offence. Relations with spirits do not conform to trance, revelation or moments of ecstasy – that is, they are not exceptional in this sense. Instead, as mentioned earlier, the shamans undertake lengthy and often dramatic negotiations, conducted primarily through the means of sounds. These sounds both irritate and excite the spirits while forcing them to give in to the shamans' requests. However, their responses and willingness to work with the shamans are primarily contingent on how the shamans can manage this soundly diversified landscape and adjust their voice. Such techniques echo, for example, Amerindian shamanic practices, where shamans can heal their patients through songs as the spirits are attracted by the aesthetics of the music (see Gow 1996; Hugh-Jones 1996), or when songs become distinct shamanic paths (Townsley 1993). Nevertheless, there is no sense of 'other-becoming' among the shamans in Tuva, understood as the appropriation of the spirits' perspectives as in the context of Amazonia (Viveiros de Castro 1998) or spirit possession as in Southeast Asian shamanism (Arhem 2016). In a rather different way, the shamans in Tuva never allow the spirit to overtake their bodies and use it as a vessel. Sudden physical

66 *The artisans of curses*

movements intended to represent the instances of trance or spirit possession, such as falling on the ground or spitting, are immediately dismissed by shamans, and ordinary people perceive them as a part of 'shamanshow' aimed at financial profit making. In fact, such incidents often become part of anecdotes that circulate in Kyzyl among shamans and their clients. For example, Hovalygmaa once described to me how she felt shocked by the work of the shaman and chairman of one of the shamanic societies, who was performing a ritual for a big group of tourists from the West.

> I observed him rolling on the floor and spitting all over his mouth. The audience was impressed; I could not help but laugh. After the show, I pulled him back and asked why he was trying to fool those people. Guess what – he tripped and did not want to look unprofessional, so he decided to pretend that he was in trance,

she said with a beaming smile.

As discussed in the case of Sulchuk, Tuvan shamans communicate with spirits, manipulate and trick them through the means of sounds. This communication constitutes an immediate (re)action, an active response situated in a given moment. The shamans constantly modulate and adapt their voice and drumming in order to please or scare the spirits and thus ensure curse removal or infliction. The shaman's actions, centred on the production of sounds, constitute a creative process of voicing into being a fragment of sociocosmic drama that brings together spirits and humans. Real shamans are considered, then, unique artisans of sociocosmic politics and distinct sonic beings rather than passive 'receptacles for spirits' (Atkinson 1992: 317). In this way, shamanic practice in the ethnographic context of Tuva challenges the understanding(s) of shamanising as involving significant and noticeable alternations in the states of consciousness, contributing further to conceptualisations of trance and mediumship in anthropological studies overall.

As discussed in the first two chapters, the mechanics of curses in most cases require the presence of the shaman and the help of spirits. Nevertheless, in order to fully grasp the implications of cursing, it is essential to delineate what happens to the third participant in this drama – the victim of curse infliction – and how he or she experiences these curses. This experience expands and reflects a particular understanding of personhood – a cursed personhood. With this in mind, I focus in the next chapter on the concept of human personhood among Tuvans and discuss how its construction is partially contingent on, and interwoven with, the mechanics of cursing, producing a distinct way of being a (cursed) human.

Notes

1 It is rather unusual to have more than one shaman among a group of siblings.
2 I discuss the ways in which authentic shamanic practice is established and validated in Chapters 5 and 6.
3 A pile of stones where the spirits are meant to reside.

The artisans of curses   67

4 Interestingly, the adjective 'visible' translates as *bürülbaazyn eves*, that is, lacking invisibility, which renders the notion of visibility as somehow deficient or secondary to that of invisibility, rather than the other way round.

5 The concept of housekeeping was introduced along with the Soviet regime; therefore, there is no equivalent for this term in the Tuvan language.

6 I do not suggest here that curse infliction does not bear any consequences and it is a request executed without any considerations of harm and potential revenge. Rather, I hope to have signalled the complexity of shamanic practices and, thus, a need for attention when applying different analytical and ethical categories to the fabric of shamanism.

7 Seven days ritual (*chedi honuk*) takes place a week after one's death and commences *sünezin*'s journey from one life into the next one. Forty-nine days' ritual (*dorten tos honuk*) concludes this process and marks the rebirth of *sünezin* in the new life.

8 Moreover, outside the ritual contexts in which shamans fully rely on the power of sounds, both those produced by the drum and the shaman's voice, interactions with spirits can occur through the means of (in)audible talks accompanied by concrete visions. While spending time with Hovalygmaa, I often noticed when she was unsure of something and, whilst pointing her finger to the sky, how she was in a silent conversation with the spirit in order to obtain information. These forms of interaction would happen on a regular basis, in a taxi, in her garden, during our English classes and especially during our trips to the countryside. Most importantly though, they always occurred in informal contexts or when the shaman required a piece of 'personal' information, for instance, while cooking and completing her recipe.

Bibliography

Arhem, K. 2016. Southeast Asian animism. A Dialogue with Amerindian Perspectivism. In K. Arhem & G. Sprenger (eds), *Animism in Southeast Asia*, 279–301. London and New York: Routledge.

Atkinson, M. J. 1992. Shamanism Today. *Annual Review of Anthropology* no. 21: 307–330.

Balzer, M. M. 2002. Healing Failed Faith? Contemporary Siberian Shamanism. *Anthropology and Humanism* no. 26 (2): 134–149.

Balzer, M. M. 2005. Whose Steeple is Higher? Religious Competition in Siberia. *Religion, State and Society* no. 33 (1): 57–69.

Buyandelgeriyn, M. 2007 Dealing with Uncertainty: Shamans, Marginal Capitalism, and Remaking of History in Postsocialist Mongolia. *American Ethnologist* no. 34 (1): 127–147.

Eliade, M. 1972. *Shamanism: Archaic Techniques of Ecstasy*. London: Routledge & K.Paul.

Ellis, J. 2015. Assembling Contexts. The Making of Political-Academic Potentials in a Shamanic Workshop in Ulaanbaatar. *Inner Asia* no. 17: 52–76.

Espirito Santo, D. 2012. Imagination, Sensation and the Education of Attention Among Cuban Spirit Mediums. *Ethnos* no. 77 (2): 252–271.

Fausto, C. 2004. A Blend of Blood and Tobacco: Shamans and Jaguars among the Parakana of Eastern Amazonia. In N. Whitehead & R. Wright (eds), *In Darkness and Secrecy the Anthropology of Assault Sorcery and Witchcraft in Amazonia*, 157–178. Durham, NC: Duke University Press.

Gow, P. 1996. River People: Shamanism and History in Western Amazonia. In C. Humphrey & N. Thomas (eds), *Shamanism, History, and the State*, 90–114. Ann Arbor: University of Michigan Press.

68   The artisans of curses

Hamayon, N. R. 1993. Are "Trance", "Ecstasy" and Similar Concepts Appropriate in the Study of Shamanism? *Shaman* no. 1 (1–2): 17–39.

Heusch, de L. 1981. *Why Marry Her?: Society and Symbolic Structures*. Cambridge, New York: Cambridge University Press.

High, C. 2012. Shamans, Animals and Enemies: Human and Non-human Agency in an Amazonian Cosmos of Alterity. In M. Brightman, V. E. Grotti, & O. Ulturgasheva (eds), *Animism in Rainforest and Tundra: Personhood, Animals, Plants and Things in Contemporary Amazonia and Siberia*, 130–145. New York; Oxford: Berghahn Press.

Holbraad, M. & Willerslev, R. 2007. Transcendental Perspectivism: Anonymous Viewpoints from Inner Asia. *Inner Asia* no. 9: 329–345.

Hugh-Jones, S. 1996. Shamans, Prophets, Priests and Pastors. In C. Humphrey & N. Thomas (eds), *Shamanism, History, and the State*, 32–75. Ann Arbor: University of MichiganPress.

Humphrey, C. 2007. Inside and Outside the Mirror: Mongolian Shamans' Mirrors as Instruments of Perspectivism. *Inner Asia* no. 9 (2): 173–195.

Humphrey, C. & Onon, U. 1996. *Shamans and Elders: Experience, Knowledge and Power Among the Daur Mongols*. Oxford: Clarendon Press.

Ingold, T. 2011. *Being Alive. Essays on Knowledge, Movement and Description*. New York: Routledge.

Kara, S. & Kunkovacs L. 2014. Black Shamans of the Turkic-Speaking Telengit in Southern Siberia. *Shaman* no. 22 (1–2): 151–161.

Lavrillier, A. 2012. 'Sprit-Charged' Animals in Siberia. In M. Brightman, V. E. Grotti, & O. Ulturgasheva (eds), *Animism in Rainforest and Tundra: Personhood, Animals, Plants and Things in Contemporary Amazonia and Siberia*, 113–129. New York; Oxford: Berghahn Press.

Lewis, I. M. 1971. *Ecstatic Religion*. Charmondsworth: Penguin Press.

Lindquist, G. 2005. Healers, Leaders and Entrepreneurs: Shamanic Revival in Southern Siberia. Culture and Religion. *An Interdisciplinary Journal* no. 6 (2): 263–285.

Pedersen, A. M. 2006. Talismans of thought: shamanist ontologies and extended cognition in northern Mongolia. In A. Henare, M. Holbraad, & S. Wastell (eds), *Thinking Through Things*, 141–166. London: Routledge.

Pedersen, A. M. 2011. *Not Quite Shamans*. Ithaca; London: Cornell University Press.

Pedersen, A. M. & Willerslev, R. 2010. Proportional Holism: Joking the Cosmos into the Right Shape in North Asia. In T. Otto & N. Bubandt (eds), *Experiments in Holism*, 262–278. Chichester, West Sussex; Malden, MA: Willey-Blackwell.

Pimienova, K. 2013. The "Vertical of Shamanic Power": The Use of Political Discourse in post-Soviet Shamanism. *Laboratorium* no. 5 (1): 118–140.

Pocock, D. 1983. Unruly Evil. In D. Parkin (ed.), *The Anthropology of Evil*, 43–56. Oxford: Blackwell.

Sneath, D. 2009. Reading the Signs by Lenin's Light: Development, Divination and Metonymic Fields in Mongolia. *Ethnos* no. 74 (1): 72–90.

Stepanoff, Ch. 2004. Chamanisme et transformation sociale à Touva. *Études mongoles et sibériennes, centrasiatiques et tibétaines* no.35: 155–183.

Stepanoff, Ch. 2015. Transsingularities: The Cognitive Foundations of Shamanism in Northern Asia. *Social Anthropology* no. 23(2): 169–185.

Strathern, J. A. & Stewart, J. P. (Strathern). 2016. Dark and Light Shamanisms: Themes of Conflict, Ambivalence and Healing. In D. Riboli & D. Torri (eds), *Shamanism and Violence. Power, Repression and Suffering in Indigenous Religious Conflicts*, 11–24. London; New York: Routledge.

The artisans of curses   69

Swancutt, K. 2008. The Undead Genealogy: Omnipresence, Spirit Perspectives, and a Case of Mongolian vampirism. *Journal of the Royal Anthropological Institute* no. 14 (4): 843–864.

Townsley, G. 1993. Song Paths The Ways and Means of Yaminahua Shamanic Knowledge. *L'Homme* no. 33 (126–128): 449–468.

Tsintjilonis, D. 2006. Monsters and Caricatures: Spirit Possession in Tana Toraja. *Journal of the Royal Anthropological Institute* no. 12: 551–567.

Vitebsky, P. 2003. From Cosmology to Environmentalism: Shamanism as Local Knowledge in a Global Setting. In G. Harvey (ed.), *Shamanism: A Reader*, 276–298. London: Routledge.

Viveiros de Castro, E. 1998. Cosmological Deixis and Amerindian Perspectivism. *Journal of the Royal Anthropological Institute* no. 4 (3): 469–488.

Whitehead, L. N. & Wright, R. 2004. *In Darkness and Secrecy: The Anthropology of Assault Sorcery and Witchcraft in Amazonia*, 1–19. Durham, NC: Duke University Press.

Willerslev, R. 2007. *Soul Hunters: Hunting, Animism and Personhood Among the Siberian Yukaghiris*. Berkley, Los Angeles, London: University of California Press.

Wright, R. 2004. The Wicked and the Wise Man: Witches and Prophets in the History of the Northwest Amazon. In N. Whitehead & R. Wright (eds), *In Darkness and Secrecy the Anthropology of Assault Sorcery and Witchcraft in Amazonia*, 83–108. Durham, NC: Duke University Press.

Zorbas, K. 2013. Shirokogoroff's "Psychomental Complex" as a Context for Analyzing Shamanic Mediations in Medicine and Law (Tuva, Siberia). *Shaman* no. 26 (1–2): 81–102.

Zorbas, K. 2021. *Shamanic Dialogues with the Invisible Dark in Tuva, Siberia: The Cursed Lives*. Cambridge: Cambridge Scholar Publishing.

3 Cursed person(hood)

When you arrive in Kyzyl, you cannot help but notice two cemeteries: one situated on the hill just on the left side of the gate to the city, and the other in the heart of the capital. The first one is separated from the rest of the territory by a ditch carved into the ground. The other remains cut off from any unwanted observers with a high metal fence. Both of these places were of great interest to me beyond the academic intrigue, especially at the beginning of my fieldwork. Prior to my trip, I had read about notorious conflicts between Russians and Tuvans due to the Russians' tradition of putting photographs of the deceased on their tombstones, a practice which terrified Tuvans and resulted in the repeated destruction of the cemeteries. Filled with adventurous excitement, I encouraged a few of my friends to come with me to visit either of the two places. They welcomed my proposition with horrified expressions and pondered why I would want to do such a thing. Among Tuvans, images, thoughts and encounters with the dead trigger a particular fear. When a person dies there are two essential rituals which are performed in order to allow *sünezin* to be reborn. The first one, seven-day ritual (*chedi honuk*), usually takes place in the garden of the relatives' house. At this time, the deceased is informed by the shaman that he has died and has to prepare for a trip between different realms (those of spirits, gods and also humans) in order to be reborn. After 49 days (*dorten tos honuk*) the second ritual, which is performed in the steppe, takes place. During the ceremony, the shaman completes the journey with *sünezin* and reveals to the relatives where the deceased will be reborn. As the ritual proceeds, the shaman can also reveal stories from the deceased's life, potential secrets (such as love affairs) as well as advice for relatives in their future endeavours. While awaiting the rituals, people employ an array of practices in order to protect themselves from any possible harm from the deceased who might become aggressive and dangerous. While awaiting the seven-day ritual, the relatives' house is continually cleansed with blessed juniper. During the 49-day ritual participants eagerly look for any footprints emerging from the fire's ashes. If the footprints are turned outside, it means *sünezin* has found a new place to be reborn. If they, however, are turned inside, this implies *sünezin* still lingers around and might claim more lives. Getting rid of photographs and belongings of the deceased is another common practice which is intended to offer protection. After

DOI: 10.4324/9781003245391-5

Cursed person(hood) 71

the 49 days' mortuary ritual is performed, the deceased are meant to be forgotten and not spoken about which concludes the process of being reborn into a new life.[1]

While Tuvans offer elaborate accounts of what happens to *sünezin* once a person dies, very little is said about what happens with the body. This led me to wonder about the significance of the bodily physicality and physical presence in Tuva in general. I wanted to know what happens to the body after people die. Surprisingly, most interlocutors would give me a perplexed look and talked about *sünezin* or, when asked about the burial practices, shrugged their shoulders and said, 'we bury them like in the Orthodox Church'. In a similar way, the shamans I worked with, when asked how people die, tended to describe in detail a complex process during which *sünezin* travels to different 'countries' before being reborn after 49 days. When repeatedly questioned about the body, even with the help of my translator, who eventually grasped the essence of my enquiries, the shamans seemed not to understand what it was that I was so keen to know. This initial vagueness that appeared to surround my questions about corporeality and physicality led me to a more thorough engagement with the idea of personhood and the ways people talk about themselves as humans (*kizji*) in Tuva. The notion of personhood in Tuva, often skewing towards the questions of identity, has constituted one of the central themes in the anthropological treatment dedicated to this region. What does it mean to be Tuvan? How should Tuvaness be conceptualised now and how has it changed throughout recent history? Some of these and similar questions have been explored from the vantage point of kinship and clan structure (Vainshtein 1981), ethnic stereotypes (Ballkina 1994), the position of males and females in the family and society, as well as the reconstruction of 'Tuvaness' in the wake of post-Soviet disintegration (Mongush 2006; Pimienova 2009). I was looking for the answer to a slightly different set of questions. What particularly interested me was the ways in which we come to know that we are alive and that we are a human being and not, for example, a spirit. In the previous chapters, I explored the phenomenon of cursing and discussed the characteristics of shamanic practice as central to the mechanics of curse. I would like to focus now on the final element of this tripartite system and discuss firstly, what it means to become a human being as opposed to another kind of persons in Tuvan ontology, such as an animal, plant and spirit. Secondly, I shall discuss how this process is shaped by, and continually intertwines with, instances of cursing, opening up a further question about what it means to have a cursed personhood.

One day, I was observing Hovalygmaa conduct her divination practices in order to detect curses inflicted on one of the secretaries from the University of Kyzyl. It was a hot day, the windows to the shaman's 'office' were wide open and the client was getting impatient, nervously clenching her fingers and looking at the shaman. Hovalygmaa, despite her overwhelming fatigue, sat in her chair and kept on smoking. Suddenly, she opened her mouth and said, 'your *sülde* is very low, you can be cursed. I can see your *sünezin* will leave soon'. The client's face did not change its expression, despite the ominous words of the shaman. She paid Hovalygmaa 200 roubles (approximately 2 pounds), and they agreed on the cleansing ritual. When the woman left I asked the shaman what she meant by

72 Cursed person(hood)

sülde being very low. 'It is simple', she explained calmly, 'In Tuva people have many layers, they look like the rings in the trunk of an old tree'. Expanding on the shaman's comment above, humans in Tuva are said to be constructed from multiple layers organised around a centre – *sünezin* ('soul'), producing thus a distinct concentric structure (I discuss this further under the heading *Like growth rings in the trunk of a tree*). This process emerges from a matrix of complex interactions which reverberate with previous lives whilst being contingent on the characteristics of spirits and the lives of relatives and ancestors. In this way, personhood is equally conceived of in a cosmocentric way, tying together spirits and humans in a relationship of complementarity. Crucial to the structure of personhood are also curses. As I will demonstrate, curses induce 'bodily' changes which engage physical, emotional and cognitive processes, whilst shifting humans from a fragile condition of 'homeostasis' (Cannon 1932: 24) to turbulence. Cursed bodies produce concrete images and physical deformations that are recognised by shamans during the rituals. Applying the analytical lens of cursing practices, brings, therefore, the concepts of 'body' (*et-bot*) and 'soul' (*sünezin*) together in an explicit fashion, allowing for the rethinking of these notions in a way that, firstly, avoids flattening them into bounded, discrete substances, such as spirit and matter, prevailing in the Cartesian concepts of the autonomous 'self' and 'individual', and, secondly, enables us to engage with the particularities of being a human as opposed to other kinds of persons in the ethnographic context of Tuva.

Exploring the materiality of curses, I follow Latour's point concerning bodily existence as 'learning to be affected' (2004: 205). In this way, while discussing the shamans' visions, I approach a (cursed) body not as a 'provisional residence of something superior – an immortal soul, the universal, or thought – but (…) a dynamic trajectory by which we learn to register and become sensitive to what the world is made of' (2004: 206). While concentrating on the bodily images of curses, I do not suggest that the Tuvan concept of personhood is predicated upon the trichotomies of body, mind and soul as these categories do not pervade Tuvan imagery in the form of independent, isolated concepts.[2] Whilst cursed bodies provide concrete images of curses, they do not constitute bodies abstracted from the social situation in which bodily acts are involved (Bird-David 2004). Rather, they are part of the overall evidence of the presence of a cursed person(hood). In other words, curses transform people into a particular stage, upon which complex interactions between humans and non-humans are instantiated and played out. In order to frame my discussion, I turn now to a brief exploration of personhood in the wider context of animistic cosmologies.

Ontological dimensions of being human

In animistic ontologies, humanity constitutes a condition where different species share a kind of universalised subjectivity) and can appear as intentional subjects (Brightman, Grotti & Ulturgasheva 2012). As discussed in the earlier chapters, in Tuva humans and non-humans are able to interact and communicate with each other within an 'intersubjective field of relations' (Arhem 2016a: 5). In other

Cursed person(hood)   73

words, diverse beings, including humans, spirits, animals and insects,[3] have *sünezin* ('soul') that is 'eternal' (*mönge*) and travels through multiple lives, each time acquiring different physicality. Within this system, similar to other animistic cosmologies (see, among others, Pedersen 2001; Viveiros de Castro 1998; Willerslev 2007), body and soul are not understood in terms of essence and appearance, where the latter becomes a vessel for the former. Instead, a prototype of a person is defined by 'a variable outer physical covering and a constant inner being' (Arhem 2016a: 14). This fluid intertwining between 'body' and 'soul' or 'interiority' and 'physicality' (Descola 2013) has particular implications for the ways in which personhood is defined in Tuva and how humans are differentiated from other species.

The cross-cultural diversity of assumptions about animism in Siberian, Amerindian and Southeast Asian context has intrigued many anthropologists (Arhem 2016b; Brightman & Grotti & Ulturgasheva 2012; Humphrey & Pedersen 2007) with numerous debates focusing on the question of personhood (Safonova & Santha 2012; Willerslev & Ulturgasheva 2012) and the notion of perspectivism and its applicability to ontologies outside of Amazonia (Arhem 2016b; Pedersen 2001; Humphrey & Pedersen 2007). For the purpose of my analysis of cursed personhood, and in order to introduce the ontological dimensions of being a human in Tuva as opposed to other kinds of persons, I am going to briefly explore the significance of some of the themes discussed in the aforementioned works. In particular, I would like to focus on the notion of (im)materiality of the soul (Willerslev 2009), the role of karma and fortune (Broz 2007), as well as the implications of certain limitations imposed on inter-species transformations (Broz 2007; Arhem 2016a).

As mentioned earlier, in Tuva *sünezin* constitutes an inalienable aspect of most beings. *Sünezin* is originally a Mongolic term (cf. Classical Mongolian *sunesun*) with which the Turks of Southern Siberia (including the Tuva-Uriankhay group) replaced the word *kut* ('soul'), used initially among all of the Turkic-speaking peoples (Kara & Kunkovacs 2014). Among Tuvans, however, the concept of the soul does not refer to an ontologically discrete, immaterial 'spirit' as opposed to matter as, for instance, in the Christian understanding of the concept. When I asked one of the shamans if she could describe what *sünezin* is like, she provided me with this short description:

> *Sünezin* is like a grain. It has traces from your last life. Then you are planted in the ground, you grow, have branches and leaves, you collect juices from this life. Then, when you die, you shrink and the juices go back to the grain and the traces of it are taken on to the next place, next soil.

Rather than representing an invisible substance, *sünezin* constitutes an entity that can take on different shapes and colours. It can always be recognised by shamans and occasionally be noticed by laymen. It is usually described as a grey cloud or a shadow that moves very quickly, leaving a gust of cold wind behind. Moreover, *sünezin* remains interconnected with other 'soul-like concepts' (Pedersen &

74   Cursed person(hood)

Willerslev 2012) or layers that produce a human in Tuva (I come back to this point in the following section). One of these layers, *sagysh-satpa* ('emotions, dreams'), can under certain circumstances become a physical image of the deceased. In this way, body and soul work as the flip side of each other (Willerslev 2009), challenging any differentiation between spiritual 'essence' and physical 'appearance'. The interchangeability of body and soul conveys in the other ethnographic contexts of Siberia (Ulturgasheva 2016; Willerslev & Ulturgasheva 2012). Close to the Tuvan experiences are Chukchi's understandings of body and soul. Willerslev (2009) shows how Chukchi turn themselves inside out, in that 'inner substance' and 'outward form' cross over, each becoming the other, so that it is impossible to specify which is their body and which their soul. In Tuva, in the instances of sudden death, *sagysh-satpa* separates itself from *sünezin* and lingers in the realm of humans awaiting *sünezin*'s rebirth. If the ritual dedicated to reincarnation of *sünezin* is not conducted properly, for example, due to the shaman's lack of experience, *sagysh-satpa* becomes the body of the deceased, which is then used by spirits, like an envelope, in order to torment and curse the living relatives.

The materiality of *sünezin* and corporeality of *sagysh-satpa* echo further the Amazonian concept of the 'eye-soul' (Taylor 1996) embedded in the notion of reversibility, the essential premise of perspectivism (Viveiros de Castro 1998). This key elaboration on 'humanized nature' (Arhem 2016a: 7) constitutes one of the crucial analytical parameters which allows the process of producing persons and recognising 'the Other' in Amerindian animistic systems to be understood. Perspectivism proposes that all living beings are subjects imbued with a point of view and can take on the viewpoints of others (Viveiros de Castro 1998). Within this system, possessing a soul implies the ability to adopt a point of view whereas having a body, defined as a bundle of capacities, affects and dispositions, facilitates differences between the viewpoints (Viveiros de Castro 1998: 480). While overlapping with numerous traits of perspectivism and personhood in other Siberian contexts (Lavrillier 2012; Skvirskaja 2012; Stepanoff 2009) in Tuva, perspectival exchange interweaves with notions of karma and good fortune whilst bearing certain implications for the process of becoming and being a human.

According to Tuvans, any existence remains contingent on perpetual rebirth. As mentioned in my interlocutors' description, in each new life *sünezin* becomes 'planted' within a different domain, which belongs to humans, spirits or animals, while retaining the traces and elements of its previous lives. As such, *sünezin* constitutes a form of 'immortal consciousness' (Pedersen & Willerslev 2012: 480), which functions beyond the body and retains its identity rather than its identity being perceived as purely relational as in some Amerindian ontologies (Rivière 1999). Whether *sünezin* is reborn as a human, spirit, animal or god is strictly dependent on how much pollution (*nugul*) or 'good' (*samaa*) it has accumulated in previous lives. Moreover, spirits may decide to spontaneously reveal themselves to people who are considered to be particularly fortunate or who perform many good deeds. Very often, these processes are also described by Tuvans as contingent on good or bad karma and one's position in the cycle of reincarnation.[4] This, in turn, has certain implications for the ways in which perspectives shift between different species. For example, in the instances of cursing that bring significant imbalance into the field of fortune, the victims may sometimes slowly begin to turn into animals, such as dogs or mice, or acquire the physique of certain spirits, thus partially losing their human personhood. In other contexts, when death is expected to occur, Tuvan shamans may organise specific rituals for their clients during which the client is introduced to a spirit as his or her future son or daughter (see Figure 3.1). If the client has accumulated enough good fortune, the spirit may agree for the human to be reborn as a part of the spirit's family. In these cases, the client is offered a quick glimpse into their future life and future family. Therefore, in Tuva the ability to shift perspectives does not seem to be restricted to people who have mastered a particular skill, such as shamans, but rather constitutes a 'temporal capacity' (Humphrey & Pedersen 2007: 146) contingent on fortune and karma that pertains to everyone. Thus, it can be suggested that, to a certain extent, humans in Tuva can control perspectival exchanges with spirits through proper conduct and accumulation of good deeds and good fortune. This, in turn, provides them with some degree of agency in the process of becoming a particular kind of person and acquiring or maintaining a particular kind of personhood.

Following on from this, there are, however, certain constraints imposed on the potentiality for reversibility between humans and non-humans. For example, being a human and having a human personhood is considered as the highest possible privilege, whereas becoming *Chetker* (responsible for cursing) or an animal, such as a dog, constitutes a form of punishment and might be associated with curses. Interestingly though, more stress seems to be placed upon perspectival exchange with spirits rather than animals or other humans. Relations between humans and spirits, especially the masters of places and gods, are strictly hierarchical and

Figure 3.1 Ritual during which the client (the man on the left) is introduced to the spirit – his future mother

76 *Cursed person(hood)*

often include elements of penalty and reward depending on humans' conduct. This dovetails with animistic systems in Southeast Asia, where hierarchy and interactions with spirits constitute fundamental structuring principles of the cosmos (Arhem 2016a: 12–13), as opposed to venatic animism typical of Amerindian perspectivism, where humans and non-humans can exchange perspectives in an equal, that is, horizontal way. Lastly, in Tuvan ontology not all spirits and animals have *sünezin*, which complicates further understanding of what unites or separates humans from other species. For example, many animals are understood as distinct creations of gods, such as *Kudai* or *Erlik*, rather than humans. In a similar fashion, many spirits do not present concrete traits like Amazonian spirits, who have clear qualities such as non-human essence or vital principle (Viveiros de Castro 2007: 155). There is not much known about the realm where the spirits live and whether it in any way resembles the realm where humans exist, which is also characteristic of other ethnographic contexts in Siberia (Broz 2007; Humphrey 2007). When spirits present themselves to shamans or laymen, they can take animal or humanoid forms. They can be anthropomorphic, with many human or animal traits, but not necessarily be a reincarnation of ancestors. Instead, they often have unknown origins. Therefore, as pointed out by Humphrey (2007: 183), spirits do not form an ontologically unified category in Siberian cosmologies and usually have diverse characteristics and names which also pertain to Tuva. Finally, different rivers, mountains or trees, as well as objects, rather than being animated by the shared essence, are often perceived as artefacts that belong to someone (see also Broz 2007). In other words, they constitute indexes of their masters of places (*eezi*) or other spirits which control them. Thus, the notion of human personhood in the ethnographic context of Tuva dovetails with understandings of being a human as contingent on the fluid intertwinement between the notions of body and soul characteristic of animistic ontologies. Nevertheless, the contrast between human personhood in Tuva and the notion of perspectivism illuminates certain limitations of this intertwinement, exemplified through the influences of other religions, in particular Buddhism, the role of fortune and the complex and uncertain characteristics of spirits. Having discussed some of the ontological features of being a human in Tuva with brief references to the wider contexts of Amerindian and Southeast Asian animism, it is now time to focus on the most essential dimension of human personhood among Tuvans: its concentric structure.

Like growth rings in the trunk of a tree

In order to understand what 'concentric structure of personhood' means, Hovalygmaa's comment that 'in Tuva people look like rings on the trunk of an old tree' needs to be taken seriously. Every human, as opposed to other kinds of person (animals, spirits, plants and insects), is meant to be constructed from numerous interdependent layers, which can be understood as different souls, gathered around and turned in on a central point: *sünezin*. While *sünezin* is considered static (*shimcheer chok*), different souls can move (*shimcheer*) and, thus, become high (*bedik, uzun*), meaning robust, or low (*kyska, chavys*), that is, weak,

Cursed person(hood) 77

depending on a variety of factors, including the presence of illnesses and curses. Every *sünezin* remains strictly connected with *sülde* ('emblem'), the following layer. *Sülde* is always meant to be high and strong and indicates whether a person finds him/herself in a condition of overall balance or disturbance. Often, if *sülde* is decreasing, people become particularly clumsy and lose the ability to work with their hands. If *sülde* is low, it indicates that a person is vulnerable and easy to manipulate, can quickly become sick, commit crimes or turn into an alcoholic. Another layer, *sülde-sünezini* ('the state of the body'), indicates whether the person is healthy or suffering from a physical illness. The next layer, *kudu-sünezini* ('consciousness'), reveals illnesses that in biomedical vocabulary would be associated with the mind, such as depression. Finally, the *tura-soruu* ('physical appearance') layer refers to peoples' general conduct in everyday life. If it is low, the person stops taking care of him/herself, becomes 'dirty' (*hirlig*) and wears shredded clothes. Low *tura-soruu* leads to further problems with education, work and communication with other people. When Tuvans describe what constitutes a human, they also mention *sagysh* or *sagysh-satpa* ('plans', 'dreams'), a layer that indicates the person's ideas and goals as well as unfulfilled plans or promises. Apart from *sagysh-satpa*, Tuvans recognise *setkil* ('mind'), which refers exclusively to thoughts, and *setkil endeves* ('emotions'). All of these layers are held together by breath (*thyn*). Coloured breath usually indicates the person is nearing death (*olur*). The shamans recognise silver breath (*serch thyn*), which indicates that *sünezin* is about to leave the human being, as well as gold (*ak*) and red (*kyzyl*) breath, which imply imminent death or the presence of curses. People can still breathe without *sünezin*; nonetheless, in such cases immediate death is expected. Once the breath is cut off, each layer of the person begins to separate. *Sünezin* and *sagysh-satpa* linger between the spaces of humans and spirits whilst the rest of the layers vanish and the physical body is disposed of and forgotten. After *sünezin* leaves the body, as I have discussed earlier in this chapter, it takes seven days for it to realise it has been separated. It then embarks on a journey, usually guided by a shaman, to seek a place where it can be reborn. During the 49 days ritual the gates to the previous life are closed by a shaman, and *sünezin* is reborn as either a spirit or a human being or an animal, and the person who passed away is not to be mentioned again. Whilst the numerous layers producing a human remain perpetually fluid and mobile, *sünezin* constitutes a static centre in a given life which maintains the rest of the layers in a relationship of interdependency. In this way, it can be argued that people in Tuva are concentric, in a sense that they are turned in on their centre (Poulantzas 1980: 101) or point of origin (Errington 1983: 547). In order to illustrate the idea of concentrism as pertinent to Tuvan personhood, I briefly turn to Errington's analysis of the body in Luwu (1983) and the notion of *sumange*.

Errington shows how *sumange* constitutes the vital energy, which pertains to everything and renders people conscious, healthy and effective. The body is shaped, therefore, in a way that it has a source of power or point of origin. This structure can also be found in the organisation of other kinds of places, such as houses and kinship groupings. Like *sumange*, which, when properly attached and

78   *Cursed person(hood)*

concentrated, remains a sign and cause of good health (1983: 548), *sünezin* constitutes the centre of a person, rooted and thus immobilised in a domain of humans. In other words, in order for life to happen people have to be centred. The process of growth and life development is then characterised by the fluid movement of the remaining layers, concentrated around static *sünezin* and described through the opposites of high and low, which indicate shifts in emotions, states of mind, health, relations with other people and the presence of curses among others. In a similar way to *sumange*, once *sünezin* leaves the body due to nearing death or curses, humans become quickly unconscious or extremely weak. The rest of the layers or soul-like elements dissolve while *sünezin* becomes reborn and thus 'grounded' again in a new domain, be it the domain of humans, spirits or animals.

The concentric structure of personhood illuminates, then, how people are not construed from clearly differentiated dimensions like the inside and outside, but rather remain turned in on their own point of origin or, to quote Poulantzas, 'turned in on their own centre' (1980: 101). As a result, they continue to stay perpetually open and thus susceptible to the feelings, wishes and actions of others. In consequence, social interactions become a key contributor to the individual's conditions, such as health and fortune, rather than being discontinuous with it. Once centred, *sünezin* initiates a condition of relatively constant homeostasis within a newborn human, dominant in the absence of new curses or other misfortune. Any changes to the layers organised around *sünezin* instantiated, for example, through occult practices, indicate transformations within the whole person. The concentric structure of human personhood illuminates, therefore, how soul and body, even though differentiated among Tuvans, are not perceived as independent or isolated from each other. Rather they remain intimately interlinked within a multilayer structure. This, in turn, sheds some light on my friends' difficulties and confusion to address questions of corporeality and physicality as individual notions.

This interdependence becomes particularly evident in the process of production of everyday sociality in Tuva, where the body is not separated from the mind and the emotions, but is embedded in the social situation that includes particular bodily moves (Bird-David 2004). Among Tuvans the notions of care, love and respect are expressed through a variety of physical moves. Rich body language, especially in the presence of children or a newly encountered group of people, constitutes for Tuvans an indication of good will and openness. Within this social context, an interesting ethnographic fact reflects the parents' tendency to show love towards their offspring through sniffing them. In a similar manner, during the rituals, bodily actions illuminate both a form of protection from the spirits and an indication of respect and gratitude. The participants are expected to cover their bodies with clothing and jewellery in order to protect themselves from losing *sünezin*, to please the spirits and express their attentiveness and esteem. Lack of hygiene, long nails and messy hair are associated with the presence of spirits who try to curse or take away something from people, such as good fortune. Having established the basic, concentric structure of personhood, which pertains only to humans in Tuva, I shall turn now to the characteristics of human personhood and how they emerge from a combination

Cursed person(hood) 79

of spirits' and relatives' influences as well as shadows of previous lives. This seems to suggest that, beyond thinking of personhood as concentric, we need to understand people and Tuvan personhood as cosmocentric, a difference I shall be explaining in what is to follow.

Residues of the past and juices of the present

In animistic cosmologies, the process of construction of personhood often intertwines with different bodily arrangements as well as forms of social exchange and contact (Bird-David 2004; Conklin & Morgan 1996; Strathern 1988). Bodies and persons are distinct products of a social and cultural milieu with personhood perceived as an ongoing project contingent on, and representing the matrix of, social relationships (Bird-David 2004; McCallum 1996). In short, rather than being about an individual, personhood reveals something about the societal patterns of interactions and existence within a group. In this sociocentric structure, interactions with spirits are imbricated in the wider realm of the social in the sense that they become a broader expression and reinforcement of the society. As discussed earlier in the context of animistic ontologies and the notion of perspectivism, in Tuva the condition of being a human constitutes a complex process that is spatially and temporally predicated upon a cosmic chain of events and reflects a gradual, lengthy procedure of transformability contingent not on one, but multiple lives. Human personhood is moulded over the course of many existences and remains intertwined with the wider web of relations with spirits and kin that fluctuate between the residues of the past and, as a friend remarked, the 'juices' of the present. In this way, the ethnographic context of Tuva makes one think about personhood in a cosmocentric rather than sociocentric fashion. In short, rather than being an inscription of the social which binds together humans, gods and spirits in a relation of representation and hierarchy as connected to 'society', the process of producing personhood in Tuva elucidates cosmic dynamics of complementarity, with the society being an integral part of the wider cosmos. In this system, to draw on Ingold's (2006) point about animacy, interactions with spirits go beyond the process of projecting the social onto the surrounding things. Rather, they constitute 'the dynamic transformative potential of the entire field of relations within which beings of all kinds continually and reciprocally bring one another into existence' (2006: 10). In order to demonstrate the cosmocentric characteristics of personhood in Tuva and illustrate my point more thoroughly, I turn to Desjarlais (2000) and Ulturgasheva (2016); their insights on the ideas of shadow and echo as linked to personhood will be developed and applied to an understanding of the Tuvan case.

Desjarlais (2000) discusses the phenomenon of *bhaja* as experienced in the context of death among Yolmo Wa. *Bhaja* reflects a particular relation between the person and their shadow also known as echo. Desjarlais shows how echo can not only sound but can also be seen and how it indicates an absence of something that was present and therefore contains traces of its predecessor. There are particular similarities between the concept of *bhaja* as echo and the way

80   *Cursed person(hood)*

the production of a person is described among Tuvans. In Tuva, once a person is born, they carry with them residues or echoes of their past lives, such as traces of the good (*saama*) or pollution (*nugul*). However, it is mainly the latter that can materialise and is usually associated with curses. This relates primarily to clan curses, such as *doora nugul* and *doora dostug*, which can be carried on for seven generations and are considered as a form of the residues of past lives (Chapter 1). Nonetheless, it is common to carry the residues of other curses experienced in previous lives too. Like in the case of *bhaja*, these 'traces' (*chyrtyk*) of past lives are mainly visual, that is, they materialise in the form of prolonged illness, bodily deformations or pre-mature deaths, rendering bodies an integral element of the wider image of cursed personhood. On a few occasions, I met families in which one of the children suffered from autism or Down's syndrome. The parents of the child would explain that their offspring's condition was tangible evidence of the presence of curses from previous lives. These diverse visual deformations were, in other words, a form of reminder of the deeds performed by the *sünezin* of the child in previous lives. In short, the visual residues of curses exemplified in bodily transformations constituted a mimesis of the previous life, although in the sense that repetition was not about repeating but turning into something else (Melberg 1995). The visual traces of engagements with curses in previous lives dovetail further with the Yolmo Wa's understanding of good death and bad death, where a good death (or in the case of Tuvans rather a good life) does not leave a dangerously strong 'echo' behind (Desjarlais 2000: 267).

The partible construction and transformation of personhood, dependent on residues of the past or future, reverberates with the notion of *djuluchen* as experienced among the Eveny (Ulturgasheva 2016). Ulturgasheva shows how *djuluchen*, the form of a shadow, imitates the body of the person. It can be separated from the human and sent into the future as a way of foreshadowing it along the desired life trajectory. As in the cases of *djuluchen*, the idea of a shadow as part of the person prevails in Tuvan imagery. For instance, *sünezin* is described by people and shamans as a grey cloud that appears after the person dies and disappears instantly. More than that, shadows of the deceased might visit the living relatives in dreams before the final ritual of 49 days when *sünezin* is reborn. Occasionally, children can see shadows of ancestors lingering in the streets or wandering around the flats, usually resembling black clouds in the shape of a human. Although Tuvans do not split their personhood like the Eveny, each life involves conscious projects of securing prosperity and health in the future lives of *sünezin*. In short, people make sure they do not accumulate too much *nugul* and preserve enough *saama* and, in this way, similar to the notion of *djuluchen*, the process of constructing personhood becomes, to an extent, contingent on the shadows of the future.

Apart from the residues of past lives, personhood in Tuva emerges from 'the juices' of the present, to use shaman analogy again. These include, firstly, the characteristics of the spirits that inhabit the region where *sünezin* is reborn. For example, spirits from the Cut Hol region in the west of Tuva are meant to be wise, patient and brave, qualities that they share with people born in their vicinity. The

Cursed person(hood) 81

inhabitants of the Ylug Hemhijskij region are great speakers and always say what they think and feel. Conversely, people from Erzin in the south of Tuva are modest, usually uttering just a few words, but remain very hospitable. This form of behaviour is also expected by the shaman from the spirits who partake in the rituals in this region. In this way, people come into existence both with and through spirits, illuminating how life is more about producing and going beyond, rather than just reflecting a given matrix of interactions.

The course of every human being's life is further predestined by the residues of the lives of both their parents and grandparents. Interestingly, each *sünezin* decides in which family they want to be reborn. Consequently, Tuvans are not meant to blame their relatives for any misfortunes, such as curses, inherited from their kin. Another crucial element of the cosmocentric structure of human personhood among Tuvans involves the concept of 'fate' (*uule, chol, salym chol*). *Uule* refers to the individual eternal course of being of each *sünezin* that can be improved or worsened depending on how each life is lived. Apart from *uule*, each human being has *chol*, which is generated by *uule*. For example, one's *chol* in a given life can be an only child. Every human being has simultaneously *salym chol*, which constitutes a course of events prescribed for one particular life. Finally, every Tuvan has *salym-chajan*, which alludes to talents or skills imbued in every human being at birth. Very often Tuvans say: 'in this life his *salym-chajan* is to be a musician' (*sen aki muzykant salym-chajan sen*).

Thus, the construction of human personhood in Tuva emerges from a distinct matrix of social and cosmic elements and undergoes transformations that exceed one individual life span. In other words, rather than being gradually modelled through different forms of sociality or bodily actions, *sünezin* is reborn with a particular ('already given') repertoire of elements and residues, a form bestowed-upon-personhood that can be further strengthened or weakened. Instead of taking shape only through engagement with the social world, Tuvan human personhood precedes it and involves a set of relations with spirits and the cosmos as a whole. People, concurrently, grow and they enhance their *saama* or *nugul* through daily interactions, which are then carried on into the next life. Within this process, curses, while introducing overall vulnerability to the feelings, wishes and actions of others, make people susceptible to social and cosmic relationships as key contributors to individual well-being and prosperity or suffering endured in this and their next lives. In other words, while weaving the relations between humans and spirits together, the phenomenon of cursing is also intimately associated with the ways people grow in a given life as human beings. Let me now extend my discussion on how cursing influences the production of human personhood and show how new curses bring cognitive, physical and emotional processes together in an explicit fashion whilst instigating a state of turbulence. In so doing, I shall place particular emphasis on how curses (de)form bodies, transforming them into neither an object nor a text nor a centre of subjectivity but, as Latour puts it, 'a dynamic trajectory by which we learn to register and become sensitive to what the world is made of' (2004: 206) and thus a materialised arena of socio-cosmic dynamics.

Cursed personhood

When discussing the issues of luck and good fortune, Tuvans would often portray 'good fortune' (*aac-kezzik*) as a condition or a trajectory (rather than a state) of relatively continuous socioeconomic cohesion, such as having a lot of animals, many children and good health. In a similar way, a healthy person is said to be someone who remains in a condition of continual overall homeostasis or balance. Within this structure, all the layers which produce a human continue to be intertwined with *sünezin* in a roughly regular manner without being dislocated through any disturbances, such as, cursing. In short, curses constitute types of disturbing agents, which, with sudden immediacy and speed, introduce disturbance into the fragile condition of balanced personhood. As the shamans explain it, once cursed the victims begin to behave in unpredictable ways, comparable to erratic waves of wind. All the layers that produce a person start to tremble while the cursed victim is said to experience a kind of uncontrolled turbulence. The implications of curses as turbulence are diverse. Once spirits attack their victim, they begin to interfere with the client's health, emotions, thoughts and relations with people. The victims abruptly change their behaviour, as well as the way they feel. They become unpredictable in their decisions and reactions, doing and saying things uncommon for them and outside of their usual behaviour. The victims are often unaware of their actions whilst feeling paranoid. Sometimes people feel depressed or particularly sad and weak. Other symptoms involve sudden illnesses (occasionally, at exactly the same time each year) such as a coma or strokes, which pass equally abruptly after a few days (like Shonchalgaj, whose story opens this book). Sudden alcoholism, clumsiness, violence and aggression, as well as vivid dreams in which spirits might try to kill the victim, are very common. Many of these changes are instantiated in the way the body of the cursed person is seen as changing. Such materiality of curses is often recorded by shamans in forms of complex drawings produced during rituals, like that in the case of one of Hovalygmaa's regular clients, Katija.

Hovalygmaa and I visited her dear friend, Katija, a policewoman, in early spring, right after she had returned from a holiday. Upon her return, Katija began to feel depressed and lethargic and seemed particularly unhappy at work, with people constantly gossiping about her. She lost energy and suspected severe illness. As it turned out, she was cursed by one of her colleagues, an otherwise very friendly next-door neighbour desperate for promotion. The shaman described her body as completely deprived of bones. Everything was moved around, and her organs were falling apart. The spirit inflicting the curse turned on an image of a huge bird with a long, curved beak. It was slowly breaking the woman's bones, smashing her organs and making her feel paranoid and anxious. Whilst providing both myself and the client with this vivid description, the shaman sat on the floor, took out a square white piece of material and vigorously began to draw with a red marker what she was seeing. Afterwards, she encouraged me to take a photograph of her drawing, implying it would be useful for my and others' educational purposes (see Figure 3.2). The top-right image presents what the victim looked like to the shaman and what the curse had done to her. The second image on the

Cursed person(hood) 83

Figure 3.2 The shaman's drawing

bottom-right presents an angry bird; the shape of the spirit inflicting the curse. The upper-left square shows a mouse, which was supposed to carry the counter-curse to the client's rival. The final square shows the name of the neighbour who requested curse infliction, written in signs that were dictated to the shaman by the helping spirit. After the shaman finished her drawing, the material was burned and the ashes of it were thrown out the window.

As already discussed, the shamans in Tuva are well-known for their ability to see things which cannot be otherwise noticed. Every time the shaman meets a client, they are instantly exposed to concrete images, such as animals, birds or insects, as well as different forms of bodily deformations that signal the presence of curses. Spirits responsible for curse infliction enter the body of the victim through the head (*besh*) and nest in the stomach (*hyryn*), intestines (*shojyhny*) or chest (*hörek*), bringing with them curses in the form of disturbing energy. Sometimes, the spirits sit on the shoulder (*egin*) or randomly chose a part of the body to which they attach (*hyrbalanyr*) themselves. They often turn into serpents, mice, birds or dogs and like to entangle or weave around the client's organs. They can either remain still in their chosen place or they can bite flesh (Rus. *telo*), break bones (*söök*) or, in severe cases, attempt to initiate the transformation of a client into, for instance, a dog. Children and foreigners are particularly at risk from the attacks of spirits, as they are seen by spirits as 'thin' (*dygysh chok*) people. In the case of the former, the adjective 'thin' refers to 'pure' (*aryg*) creatures with thin hair and skin. In the case of the latter, it describes being unaccustomed to interactions with spirits and thus especially susceptible to their powers and tricks. In order to protect newly arrived guests and children, the shamans always make sure

84 Cursed person(hood)

their heads are covered with a hat in the presence of spirits and during the rituals. The head constitutes the thinnest part of the body and, as such, allows *sünezin* and spirits to freely move through it. On some occasions, rather than entering the body, the spirits begin to live with the victims in their flats, observing them while casting nasty looks and following them in their everyday routines. These spirits often appropriate the physique of deceased relatives, although it is common for them to also transform into a beautiful woman with her breasts at the back or a man with an iron nose (see also Lindquist 2008).

A very typical symptom of curse is mud (*hir*) that accumulates in different parts of the body, although the shamans often point to head, stomach and shoulders while revealing their visions. *Hir* constitutes a residue and a consequence of curses present for lengthy periods of time. The process of accumulation of *hir* as a result of curses is indexical of other ways of polluting the everyday lives of Tuvan people. For example, a type of heating used in flats mainly during the winter, as well as nearby coal-powered factories, generates dark clouds of soot that can be seen for miles. This soot accumulates everywhere – inside the flats, on furniture, on clothes – and constitutes an integral, irritating element of life in the city in winter. People find it on their hands, faces and noses and always complain about it, repeating *saasha, saasha* ('soot, soot'). As a result, in the summer, it is very common for people to dispose of destroyed furniture, paint their flats and clean their houses. Also, it is common to invite the shamans to conduct cleansing rituals and remove dirt that has accumulated in people, including curses (I have also discussed this in Chapter 1). Once a cursed client visits the shaman, they can see how much mud has been accumulated and to what extent curses have disturbed the person.

The material symptoms of curses are diverse; however, the most common are different smells, changes in skin colour (skin may become yellow) and bags under the eyes. Some people may have red, silver or gold breath (especially when they are near death). The organs might be disturbed or moved, and sometimes they may turn black. On other occasions, especially with strong death curses, bodies may dry out. Once the shamans engage in divination practices or commence the curse deflection rituals, they provide the clients with vivid images of curses and the spirits inflicting them. After each ritual the shaman imposes particular restrictions on the victim that involve fluid control and exchange. The most common restriction, usually lasting seven days, is a limitation on the consumption of alcohol, sexual abstinence and forbidding the consumption of certain types of food, the choice of which depends on the shaman and the expectations of the spirits. In the presence of a death curse, the shamans provide the victim with a glass of water in order to alleviate bodily dryness. At the end of each ritual, which involves the deflection of curses, everyone present is asked to drink tea with milk in order to maintain health and ensure the surge of good luck.

The accurate recognition of cursed personhood is contingent on the concrete images of bodily (de)formations that the shamans perceive and present to the clients. Nevertheless, these bodies are not regarded as discrete material substances. Rather, as in other animist ontologies, they are perceived as 'a dialectic arena where the natural elements are domesticated by the group and the elements of the group (social elements) are naturalized in the world of animals' (Brightman, Grotti & Ulturgasheva 2012: 4). In this way, cursed bodies can be approached as sites where relations to others are created, transformed, validated and destroyed, whilst being perpetually affected by a variety of processes that occur near or within them and thus deprived of the strict 'inside/outside' distinction inherited from Cartesian philosophy. The ethnographic context of Tuva illuminates, therefore, how having a particular kind of body (in this case a cursed body) '*is to learn to be affected*, moved, put into motion by other entities' (Latour 2004: 205, original emphasis). In short, curses, while introducing turbulence to a victim, transform bodies into active trajectories that produce both a concrete kind of turbulent person and a particular kind of turbulent cosmos. As presented earlier, curses make people and their personhoods vulnerable to the wishes and actions of others, including spirits and humans, a process that materialises itself in concrete bodily images, visible to a certain extent to other people (in the form of bodily deformations, particular smells and skin colours) and fully accessible to shamans (in images of mud and changed organs). In this way, from the perspective of the mechanics of cursing, acquiring a (cursed) body constitutes, what Latour (2004: 206) defines as, a progressive enterprise through which one learns to register and becomes susceptible to the fabric of the world. Rather than focusing on direct definitions of the body, approaching bodies from the angle of curses allows us to concentrate on 'what the body has become aware of' (2004: 206). Given this, cursed bodies are not a temporary residence of something superior, like an immortal soul, but instead are the arenas of complex actions. Cursed bodies come into being through the ongoing encounters with the world(s) and persons within it. While constituting a catalyst for curses to acquire materiality, bodies remain, therefore, critical to the affirmation of the overall presence of the cursed person(hood).[5]

Curses are dramatic events which push together shamans, clients and spirits into a matrix of sociocosmic interactions while unearthing traces of what it means to be a shaman or to have a cursed personhood in Tuva. While situated within the zones of cosmological uncertainty, they reveal entangled trajectories through which people and spirits relate to one another engaging all three temporal variables – past, present and future. Working with curses, both for shamans and those courageous enough to inflict curses themselves, involves an efficacious use of sounds. Tuvan shamans employ in the rituals an array of sonic phenomena ranging from instrumental sounds, music, singing to gasps and shouts, while individuals wishing to curse independently have to pronounce words with specific intonation and rhythm. Thus, Tuvan cultural arrangements of curses and the sonic throw an important question back at us. What is the relation between the efficacy of shamanic practice, curses and sounds? What does it mean to say that sounds can do things? In the second part of this book, I shall extend my discussion on turbulence and move towards the potent qualities of sound and voice in shamanic rituals. In the following chapter, while concentrating on the role of the shamanic drum, I will show how curses, shamans and different kinds of persons, including humans and spirits, come together in the ritual setting and

86   *Cursed person(hood)*

produce a particular kind of semi-controlled turbulent space. In so doing, I hope to illuminate how, in a similar manner to *sünezin* in the context of personhood, the drum constitutes a centre of the ritual involving curses and thus becomes an indispensable instrument in the process of foregrounding ritual events. Along these lines, I am going to show how the notion of turbulence represents one of the core ideas in Tuvan cosmology, which pertains not only to personhood and curses but also can be traced in sounds, language and organisational structure of shamanic rituals.

Notes

1 Tuvan perception of the dead dovetails with the way in which relationships between the living and their dead relatives are conceptualised in Amazonian cosmologies where there is no metaphysical or social link between live humans and dead ones (Fausto 2007: 510; Viveiros de Castro 1998: 482–3) and the deceased is meant to be actively forgotten (Conklin 1995). In a similar way, in Tuva dead relatives become 'others', i.e. animals, spirits or different humans. There is no notion of ancestor worship. The deceased's name is not to be mentioned again, whilst their possessions are either destroyed or given to selected family members and friends. This contrasts with Southeast Asian cosmologies, where the dead and the living preserve metaphysical and social relationships of continuity (Arhem 2016b: 290).

2 The definitions of the terms 'self', 'person', 'personhood', 'individual' and 'dividual' have been the subject of numerous discussions in a variety of anthropological debates (among others, see Bloch 2011; Scheper-Hughes and Lock 1987; Smith 2012; Strathern 1988). The Tuvan language does not offer any direct equivalents to these terms, and the condition of being a particular kind of person, i.e. human or non-human, is contingent on a variety of factors. In order to avoid unnecessary entanglements in abstract terminology, I primarily use the Tuvan terms, such as *kizji* ('human being'), *amytan* ('animal'), *eezi* ('masters of places spirits') and *sünezin* ('soul') in order to elucidate the relationship between being a human and being a person in Tuvan cosmology. Thus, I engage with the characteristics of acquiring a particular kind of (cursed) personhood. I employ the term 'human personhood' (Arhem 2016a: 10) as an analytical tool to interpret what Tuvans described as a multilayered structure, characteristic only of human beings.

3 During my fieldwork, I did not come across any data implying that *sünezin* pertains also to objects or plants.

4 This illuminates how some aspects of animism, including the notion of personhood, have developed in Tuva alongside great world religions, such as Hinduism and Tibetan Buddhism.

5 Presented in this chapter are ethnographic examples of cursed personhood, and the role of spirits raise some analytical problems that look similar to the notions of spirit possession and, perhaps, exorcism. Nonetheless, the use of these interpretations does pose certain challenges in the ethnographic context of Tuva, as Tuvans never perceive such events in terms of spirit possession and most definitely not exorcism. Instead, they often find these suggestions offensive (similar to any mention of trance and spirit possession in relation to shamans and their work, as discussed in Chapter 2). In short, the spirits' involvement in cursing, rather than being understood through a rhetoric of possession, reflects instances of spirits living with and around their victims, rather than in them, whilst producing a particular kind of sociability predicated on the intrinsic notion of turbulence. Inevitably, this idea requires more investigation which could be the subject of further research.

Bibliography

Arhem, K. 2016a. Southeast Asian Animism in Context. In K. Arhem & G. Sprenger (eds), *Animism in Southeast Asia*, 3–30. London and New York: Routledge.

Arhem, K. 2016b. Southeast Asian Animism. A Dialogue with Amerindian Perspectivism. In K. Arhem & G. Sprenger (eds), *Animism in Southeast Asia*, 279–301. London and New York: Routledge.

Ballkina, F. G. 1994. Covremennaja Tuva. Cociokul'turnyj aspekt razvitija. *Sociologicheskie issledovanija* no. 10: 159–161.

Bird-David, N. 2004. Illness-images and Joined Beings. A Critical/Nayaka Perspective on Intercorporeality. *Social Anthropology* no. 12 (3): 325–339.

Bloch, M. 2011. The Blob. *Anthropology of This Century* no. 1.

Brightman, Ma, Grotti, E. V., & Ulturgasheva, O. 2012. Introduction. In M. Brightman, V. E. Grotti, & O. Ulturgasheva (eds), *Animism in Rainforest and Tundra: Personhood, Animals, Plants and Things in Contemporary Amazonia and Siberia*, 1–28. New York; Oxford: Berghahn Press.

Broz, L. 2007. Pastoral Perspectivism: A View from Altai. *Inner Asia* no. 9 (2): 291–310.

Cannon, B. W. 1932. *The Wisdom of the Body*. London: Kegan Paul, Trench, Trubner & Co.

Conklin, A. B. 1995. "thus are our bodies, thus was our custom": Mortuary Cannibalism in an Amazonian Society. *American Ethnologist* no. 22 (1): 75–101.

Conklin, A. B. 2001. *Consuming Grief. Compassionate cannibalism in an Amazonian Society*. Austin, Tex.: University of Texas Press.

Conklin, A. B. & Lynn, M. M. 1996. Babies, Bodies and the Production of Personhood in North America and a Native Amazonian Society. *Ethnos* no. 24 (4): 657–694.

Descola, P. 2013. *Beyond Culture and Nature*. Chicago, Illinois U.S.; London: The University of Chicago Press.

Desjarlais, R. 2000. Echoes of a Yolmo Buddhist's Life, in Death. *Cultural Anthropology* no. 15 (2): 260–293.

Errington, S. 1983. Embodied Sumange' in Luwu. *The Journal of Asian Studies* no. 42 (3): 545–570.

Fausto, C. 2007. Feasting on People: Eating Animals and Humans in Amazonia. *Current Anthropology* no. 48: 497–530.

Hugh-Jones, S. 1996. Shamans, Prophets, Priests and Pastors. In C. Humphrey & N. Thomas (eds.), *Shamanism, History, and the State*, 32–75. Ann Arbor: University of Michigan Press.

Humphrey, C. 2007. Inside and Outside the Mirror: Mongolian Shamans' Mirrors as Instruments of Perspectivism. *Inner Asia* no. 9 (2): 173–195.

Humphrey, C. & Pedersen, A. M. 2007. Editorial Introduction: Inner Asian Perspectivisms. *Inner Asia* no. 9 (2): 141–152.

Ingold, T. 2006. Rethinking the Animate, Re-animating Thought. *Ethnos* no. 71 (1): 9–20.

Kara, S. & Kunkovacs, D. L. 2014. Black Shamans of the Turkic-Speaking Telengit in Southern Siberia. *Shaman* no. 22 (1–2): 151–161.

Latour, B. 2004. How to Talk About the Body? The Normative Dimension of Science Studies. *Body & Society* no. 10 (2–3): 205–229.

Lavrillier, A. 2012. 'Sprit-Charged' Animals in Siberia. In M. Brightman, V. E. Grotti, & O. Ulturgasheva (eds), *Animism in Rainforest and Tundra: Personhood, Animals, Plants and Things in Contemporary Amazonia and Siberia*, 113–129. New York; Oxford: Berghahn Press.

88 Cursed person(hood)

Lindquist, G. 2008. Loyalty and Command. Shamans, Lamas, and Spirits in a Siberian Ritual. *Social Analysis* no. 52 (1): 111–126.

Mongush, M. 2006. Modern Tuvan Identity. *Inner Asia* no. 8: 275–296.

McCallum, C. 1996. The Body that Knows. From Cashinahua Espitemology to Medical Anthropology of Lowland South America. *Medical Anthropology Quarterly* no. 10 (3): 347–372.

Melberg, A. 1995. *Theories of Mimesis*. Cambridge: Cambridge University Press.

Pedersen, A. M. 2001. Totemism, Animism and North Asian Indigenous Ontologies. *Royal Anthropological Institute* no. 7: 411–427.

Pedersen, A. M. & Willerslev, R. 2012. "The Soul of the Soul is the Body". Rethinking the Concept of Soul through North Asian Ethnography. *Common Knowledge* no. 18 (3): 464–486.

Pimienova, K. 2009. The Emergence of a New Social Identity. In H. Beach, D. Funk, & L. Sillanpaa (eds), *Post-Soviet Transformations*, 161–185. Uppsala: Uppsala University Press.

Poulantzas, N. 1980. *State, Power, Socialism*. London: Verso.

Rivière, P. 1999. Shamanism and the Unconfinded Soul. In M. James & C. Crabbe (eds.), *From Soul to Self*, 70–88. London: Routledge.

Safonova, T. & Santha, I. 2012. Stories about Evenki People and their Dogs: Communication through Sharing Contexts. In M. Brightman, V. E. Grotti, & O. Ulturgasheva (eds), *Animism in Rainforest and Tundra: Personhood, Animals, Plants and Things in Contemporary Amazonia and Siberia*, 82–95. New York; Oxford: Berghahn Press.

Scheper-Hughes, N. & Lock, M. M. 1987. The Mindful Body: A Prolegomenon to Future Work in Medical Anthropology. *Medical Anthropology Quarterly, New Series* no. 1 (1), 6–41.

Skvirskaja, V. 2012. Expressions and Experiences of Personhood: Spatiality and Objects in the Nenets Tundra Home. In M. Brightman, V. E. Grotti, & O. Ulturgasheva (eds), *Animism in Rainforest and Tundra: Personhood, Animals, Plants and Things in Contemporary Amazonia and Siberia*, 146–161. New York; Oxford: Berghahn Press.

Smith, K. 2012. From Dividual and Individual Selves to Porous Subjects. *The Australian Journal of Anthropology* no. 23: 50–64.

Stepanoff, Ch. 2009. Devouring Perspectives: On Cannibal Shamans in Siberia. *Inner Asia* no. 11(2): 283–307.

Strathern, M. 1988. *The Gender of the Gift: Problems with Women and Problems with Society in Malenesia*. Berkley: University of California Press.

Taylor, A. Ch. 1996. The Soul's Body and Its States: An Amazonian Perspective on the Nature of Being Human. *The Journal of the Royal Anthropological Institute* no. 2 (2), 201–215.

Ulturgasheva, O. 2016. Spirit of the Future. Movement, Kinetic Distribution, and Personhood among Siberian Eveny. *Social Analysis* no. 60 (1): 56–73.

Vainshtein, S. 1981. *Nomads of South Siberia*. Cambridge: Cambridge University Press.

Viveiros de Castro, E. 1998. Cosmological deixis and Amerindian perspectivism. *Journal of the Royal Anthropological Institute* no. 4 (3): 469–488.

Viveiros de Castro, E. 2007. The Crystal Forest: Notes on the Ontology of Amazonian Spirits. *Inner Asia* no. 9 (2): 153–172.

Willerslev, R. 2007. *Soul Hunters: Hunting, Animism and Personhood Among the Siberian Yukaghiris*. Berkley, Los Angeles, London: University of California Press.

Willerslev, R. 2009. The Optimal Sacrifice: A Study of Voluntary Death Among the Siberian Chukchi. *American Ethnologist* no. 36 (4): 693–704.

Willerslev, R. & Ulturgasheva, O. 2012. Revisiting the Animism versus Totemism Debate: Fabricating Persons among the Eveny and Chukchi of North-eastern Siberia. In M. Brightman, V. E. Grotti, & O. Ulturgasheva (eds), *Animism in Rainforest and Tundra: Personhood, Animals, Plants and Things in Contemporary Amazonia and Siberia*, 48–68. New York; Oxford: Berghahn Press.

Part II

Sound and turbulence

4 My drum is thunder

Cursing rituals, turbulence and the sound of drums

It was a day in late spring. We were on our way to meet a client who lived on the outskirts of the city. The shaman sat comfortably in the taxi and talked excitedly about her adventures in a recent trip to the taiga. After an hour's drive, we arrived at a dilapidated residential block, a grey architectural reminder of the Soviet period in the middle of the steppe. Through a hole in the wall, which served as a gate, we stepped into the dark interior of the building. On the second floor we met Orzju, a German language teacher, who warmly invited us into her kitchen. She was cursed by a neighbour who had seduced Orzju's husband, a common cause of cursing among women in Kyzyl. After the usual exchange of news and gossip and a short meal, the shaman commenced the ritual. Once she disappeared into the corridor and we suddenly heard a long, loud cry: the howl of a wolf. The room was filled with dancing tendrils of blessed juniper smoke, and the first sounds of the drum with the shaman's soft humming followed. *Pam pam pam*, the sounds of the drum rhythmically emerged through the smoke screen. Drumming faster and faster, the shaman began to move around the room, her coat crackling and her voice getting stronger. '*Pam pam pam* … this is the sound of my drum', the shaman sang in a deep, powerful voice. 'I make tornadoes from dirt and dust. Make them swirl, make them for my children *pam pam pam*', her voice rose steadily. 'Cut off the curse, my gods. Make the curse melt away, take away the curse my gods', the voice reached its highest register. *Pam pam pam*. 'My drum makes swirls; my drum is thunder'.

Tuva is fully permeated by diverse sounds. Their presence reverberates in narratives and peoples' behaviours; it echoes through the landscape of cities, steppe and mountains. Each time I put on a record with Tuvan throat singing and hear the long cries and howls of both the singers and their instruments, or when I relisten to the shaman's chants in a ritual which offers a mixture of gasps, laughter, screams and beautiful singing, I cannot help but feel the effectuating power of sound which seemingly creates a kind of connection and bridge with another world. Tuvan friends often used to say to me that sounds have power, that they can do things. This throws back at us a number of questions. What can be unveiled if we look closer at how Tuvans theorise sound? How can Tuvan sounds disturb the frameworks in which we come to an understanding of what it means to listen and hear, to voice things, to relate to one another or even to conduct a ritual? In the previous

DOI: 10.4324/9781003245391-7

94 *My drum is thunder*

chapters, I have discussed how curses and shamanic practices are bound up with producing a particular kind of person. More specifically, I have illuminated how the interactions between humans as well as humans and non-humans, exemplified in curses, are characterised by dynamics of turbulence and balance influencing the concentric structure through which human (and cursed) personhood is articulated. From this point onwards, I would like to focus on how shamans, spirits and clients are brought together in the context of cursing rituals through the power of sound. In other words, I shall explore what comes to the surface if we take the claim that the drum is thunder seriously.

Sound in Tuva

One of the main attractions in Kyzyl is a park situated on the banks of the Yenisei River. In the main section, there is a monument designating the park as the very centre of Asia. The place attracts tourists and families who rest, play and admire the view of the wide steppe and distant Sayan mountains. At the entrance to the park a massive board informs visitors both in Russian and Tuvan languages about the ten things that are strictly forbidden within the park; a distant reminder of the previous political system. Visits to this green square became my usual practice. One of the entertainments was music coming out of the numerous speakers situated around the park benches. The operas of Shostakovich and Tchaikovsky were combined with traditional Tuvan throat singing. The deep, vibrating voices of Tuvan singers intertwined with smooth passages from the Russian composers accompanied visitors throughout their walks and conversations, creating this unusual mélange of sonic experience. One day, I shared my musical observations with a friend, an ethnomusicologist and a rare expert on the practice of throat singing – Valentina Süzükei. Valentina and I met regularly to study the Tuvan language and talk about life in Kyzyl. She has been a devoted language teacher to all aspiring researchers and ethnographers who have visited Kyzyl since the collapse of the Soviet Union. Valentina would always wait for me in her office on the second floor of the Tuvan Cultural Centre, next to the room where the Tuvan National Symphony Orchestra rehearsed. Each time, after a round of empathetic smiles while observing my struggle with verb conjugation in the Tuvan language, Valentina would alleviate my suffering with conversations about music and the theory of sound in throat singing.[1] Encouraged by my brief research on throat singing and sonically dense experiences in the park, I asked Valentina to teach me how to listen in a Tuvan way. 'I can't', she smiled. 'You will never be able to hear it properly, in our music it is not about a melody that you can grasp, it is about everything that is around it, all the different smells', she said as she waved her hands towards her nose as if sniffing something delicious. 'You need to be able to hear the very nuances of the melody, the almost misty, elusive sounds and for that your ear has to be trained here, in Tuva', she concluded.

Sounds in Tuva pertain not only to the realm of music, but also emotions, the representation of landscape and animals, topography as well as communication and interactions between humans and spirits. Singing and performing is neither restricted to people exhibiting particular talents nor considered as a particular calling (see also Levin & Süzükei 2017). Rather, anyone may have the capacity for expressiveness and creativity, and everyone is assumed to possess the skills to play instruments and sing. According to Valentina, children become familiar with sound making by playing instruments made from natural materials, for example, common plants (*murgu*), bullroarers (*hirlee*), birch bark whistles (*ediski*), hunting horns (*amyrga*), wooden jaw harps (*daya-homus*) and many others (Levin & Süzükei 2017). These instruments are played simply as a form of entertainment while spending time in the steppe and herding animals. Inspiration to make music is meant to come from the deeply sounded surroundings which are constantly filled with winds, thunder, rain, bird calls or the cries of animals. In pre-Soviet times, sound played an essential role in hunting, allowing hunters to locate prey and orient themselves in space. For instance, through listening to the sound of a horseshoe, a hunter could quickly recognise a type of ground (stones, sand, moss) (Darzaa 1998). Bird sounds and rodents would inform him about heights and changes in the landscape. Some hunters used to have a *hirileesh*, a specific device employed to transform kinetic energy into sound energy. These sounds were easily sensed by animals and were expected to tame and control lightning and wind (Darzaa 1998: 177). A very common way of orientating in space was provided by sound calendars, where sounds of winds, water, trees and animals would inform the pasturing groups when it was time to move their *aal* (Süzükei 2010). One of the few remaining reindeer breeders, with whom I worked at the beginning of my fieldwork, vividly described how she never got lost in the taiga and never needed a map. What helped her was a form of 'sonic memory'. Through carefully listening to the forest she was always able to find her way home. One of the most important aspects of sound and music in Tuva, and the one which I closely explore in this and the following chapter, is that sounds facilitate interactions and communication between humans and non-humans. For example, diverse forms of music making, including throat singing, performed in the steppe are considered as intimate ways of conversing with spirits. Moreover, listening and voicing particular sounds have potency to facilitate intermittent encounters with spirits during rituals. Sounds constitute also an essential tool for shamans in negotiations with spirits during the ritual proceedings. Thus, as we shall see, sonic production and perception in Tuva have the power to bridge an important ontological border between visible and invisible, between human and non-human.

By choosing to engage with sounds in Tuvan shamanic practice, in this chapter I also seek out to problematise the role of shamanic drums and the notion of turbulence. Contextualising the central role of the drum in the shamanic ritual, I explore how the shaman, the spirits and the clients along with the course of events in the ceremony are brought together and organised around the drum and its sounds in a centripetal fashion (reflecting some of the conceptual similarities between drums and *sünezin* – the centre of human personhood). Through unsettling cosmic fragile configurations, the drum opens up and produces a distinct semi-controlled turbulent space indispensable to conducting further negotiations with spirits and establishing new arrangements in a form of curse deflection or infliction. The

96　*My drum is thunder*

notions of turbulence and centripetalism are also structural properties of sound as discussed and presented in Tuvan theory of sound in *khöömei* – throat singing. As I will show, the process of sound production in Tuvan musical tradition is homologous to the structure of events occurring during shamanic rituals involving curses. I would like to begin my analysis by introducing a broader discussion on how turbulence is one of the fundamental concepts among Tuvans, which calcifies around a specific set of ideas and experiences beyond cursing events.

Ezinneldir and düvülendir

I have discussed earlier in the context of cursed personhood the ways in which curses create in their victims the experience of dangerous turbulence. Indeed, the notion of turbulence precipitates in Tuvan ontology while pertaining not only to the event of being cursed but also to, for example, certain aspects of language, shamanic rituals, singing and drumming or the spirits' moods. As briefly mentioned in the opening vignette, at the beginning of each ritual, the shaman addresses the spirits by saying that the sound of the drum creates whirls and thunders (*düvülendir dingmirej beer dungurumnu, ezinneldir edip turar dungurumnu*). These terms *düvülendir* ('whirls') and *ezinneldir* ('swirls') refer to the notion of turbulence (see also Levin & Süzükei 2017) and turbulence-like effects, such as disturbance and dispersion. Interchangeably, especially in the context of music making and sound in throat singing, Tuvans also employ the Russian term *turbulentnost'* (turbulence).[2]

Ezinneldir and *düvülendir* constitute key ideas without which the role of sound in Tuvan onto-epistemic systems cannot be fully understood. As mentioned in the Introduction, *ezinneldir* and *düvülendir* are used when describing an abrupt experience of being cursed. Both terms can also be employed to refer to sudden changes in behaviour as well as unpredictable or disturbing events and forces not necessarily triggered by the instances of curse. For example, the spirits and their moods can be described as turbulent. If the spirits arrive at the ritual like *ezinneldir* and *düvülendir*, this implies they are extremely angry, and the shaman is doomed to work even harder. Subsequently, both of the terms are employed to describe someone's movement that is fast and abrupt and leaves some sort of trace, for example, a cold current. *Ezinneldir* and *düvülendir* are used in relation to the strength and unpredictability of fire, which suddenly intensifies due to shifts in the spirits' moods or needs. Both terms can also be employed in order to describe the distinct characteristics and strength of the echo. *Ezinneldir* and *düvülendir* are further referred to as metaphorized descriptions of timbre (Levin & Süzükei 2017). As Levin and Süzükei[3] show, in the Tuvan language, there is a rich lexicon of onomatopoetic ideophones, that is, ordinary words depicting sensory imagery which refer to the notion of turbulence. These words illustrate the whole pallet of different sounds that produce turbulence-like acoustic effects, thus generating a distinct image of a turbulent soundscape in Tuva. Levin and Süzükei provide a wide array of examples of ideophones, a few of which I have listed below (2017: 7).

xoluraash: sound of something banging in an empty container of any sort
xülüreesh: sound of water bubbling down a pipe
shylyraash: swishing sound, used, for instance, in relation to a young person who is trying to make words, or a drunk who is muttering
syylaash: s high-frequency whistling sound often used to describe children's voices
tyrylaash: perpetual vibration or rolling sound, such as hammering, drilling and also certain birds
dingmireeshkin: sound of a thunderous waterfall or thunderstorm

Levin and Süzükei show further how the aforementioned lexicon of ideophones depicting the effects of turbulence has particular implications for the distinct ways of listening among Tuvans too. In their discussion on timbre – tone colour – both authors coin the term 'timbre-centred listening' and show how timbre and, associated with it, turbulence are not merely a reflection of musical taste or aesthetic preference, but rather represent a psychoacoustic calibration that emphasises a distinct kind of listening (Levin & Süzükei 2017: 1). Given this, Tuvans are able to draw inspiration for their music and construct knowledge about the surrounding world through listening in a timbral way, that is, the manner in which the listener notices and pays careful attention to different tints or colours of the same sound. Through this particular kind of listening, Tuvans can recognise weather patterns, seasonal changes, hunt and differentiate between animal species and birds with great precision. Levin and Süzükei also show that timbre as a concept and an integral element of sound has very rich descriptions in the Tuvan language. It is often characterised as *haash* (nasal), *choon* (thick), *chinge* (thin), *ötküt* (clear, piercing), *chidig* (sharp), *chymchak* (soft) and *hos* (free, loose, relaxed, empty), as well as *kudaranchyg* (sad or wistful), *orgu, cuuk, kylash* (smooth) or *chylyg* (warm) (Levin & Süzükei 2017: 8). Moreover, according to the authors, timbre-like qualities are also ascribed to the way in which the shamanic costume is sometimes organised. Different elements of the shaman's gown, such as a metal mirror used to diverge the spirits, the strings (*syr-òk*) symbolising the tips of the shaman's arrows, multiple strings (*kyngyraa*) attached to the shaman's hat and small metal balls (*konguraa*) produce during the ritual a form of timbral dissonance caused by the shaman's movements (Levin & Süzükei 2017: 5). Finally, the notion of turbulence, as I will show, constitutes an intrinsic element of sound production in throat singing in Tuva. This, in turn, has particular implications for understanding the role of drums and their sounds in shamanic rituals involving curses. The process of sound production in Tuvan musical tradition bears certain homologous features to the structure of events occurring during shamanic rituals involving drums.

What is then the link between drums, turbulence and throat singing? I propose to employ an understanding of the sound unit in *khöömei* as a discrete analytical framework to explore the turbulent characteristics of the ritual event as it is framed and focused on shamanic performance. I argue that the particular production of the sound unit in throat singing, whilst being contingent on the notion of

98 *My drum is thunder*

turbulence generated by a central sound, constitutes an effective model to understand the structure of events in shamanic rituals organised around the drum. In my analysis, I concentrate exclusively on a musical tradition of throat singing known worldwide as *khöömei*, as it is in this tradition that the specific features of the Tuvan sound ideal can be delineated in their most refined form. To explain my argument, I shall begin with a brief contextual outline of the Tuvan music tradition and throat singing practice in order to illuminate the structural characteristics of sound in *khöömei* and its conceptual similarities with the ways in which shamanic rituals are organised and experienced. Therefore, I mean to show that particular traits of sound structure in *khöömei* explored by Tuvan ethnomusicologists, like my friend Valentina, refer to and draw on wider ideas, and potentialities, of Tuvan ontology that can be traced to important factors outside the realm of music and thus become informative of Tuvans' ways of engagement with the world.

The art of *khöömei*

Defined in Tuva as the art of playing the throat, *khöömei* is widely known as the Tuvan tradition of throat singing (Süzükei 2010: 223). Indeed, Tuvans are famous for this particular form of musical performance that has attracted people from all over the world, both as a theoretical and practical phenomenon. *Khöömei* constitutes one example of timbre-centred music practices in Tuva and is defined by some ethnomusicologists as an auditory and visual perception of the environment (Hodgkinson 2005/2006; Levin 2006). Despite being referred to as singing, *khöömei* is a highly specific and autonomous phenomenon that, although produced by the human vocal apparatus, has very little in common with what is defined as singing. Essentially, the vocal apparatus is considered a separate musical instrument rather than a part of the physical body. *Khöömei* constitutes a particular form of performance, which involves only the singer and their voice.[4] Tuvan music experts often stress the fact that, rather than throat singing, *khöömei* should be translated as the art of playing the throat, as already mentioned above. While performing *khöömei*, a singer produces one main sound (drone) which is then split into its numerous parts (overtones). In order to produce melody, drone and its overtones have to be sung simultaneously. The innate simultaneity of sound(s) leaves the singer and their voice in a state of constant controlled turbulence (Süzükei 2010: 34).

The Tuvan musical tradition managed to retain its continuity until the Soviet regime. After that, the Soviets enforced its codification according to academic standards. Tuvan musical practices were thus evaluated and transformed through unfamiliar rules of academic music. Despite this process, the throat singing debuted in its pure, non-professionalised form in 1934 in records produced by the Moscow Sound Recording Factory at the request of the government of the Tuvan People's Republic. It was welcomed warmly as 'an extraordinary example of creative human fantasy in the realm of sound' (Süzükei 2010: 212–213). Today, the tradition of throat singing and Tuvan music flourishes mostly on the international scene, with an annual international festival of *khöömei* that attracts primarily foreign musicians from the United States and Europe. There are numerous professional groups of throat singers in Kyzyl, such as Alash and Hun-Hur-Tu; however, their performances in Kyzyl are rather sporadic. Most of the time they tour around the world, with recordings and distribution occurring primarily outside of Russia.

The elusive characteristics of Tuvan throat singing have challenged numerous ethnographers who have attempted to delineate the production of sound in *khöömei* through concepts such as aesthetics, mimesis or folk philosophy (Hodgkinson 2005/2006; Levin 2006; Levin & Edgerton 1999). Levin and Edgerton (1999) argue that throat singers interact with the natural sound world by imitating the sounds of places and beings. In particular, they copy those sounds of nature that offer rich harmonics, such as wind or water. Consequently, throat singing is like drawing a picture of the landscape (an image), and thus its essence lies in a mimetic faculty, with the 'mimetic impulse' being triggered by 'perceptual immediacy' (Levin 2006: 78). Conversely, Hodgkinson argues that throat singers are not mimetically replicating the sounds of nature and thus creating images, but rather 'transmitting their inner experience triggered by what they see' (2005/2006: 7). In this way, music is said to converge into an aesthetic concept equivalent to what in the European framework could be called a kind of philosophy. However, rather than concentrating on what throat singing is about, I would like to draw attention to the unique structural aspects of the sound unit in *khöömei*. As I will illustrate, the way in which Tuvans theorise sound in *khöömei* opens wider avenues to explore how it precipitates knowledge and experience of the world and relations within it. First of all, however, let me introduce how sound is constructed in *khöömei*. A comparison between the throat singing tradition and classical, academic treatments of music and musical composition will allow us to extrapolate the distinct features of Tuvan sound.

Classical theories of music and Tuvan throat singing

In classical music, based on the 12-note system and equal temperament (Babbitt 1960, Duffin 2007), styles, theories and performances are based on the concept of tone. Tone constitutes a pure sound with precisely defined stable pitch and strength. Each tone occupies a strict position on the pitch scale; if changed, the position may lead to the destruction of the purity of the sound (as in the instances when a singer suddenly begins to sing out of tune). Subsequently, any composition is organised around a specific conception of rhythm. In short, tones progress through a clear form that has a certain duration and that moves towards the prepared conclusion. Moreover, in classical music composition, in order to produce melody, a new sound has to be produced each time from a different source, and to move from one sound to another one needs a physical movement – changing pitch by, for example, pressing strings (Süzükei 2010: 33). In this way, melody is constructed from discrete sounds, sounds coordinated through independent

100 *My drum is thunder*

row-organised pitch scales (see Figure 4.1). In very simplistic terms, sound is packed into isolated independent tones and oriented outwardly. Most importantly, any composition constitutes a unified structure that can easily be copied and learnt and which is arranged into fixed music notations.

The essential difference between the classical or academic conception of sound and sound in throat singing is that Tuvan music cannot be correlated with row-organised and linear structuring; it does not constitute a unified and copyable structure. In *khöömei*, the sound emerges from a drone–overtone system, a system in which a central sound, the drone, is being split into its partial overtones (see Figure 4.2). It is a system based on the subordination and coordination of the fundamental sound and its parts. Therefore, music in throat singing is timbre-centred rather than pitch-centred (Süzükei 2010). In short, the basic sound opens up and produces a variety of overtones; thus, drone and overtones become an inseparable whole. They are mutually dependent. In this way, any sound unit or sound 'atom' in *khöömei* resembles a spreading fan. Inside, there is a whole acoustic world created by the spray of overtones. In other words, as emphasised by Valentina, sound in throat singing avoids any strict motif, regular rhythm or melody in order to establish the timbral qualities of the drone–overtone sound. Rather than repeatedly producing a new sound from a different source, the melodic alternation of overtones occurs against the background of uninterrupted and constantly sounding drones. In this way, sound in *khöömei* is centripetal, which means that the parts (overtones) are directed and drawn towards the centre (drone) (Süzükei 2010). The drone and its overtones exist simultaneously. This simultaneity constructs a

Figure 4.1 Sound unit in the classical (12-tone) musical system

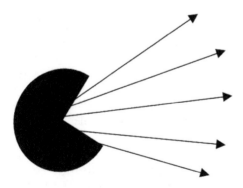

Figure 4.2 Sound unit in throat singing

space of turbulence in which the singer and their voice are constantly enmeshed whilst performing *khöömei*. What the audience hear is not a unified structure of pure tones, but rather timbral richness and a wide range of free overtones.

As a result, *khöömei* constitutes a distinct form of music with particular and unique features, each melody is different. It cannot ever be repeated in exactly the same way, and thus cannot and should not be codified in any written form. Given this, throat singers are recognised not by the pieces they sing, but rather by their voices. As Valentina put it, sound in Tuva becomes a holographic rather than a photographic image and is akin to a snowball; when thrown, one can notice how the snow sprays. Alternatively, one can think about the sound unit as a diamond with multiple reflections on its surface, or a snow globe. In other words, to hear things the Tuvan way is to be able to sense and appreciate these delicate nuances of sounds, to notice each evasive spray of the drone and to grasp every multi-faceted reflection.

Given these complex and context-dependent characteristics, Valentina was always disturbed when people suggested that throat singing could be codified and learned from musical notation: 'you cannot put this into a unified equation' she would always insist, as *khöömei* is supposed to be learnt only by listening.

> People always need an image, something tangible you can rely on. Throw yourself into the sea of throat music and you become disoriented. You try to get out by calling it an imitation, a picture of landscape or even an independent music genre or avant-garde music, otherwise, you are lost,

she would always conclude our heated discussions. Indeed, the theoretical understanding of music in Tuva disrupts, to a certain extent, academic or classical thinking about sound, turning it upside down and instead embodying the lack of 'logical' and universally codified ideas about musical composition. Tuvan music can serve as an example of a non-linear or variant system, divested of an ordered sequence of tones. Rather than a sequentially organised structure, the essence of sound production in *khöömei* lies in the opening up of a drone into multiple overtones. Thus, sound in throat singing offers the structure of dispersion and centripetalism,[5] a cluster of interdependent parts that, in order to exist, must remain immersed in the state of controlled turbulence, that is, interrelated with and through the fundamental sound, the centre. Having established the distinct features of the sound unit in *khöömei*, the properties of centripetalism and turbulence, I will now show how this structure of sound is homologous to the structural organisation of shamanic rituals involving curses. As will be seen, in the ritual event the drum with its sounds occupies a focal position within this structure similar to the position of the drone sound in *khöömei*.

The role of the drum in shamanic rituals

Shamanic drums (*dünggür*) are an essential element of the shamanic instrumental repertoire in Tuva. Before each ritual, the drum is placed in a designated

102 *My drum is thunder*

spot by the shaman, where it is meant to dry in order to produce loud and powerful sounds. The shaman always chooses the person who is asked to take the drum, and it is considered a form of privilege and recognition. Tuvan shamans often stress how most of their practices can be conducted without certain elements of shamanic equipment, such as the costume, the shamanic hat (*burt*), brass scissors (*ches hachy*) or different shamanic tokens (*eeren*). Nonetheless, this does not seem to apply to drums, without which any of the major rituals (curse deflection, acquiring good fortune) cannot be conducted. In Tuva, it is precisely through the use of drums that the shamans are distinguished from other practitioners. Drums used to be made out of different skins according to the different purposes they served. For instance, bull skin was utilised in the time of Mongolian and Chinese invasions, when stealing was common. Skin from a bull was supposed to be the most efficient for detecting and casting *kargysh-chatka* when dealing with cases of theft. Drums made out of horse skin were meant to work faster. Drums made out of wolf skin were designed to kill the shaman. Officially, shamans refuse to inflict death curses and kill their rivals today. They only admit to divesting someone of their powers or taking away their energy. Given this, drums used by the shamans nowadays are made from goat or deer skin and have less strength to kill and are only meant to harm. In anthropological literature, drums tend to be conceptualised as symbolic instruments which allow shamans to communicate with spirits and travel to different worlds (Eliade 1972; Li 1992; Shirokogoroff 1935); as mythological and cosmic representations (Pentikainen 2010); and as healing or therapeutic tools (Van Deusen 2004). The idea of turbulence used in relation to the sounds and powers produced by shamanic drums during the rituals allows an important spin to be added to the ways in which the role of drums in shamanic practice has been anthropologically approached. In other words, taking the assertions that the drum is thunder seriously permits us to go further and problematise both drums and their sounds as ontologically driven phenomena which can profoundly contribute to our understanding of ritual dynamics.

Once the shaman begins drumming during the ritual, the sound of the drum is understood as a particular power (*kysh*) that creates whirls as well as thunder or tornadoes. In this way, the drum opens a particular event and unsettles cosmic configurations, creating a distinctly turbulent space. This cosmic unsettlement is indispensable for the shaman to undertake negotiations with spirits and (re) arrange things afresh through inflicting or deflecting curses (an important point to which I shall return in the following chapter). Throughout most of the ritual, the shaman sits still while continuously drumming which illuminates how, in a similar fashion to *sünezin*, the drum constitutes the centre that is rooted in a given event. The drum is perceived as the beginning and the central element of the ritual proceedings, around which all the other elements are arranged and kept in a relation of interdependency. In other words, the drum affects the space of the ritual and the elements it entails in the same way that shaking affects a snow globe – lifting diverse pieces while creating an arena for reconfigurations. In order to illustrate this, I turn again to ethnography.

My drum is thunder 103

On one occasion, I went with Hovalygmaa to visit her two nephews, Sajan and Bajlak. As I mentioned earlier, Tuvans often arrange meetings with a shaman in order to get a type of 'check-up' to deflect any possible curses. This was the case with the brothers we were about to visit. Departing in the early morning, we left the arrays of blocks of flats behind us and arrived at the outskirts of the city, populated with dilapidated wooden houses where the brothers lived. The older brother, Bajlak, described himself as a 28-year-old local 'mafioso'. He was recently divorced and had a particular weakness for drinking, which resulted in constant fights and problems with the police. The younger brother, 23-year-old Sajan, was a rising star in wrestling and was about to represent Tuva in a national wrestling competition in Mongolia. The house they lived in had low ceilings and gave the impression of randomly organised boxes that someone had put together and turned into a living space. We all sat in the living room where we were given food, take-away noodles from the nearby canteen. Curious neighbours and relatives looked into the house and, encouraged by the shaman, decided to join us for the ritual. The room filled with people, as the shaman focused on the two brothers. In the end, we were joined by four men and a woman who carried a newborn baby. One of the men, however, was asked to leave as the shaman found him 'clean' (*aryg*), in the sense that he did not suffer from any curses. After an hour of preparation and chatting, the shaman began the process of cleansing the brothers. Everyone, with the exception of myself was asked to remove their hats as the shaman was about to deflect any curses from the spectators as well. The shaman lit juniper and directed smoke towards each person while spitting under their arms. She also used blessed juniper to mark certain areas of the room separating the space in which spirits were expected to arrive from the rest of the flat. Then, she took her drum and sat on a chair, humming softly and very quietly. *Düvülendir dingmirej beer dungurumny* – 'the drum (the sound of the drum) creates thunder and loud lightning', she began to sing. Her voice strengthened abruptly and turned into gurgling laughter. Then, she relapsed into humming as if nursing a child to sleep. A moment later, she jumped and shouted: *hyshh hyshh* as if pushing away a nasty animal. Her voice became stronger as she began to drum loudly and to sing *algysh* – a shamanic hymn. Suddenly, someone aggressively knocked on the door. No one responded. The shaman remained focused on the clients. She was drumming louder and louder, her voice at its highest pitch and strength. I knew this was the moment when she was forcing the spirits that brought curses to leave. The baby on the woman's arm started to cry and she had to breastfeed it, which irritated the shaman. A few minutes later, one of the brothers' cousins arrived and decided to join the ritual. The shaman continued playing the drum and, now gently humming, asked the spirits for their blessing and good luck for the brothers. In between the chants, she revealed there was a spirit living in the flat intending to curse Sajan, which forced her to prolong the process of deflecting the curse as she had to summon more spirits and adjust her chant. After a short break, the shaman concentrated on the remaining clients. As she had instructed me on a number of occasions, regardless of her physical state she was not allowed to stop a ritual halfway through or refuse to help a member of the community who asked her

104   *My drum is thunder*

for help. She performed a short song in front of the next client and moved along towards the cousin who had arrived halfway through the ritual. Suddenly, her voice became faster and louder. She started screaming and shouting at everyone to step back. We sprang to our feet and gathered in a corner while observing the scene. The shaman began spinning and crying out loud. We heard her singing:

What is this?
Black stamp has been marked.
(…) Get rid of the black stamp! Tears have been shed/hidden.
Someone on the horse is stalking from behind.
From way behind the mountains and hills
there is a bitch (a woman) crying a blood tear
waiting for the child!
Her cold arm stretching towards
your child!
What is this?
There is a danger of a curse
what do we need this evil for
there is something else coming from another place
something that has been summoned!
Kandaaj chüvel? Tölüngerge kara tangma bazyp kaap dyr.
Bazyp kaany kara tangma hajladyngar!
Karyg chatka kylyp kaap dyr, dengerlerim!
Karak chazjyn kaap dyr. Kara sungu chazjyp kaap dyr.
Azjyg cungu chazjyp kap dyr.
Tölüngerning artynajdan, Attyg kizji kedep choruur.
Artar-cynnar artynajda. Eshpi kizji yglap orar. gerni manap orar.
Cook holun cunup algan tölünerzje!
Kandaaj chüvel?
Kargysh-chatka ajyyly-dyr! Aza-buktung heree-le dir!
Öcke churttan kelgen chüve dir. Kygyj-bile kelgen chüve dir.

The shaman sat next to the terrified man who cringed, holding his knees. His whole posture suddenly shrunk and he looked like a petrified child. The shaman hid the man's face with the drum and asked one of us to bring a glass of water. She asked him to drink it fast, as if it was the last drop of water he could get. We all stood still waiting for her to tell us what to do. The shaman reluctantly explained to us what happened. She detected a very strong curse, inflicted with mutton blood by a powerful shaman from a village. It turned out the man was a suspect in a murder case. The family of the murdered woman, convinced of his guilt, decided to send him a death curse. Water, offered by the shaman, was meant to restore energy balance within the man and prevent his body from immediate drying and subsequent death, which is one of the forms in which the strongest curses materialise themselves. We all went outside while the shaman arranged a curse deflection ritual with the frightened man. He thanked her profusely and offered 500

My drum is thunder 105

roubles (approximately 5 pounds), although the regular offering was 100 roubles (1 pound). I asked the shaman if the man was guilty. She shook her head. 'If he was, *Erlik*[6] spirits would have arrived. They did not. The man is innocent'.

As presented in the vignette, the drum marks the beginning of ritual proceedings and accompanies diverse occurrences that unfold in the wake of its sounds. In order to engage with the machinery of the curse, the shaman has to produce a particular kind of turbulent space, which allows her to unmake previous configurations and undertake negotiations with spirits while generating new cosmic arrangements in the form of curse infliction or deflection. In this way, the efficacy of the shaman's work is contingent on a kind of disturbance and uncertainty, exemplified in the semi-controlled turbulent characteristics of the event. Thus, the components of the ritual, centred on the shamanic drum, function in a structurally centripetal way, homologous to the structure of the sound unit in *khöömei*. More than that, the sudden arrival of the 'innocent' man and the way his presence is incorporated in the shamanic ritual, along with other unexpected developments such as detecting the death curse and discovering the presence of another spirit in the house, add an interesting spin to the fashion in which ritual dynamics have been, in classic approaches, discussed within anthropology. In order to illustrate my idea, I turn to some parameters for comparison of shamanic rituals and religious rituals, in particular to the ways in which ritual space and ritual events are organised in shamanic and liturgical orders.

Liturgical order versus shamanic ritual

I suggest that shamanic rituals in Tuva are characterised by a turbulent movement of different elements turned in and interdependent on the drum. In other words, the organisational structure of the ritual stemming from turbulence triggered by the drum is characterised by the elements of fluidity and unpredictability. This remains in a certain contradistinction to the ways in which the sequence of events has been conceptualised by some anthropologists in religious rituals. Rappaport's *Ritual and Religion in the Making of Humanity* (1999) opens the way for such a comparison between organisational structure in some religious rituals as contrasted with a shamanic ritual in the Tuvan context. Rappaport defines ritual form as 'more or less invariant sequences of formal acts and utterances not entirely encoded by the performer' (1999: 24). As he suggests, the most formalised behavioural patterns are expected to prevail in religious rituals. Thus, in liturgical orders events are organised around conventional elements, such as decorous gestures and postures, whilst behaviour tends to be repetitive and punctilious. These elements are arranged in time and space in a more or less fixed manner while maintaining the relations of order as opposed to chaos and disorder. Along these lines, Rappaport illuminates the importance of invariance, stressing the narrow choices participants are offered in rituals, such as whether to take communion or not. As he concludes, these are the formal options strictly specified by the performed order. Unquestionably though, as he also points out, even the most invariant liturgical orders are open to, and sometimes demand, variation. Nonetheless, what is crucial is the fact that the formal end of the ritual towards which such events are directed is not influenced or altered. In other words, variance, or what I shall call disturbances, is not blocking any transition which is key to the ultimate formal finale of the ritual. In this way, the ritual events proceed more or less coherently towards a specific final aim, such as communion or absolution, from a point A, outside the church/profane, towards a point B, the altar/sacred. As in classical music, which requires an organised sequence of tones in order to produce a melody, rituals demand 'fixed sequences of acts and utterances following each other in order' (Rappaport 1999: 35) allowing them to reach a conclusion or final destination.

I suggest that the structural organisation of Tuvan shamanic ritual is different (Figures 4.3 and 4.4). Crucially, rather than being structured around an ordered sequence of events leading to a transition from position A to position B, the ritual is characterised by a turbulent movement of different elements turned in and interdependent on the drum, which generates the opening and the unsettlement of the cosmos. The ensuing structure and the proceedings of the ritual are contingent on a receptiveness to disturbances, that is, interruptions and inconsistencies by anyone and anything, for instance, the sudden materialisation of the spirit living in the house, the unexpected arrival of the cousin or an incidental detection of a death curse. At the beginning of the ritual, the shaman addresses the spirits by saying that the sound of the drum creates thunder. Once the shaman begins

Figure 4.3 Sound theory in classical 12-tone system and in throat singing

Ritual structure in liturgical order

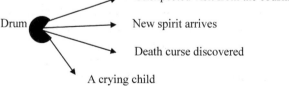

Figure 4.4 Ritual structure in liturgical and shamanic orders

drumming, the space of the ritual begins to open up in a similar way to a fan. The sounds of the drum start to instigate turbulence – 'the sound of my drum creates thunder' – sings the shaman. All of a sudden, the room becomes filled with clients, the arriving spirits, the ill-wishing ancestor and a woman with a blood tear. The shaman, as an artisan, plays the drum, and through manipulating its sounds, she subtly modulates and manages the clients, and the spirits, in other words, navigates the turbulent or 'timbral' character of the ritual. The occurrences in the ritual are further reconfigured with the sudden arrival of another cousin, abrupt knocking on the door and the child crying and demanding food. Like reflections in water or reflections in a diamond, these elements constantly position and reposition themselves, become more or less present and contingent on the work of the shaman, her interactions with sounds through drumming and the extent to which she focuses on different elements of the ritual: the clients, the spirits, curses, diagnosis, negotiations and so on. Whilst navigating the shifting elements of the ritual, she continues to sit still in one place for most of the ceremony, which reinforces the central and static position of the drum in the event. Thus, whilst remaining in the centre of unstable events, the drum binds up and maintains numerous elements in a relationship of dependency, including the shaman, the terrified client and the spirits responsible for both deflecting and inflicting curses (see Figure 4.4). Disturbance and dispersion occur through the constant interchange of the elements without any concrete, formal order – the cry of the baby, the spirit observing and plotting against the client, the arrival of the woman with a blood tear – a dispersion very similar to the mechanics of timbre and the way it develops in throat singing.[7] In other words, the space within which ritual occurs is produced through 'spatially diffused points (…) not as links in a chain, but as dispersions in a single place' (Poulantzas 1980: 101) organised around and interwoven with the central element, the drum. Rather than a transition from point A to point B, from sin to absolution or from the aisle to the altar (see Figure 4.3), the structure of the ritualistic event remains inconsistent whilst being contingent on and shaped by the (mis)management of sociocosmic relations (negotiating with spirits, protecting the client, countercursing).[8] Contrasting approaches to sound in classical music and in throat singing with the study of liturgical and shamanic orders allow us to not only elucidate how the organisational structure of shamanic ritual is generated but also illuminate the intrinsic features of uncertainty upon which this structure and the success of the ritual depend.

Shamanic ritual is about an unexpected encounter

Shamanic rituals in the Tuvan context welcome unpredictability, sudden confrontations and an abrupt turn of events in order to efficiently conduct a ceremony. In other words, the essence of the ritual is exactly the uncertain construction of the ritual setting and what occurs within it, which consequently influences the outcome. This conveys also in other shamanic contexts. The elements of uncertainty and inconsistency in shamanic rituals reverberate, for example, in Taussig's (1987) depiction of the *yage* rituals through the lens of montage, which means

108 *My drum is thunder*

they are seen as 'alterations, cracks, displacements, interruptions for shitting, for vomiting, for a cloth to wipe one's face' (1987: 441). Similarly, for Yaminahua shamans, the cosmos is never perceived as completed and therefore every ritual space is unpredictable and contains uncertainty, which is, however, expected and desired (Townsley 1993: 466). In Tuva, the space of the ritual is opened up in order to allow the arrival of new spirits and new happenings. The shamans have no certainty about what this space will contain and are prepared to find something new in it each time. Thus, the Tuvan cosmos presents itself as constantly in motion, fragile and intrinsically turbulent. It is intrinsically unstable in the sense that it remains perpetually inconsistent and unpredictable to humans. Rather than reflecting a state of cooperative organisation and social stability, it is permeated by ongoing instances of frictions and shifts contingent on the uncertainty of both human actions as well as on gods' and spirits' moods and needs, intertwined with ongoing transformations in the world, including technological development and changes in economic and political realms. Anthropologists have been keen to criticise the previous trends to depict cosmology as a state of ordered sociality emerging from chaos (Sahlins 1996) and focused on elucidating the shifting and fragmented patterns of cosmic movements (Mikkelsen 2016; Pedersen 2011; Pedersen & Willerslev 2010; Witherspoon 1977). For instance, Pedersen and Willerslev (2010) argue that in North Asia, due to a lack of ontological fullness triggered by economic and political transformations, cosmologies are more fragile and thus require continuous maintenance. Drawing on this, in an example from Northern Mongolia, Pedersen (2011) describes a broken cosmos, suffering from an ontological breakdown caused by transition to market economy in the wake of Soviet disintegration. In contrast, Mikkelsen (2016), rather than opposing chaos and order in Bugkalot cosmology, introduces a third alternative: he shows how an intrinsically chaotic cosmos becomes momentarily stabilised through human and shamanic forms of engagement. In this way, while taking chaos *seriously* (2016: 202, original emphasis) Mikkelsen attempts to approach fragmentation as a cosmic pattern rather than an exemplification of 'transitional cosmology' (Pedersen 2011). Echoing this approach to some extent, Witherspoon shows how, among the Navajo, all things are understood to be in a state of motion unless this motion has been somehow withdrawn (1977). Motion and stasis, therefore, like chaos and stability, constitute an essential opposition upon which the Navajo life is organised. In a similar fashion to the Navajo and Bugkalot examples, Tuvan cosmology never reveals itself as complete, but rather remains folding and unfolding in diverse, unforeseen configurations. It is the shamans who momentarily undertake attempts at (re)arranging this process, never knowing, however, which turn it might take. This element of the 'unexpected', along with the fact that the same structuring of the ritual event pertains to rituals dedicated to both curse infliction and deflection, illuminates additional aspects of ambiguity embedded in shamanic practice in Tuva. Crucially, there is no difference in the type of turbulence triggered by the drum that is produced for the purpose of infliction and deflection of the curse. What matters is the intention of the shaman performing the ritual and the efficacy of their performance (which I shall discuss in the following chapter).

My drum is thunder 109

Thus (to revisit my discussion on ambiguity in shamanic practice in Chapter 2), rather than perceiving shamanic practice through the lens of beautifying, curing or fixing the world as opposed to inflicting harm, the ethnographic context of Tuva illuminates how shamans simply confront the incessant flow of cosmic events, while establishing temporary arrangements in the form of curse infliction or deflection. These arrangements should not, however, be understood in a straightforward way through the opposed ideas of harm and cure as markers of (im)moral behaviour. Instead, they constitute reports on the cosmic flow and delineate what things are or are not, rather than emphasising the curing or damaging aspects of shamanic practice. It is important to notice, however, that there is a significant difference between the type of turbulence that is produced by the shamanic drum and the type that is produced by the throat singer and curses. This difference lies in the degree of control that a person has over the condition of turbulence. During throat singing, the singer produces controlled turbulence while responding to diverse surrounding impulses. Turbulence produced by the shamanic drum is semi-controlled, as it is partially navigated by the shaman but also involves the aspect of uncertainty. Turbulence associated with being cursed remains uncontrolled and leads to unpredictable behaviours that are beyond the victim's power.

Through an exploration of the similarities and connections between throat singing and shamanic practice, the significance of sound exemplifies and brings together most of the themes I have emphasised so far in this book– themes like Tuvan shamanic practice, the role of the drum, cursed personhood as well as the importance of turbulence and centripetalism. Sounds produced by the drum are indispensable in order to discompose the old cosmic configurations and confront curses. Initiating the event, they shape the ritual in a particular centripetal structure which binds up shamans, spirits and the audience in an interdependent fashion. However, while the sounds of the drum unsettle things by producing turbulence (one could say that they prepare the ground for the shaman to work), something else takes on the role of confronting turbulence and (re)arranging dynamics through curse deflection or further curse infliction. This is the shaman's voice accompanied by the sounds of certain shamanic tools. In the next chapter, therefore, I am going to take my discussion of sound a step further by concentrating on the agency of the shaman's voice – a sound upon which the successful infliction or deflection of curses and the overall efficacy of shamanic performance depends. In this way, while the sounds of the drum unsettle the cosmic arrangements through producing semi-controlled turbulence, the sounds generated by the shamanic vocal apparatus do the opposite – that is, they confront turbulence and (re)arrange things afresh through implementing curse deflection or further curse infliction.

Notes

1 Development of a 'theory' of throat singing as well as any scientific treatment of Tuvan music began in the 1940s (Süzükei 2010: 4).

110   *My drum is thunder*

2 The term 'turbulence' (Rus. *turbulentnost'*), borrowed from physics, was first employed in the context of Siberian music in the 20th century to delineate the acoustical effects produced by a jaw harp (Levin and Süzükei 2017: 14).

3 Valentina Süzükei is my close friend whose unique expertise on ethnomusicology echoes throughout this chapter both in the form of our personal conversations as well as Valentina's key publications.

4 Throat singers were mainly male due to a taboo that throat singing may cause, for example, infertility (Levin and Edgerton 1999: 82). This belief is being gradually dismissed among Tuvans although it is still rare to meet women performing throat singing (except for the female shamans).

5 This kind of structuring (centripetalism) permeates, to a certain extent, other aspects of Tuvan existence. Among Tuvans there is a particular stress placed on the movement from the whole (centre) to its parts, which today is formally most evident in throat singing. However, it used to prevail in other elements of life. Despite being 'archaic' and rarely recognised, I am including a few examples of this phenomenon in this analysis as possible proof of the wider significance that centripetalism seems to have in Tuvan ontology. For example, the significance of the shift from the whole to its parts, rather than the other way around, echoes understandings of time arrangements that become obvious when comparing the Tuvan and Russian languages. For instance, in the Russian language half past eight (Rus. *polovina deviatovo*) translates as 'the half of the ninth hour' and suggests a shift from the part to the whole. For Tuvans, this concept is confusing as they are more accustomed to the reversed logic. Eight-thirty (*ses shak thartyk*) translates as 'eight-hour half' implying a shift from the whole to its parts. This, in turn, produces many funny anecdotes about Tuvans missing their flights, buses or appointments. Another context in which the relation between the centre and its parts is exemplified in the centripetal understanding relates to musical instruments. Before the arrival of the Soviets, when playing string instruments called *byzaanchy*, Tuvans used to employ a particular technique focusing on touching the strings in order to produce music. Rather than pressing them from above, they used to place the fingers underneath the strings and, in this way, make music. In the process of the 'professionalisation' of Tuvan traditional music conducted by the Soviets, this technique was lost. Nevertheless, as Valentina suggested, this particular way of performing was based on sound production embedded in the movement from the whole – the centre of the instrument – to its parts, that is, the strings rather than the other way around, displayed in academic techniques of playing musical instruments.

6 Erlik is one of the gods sometimes compared by my informants to the Christian Satan or devil. There are also small Erlik spirits that can help as well as disturb people depending on the context, which I briefly described in Chapter 2.

7 There are other parallels between the organisational structure of a musical piece in *khöömei* and shamanic rituals. As mentioned earlier, in throat singing the melody is unique, in the sense that it cannot be repeated again in exactly the same way. As stressed by Valentina, the perception of a melodic structure is unimportant for experienced listeners. Rather, such listeners' sensory focus is on the timbral palette organised not by a melodic structure but by something that can be compared, according to Valentina, to expressionist gestures. In a similar way, the shamans claim that each chant and sound production ushered during the ritual is unique and contingent on the mood and needs of the spirits. Moreover, the shamans rarely seem to remember what they sang about and often the elements of the ritual are instantly forgotten. In this way, similar to individual pieces in throat singing, separate shamanic rituals cannot be codified and narrowed to more or less invariant sequences of events and utterances. Their efficacy is contingent on the opening up and unsettlement of the universe facilitated by the drum and demands, interruptions as well as unexpected occurrences.

My drum is thunder 111

8 One of the most variegated forms of action among Tuvans, which includes uncon-strained movement of elements similar to that of turbulence described in relation to drums and shamanic rituals, is travelling habits. When describing their trips through the taiga or the steppe, my interlocutors would rarely discuss travelling strictly in terms of reaching point B from point A. Rather, they would talk about things happening on the way and the road itself as if simply moving around. In fact, the idea of movement was often compared to an echo or shining reflections on water by my Tuvan friends. It was about being in one place and swiftly shifting to another without seeking any final desti-nation. Indeed, to a lesser extent, although in an equally noticeable way, while walking in the streets of Kyzyl, my interlocutors often gave me the impression they were not concerned about the place they were meant to be going to. During some interviews or trips to visit shamans, we often ended up meandering through the streets, which never seemed to cause any distress or concern to them. These, what one might call, 'dis-turbed' mobility habits do not pertain only to Tuva. Similar tendencies were described by Safonowa and Santha (2011) in their ethnography of Evenki. As the authors explain, Evenki wander between situations or events that provoke companionship. Their trips are characterised by the lack of a prescribed route. As they say, the breakdowns, river crossings, drunken encounters and other unexpected circumstances liberate them from the hegemony of the initial purpose. This means they can easily take risks, go some-where without having a concrete purpose and look for occasional contacts and encoun-ters (2011: 76). This seemingly random and unpredictable pattern of behaviour is also reflected in jokes and funny anecdotes that people tell about their experiences with foreigners. For example, Tuvans are infamous for being late. As a result, foreign guests often experience painful moments and little breakdowns trying to meet a Tuvan at a par-ticular time or organise some sort of activity, a trip or an interview. Their dependency on schedules and punctuality clashes with Tuvan ways of arranging meetings, which linger somewhere between making a sudden appearance and not showing up at all.

Bibliography

Babbitt, M. 1960. Twelve-Tone Invariants as Compositional Determinants. *Musical Quarterly* no. 46(2): 246–259.

Darzaa, V. 1998. *Kochevaja kul'tura Tuvincev*. Kyzyl: TCK.

Duffin, R. W. 2007. *How Equal Temperament Ruined Harmony (and Why You Should Care)*. New York: W.W.Norton & Company.

Eliade, M. 1972. *Shamanism: Archaic Techniques of Ecstasy*. London: Routledge & K.Paul.

Hodgkinson, T. 2005/2006. Musicians, Carvers, Shamans. *The Cambridge Journal of Anthropology* no. 25 (3): 1–16.

Levin, T. 2006. *Where Rivers and Mountains Sing*. Indianapolis: Indiana University.

Levin, T. & Edgerton, E. M. 1999. The Throat Singers of Tuva. *Scientific American* no. 281 (3): 80–87.

Levin, T. & Süzükei, V. 2017. Timbre-Centred Listening in the Soundscape of Tuva. In E. I. Dolan and A. Rehding (eds), *The Oxford Handbook of Timbre*. Oxford: Oxford University Press.

Li, L. 1992. The Symbolization Process of the Shamanic Drums Used by the Manchus and Other Peoples in North Asia. *Yearbook for Traditional Music* no. 24: 52–80.

Mikkelsen, H. H. 2016. Chaosmology. Shamanism and personhood among the Bugkalot. *HAU: Journal of Ethnographic Theory* no. 6 (1): 189–205.

Pedersen, A. M. & Willerslev, R. 2010. Proportional Holism: Joking the Cosmos Into the Right Shape in North Asia. In T. Otto & N. Bubandt (eds), *Experiments in Holism*, 262–278. Chichester, West Sussex; Malden, MA: Willey-Blackwell.

112 *My drum is thunder*

Pedersen, A. M. 2011. *Not Quite Shamans*. Ithaca; London: Cornell University Press.

Pentikainen, J. 2010. The Shamanic Drum as Cognitive Map. *Cahiers de literature orale* no. 67–68: 1–12.

Poulantzas, N. 1980. *State, Power, Socialism*. London: Verso.

Rappaport, A. R. 1999. *Ritual and Religion in the Making of Humanity*. Cambridge: Cambridge University Press.

Safonova, T. & Santha, I. 2011. Mapping Evenki Land: The Study of Mobility Patterns in Easter Siberia. *Folklore: Electronic Journal of Folklore* no. 49: 71–96.

Sahlins, M. 1996. The Sadness of Sweetness: The Native Anthropology of Western Cosmology. *Current Anthropology* no. 37 (3): 395–417.

Shirokogoroff, S. 1935. *Psychomental Complex of the Tungus*. London: Kegan Paul.

Süzükei, V. 2010. *Problema konceptualnogo edinstva teorii i praktiki*. Kyzyl: OAO.

Taussig, M. 1987. *Shamanism, Colonialism and the Wild Man*. Chicago; London: The University of Chicago Press.

Townsley, G. 1993. Song Paths The Ways and Means of Yaminahua Shamanic Knowledge. *L'Homme* no. 33 (126–128): 449–468.

Van Deusen, K. 2004. *Singing Story, Healing Drum. Shamans and Storytellers of Turkic Siberia*. Montreal: McGill Queen's University Press.

Witherspoon, G. 1977. *Language and Art in the Navajo Universe*. Ann Arbor: University of Michigan Press.

5 Voiced into being

The power of sound and shamanic voice in the cursing rituals

When I began observing different shamans in ritual settings I became used to a repertoire of sonic elements that most of them were incorporating in their practices. These components usually included the clanging and crackling of the shamanic coat, delicate jangling of the bells attached to different instruments and the rhythmical sounds of the drum intertwined with the shamans' singing (*alganyrar*). I came to realise how the production of sounds constituted an important element of ritual proceedings, replacing the classical ideas of trance involving speaking in tongues or rolling the eyes (Chapter 2). I was also enchanted by the role of drums as instigators of a particular kind of turbulence necessary to discompose previous cosmological arrangements and relations with spirits (Chapter 4). However, what I was particularly still perplexed by were my Tuvan friends' claims that the effectuating power of ritual lay in *how* the sounds were pronounced by the shaman and not so much in *what* the shaman was actually singing about. I was further intrigued by the claims that a 'good shaman' who sings well can allow people to momentarily encounter spirits during the ritual. How could sounds become a mode for material interactions with spirits? It was not until Hovalygmaa and I revisited Ajdyn, the client suffering from a horrific death curse inflicted by a spirit in the form of a woman with a blood tear (discussed in the previous chapter), when I abruptly became familiar with the full spectrum of possibilities that the shaman's voice and their deeply sounded performance can offer, allowing me thereby to better understand the efficacy of sounds in the processes of both inflicting and deflecting curses. In this chapter, I wish to further contribute to the readings of sound and musical performance as potent to effect change. Following Seeger's idea about musical analysis as key to the understandings of the social and cultural environments (1987: xiii), my analysis of the shamanic rituals as sounded performance is thus an in-depth exploration of how sounds act as dialogical rather than representative tools, redefining what we understand as communication and contributing to our comprehension of how people may produce, interpret and experience relationships and reality through sound. In particular, what I wish to open to ethnographic inquiry is the effectuating power of shamanic voice and the ways through which it facilitates intermittent encounters between humans and non-humans in the cursing rituals in Tuva.

DOI: 10.4324/9781003245391-8

114   *Voiced into being*

Sound in shamanic performance

Numerous anthropological accounts illuminate how sounds have the potency to create and transform the fabric of the world rather than simply represent it. For example, Brabec de Mori shows how, when adequately produced by the singer, sounds can become 'sonic substances' that linger in the patients' bodies and facilitate healing (2015: 25). Feld (2012 [1982]) discusses how among the Kaluli linguistic and musical patterns are derived iconically from natural sounds, providing a variety of communicative possibilities. Using Tuvan hunting as an example, Harrison (2004) offers a compelling analysis of sound as central to controlling prey as well as influencing weather. Bringing together sound and speech, Nuckolls (2010) and High (2018) show how in the Amerindian context ideophones can generate and control complex realignments between humans and non-humans. In many anthropological accounts, sound is looked at as an integral part of music, singing and vocal performance. In these studies, the power of song to effect change is clearly opposed to its perception as a mere system of representation. Songs and music are shown to regulate and maintain cosmological orders (Basso 1985; Seeger 1987), facilitate communication between humans and non-humans (Brabec de Mori 2015) or constitute complex processes of relating with others (Course 2009).

The power of singing and music is particularly clear in shamanic practices and different forms of shamanic singing. In many cultural arrangements, shamanic songs and chants are central to healing and curing practices (Balzer 1997; Gow 1996; Hugh-Jones 1996; Lévi-Strauss 1963; Van Deusen 2004). Shamans refer to music and singing when seeking to communicate with spirits (Levin 2006; Townsley 1993), inflict harm (Olsen 1996) or maintain balance and order in the world (Piedade 2013). The analysis of shamanic performances, chants and their function is often tightly connected with the study of language and speech, where the transformative qualities are ascribed to the very process of uttering words. This is particularly visible in Amerindian contexts (Déléage 2009; Olsen 1996; Townsley 1993) where language is often seen as the force that facilitates change (Witherspoon 1977), as well as in some of the works on shamanic performance in Siberian studies (Hoppal & Sipos 2010; Van Deusen 1997). Central to these accounts is, therefore, the 'magical power of words' (Tambiah 1968), whereas, when formally connected with words, sounds become purely 'a sonorous matter of language' (Severi 2015: 245).

How does this correspond with Tuvans' ideas that it is the power of the shamanic voice, as well as the sounds it produces, that remains key to the events in the ritual? I wish to move beyond the well-established analytical gaze on shamanic words and utterances as powerful. Although I recognise that shamanic performances often combine the sensory tools (sound, smells) with linguistic forms (words and their meaning) in a complementary fashion, I am less invested in language as the fundamental field of the sonic. My contribution aims to show instead that, in order to fully understand the potency of vocal performance in

Voiced into being   115

shamanic rituals, we have to also pay attention to the whole pallet of sounds produced by shamans. This includes not only sounds within words but also sounds considered as non-linguistic or semi-linguistic utterances (Feist 2013: 106), such as howls and cries, musical sounds as well as rhythm, tempo and intonation, all connected through the shaman's voice. Tracing a case study of a curse deflection ritual that happened to Ajdyn, I show how performing sounds remains key to human and non-human relationships while being empowered with the potency to make and unmake these relations in the presence of cursing. What happens during shamanic rituals in Tuva, therefore, theorises sound in an innovative way and draws attention to its central rather than peripheral status in both shamanic practice and ritual efficacy. As such, it emphasises an important area in shamanic studies, which (while acknowledging the role of sound), analytically tends to privilege the performative, structural and visual aspects of shamanic practice (Gow 1996; Humphrey 1996; Riboli & Torri 2016). Throughout this chapter, I investigate diverse expressive techniques used by the shaman, such as intonational shifts, gasps and humming, as central to the clients' participation and experience of the ritual as successful. I show how sounds emitted via these techniques facilitate intermittent sensory encounters with non-humans that are often described as a cold wind (*hat*), a murmur (*shimeen*) or catching a partial image (*dürzü*) of a spirit. In this way, the shaman, rather than mirroring the world of things through sound, imbues sounds with ontological potency to voice spirits into being. Following on from this, the encounters with an Other triggered via sound illuminate how people in Tuva construct and validate their relationships with humans and non-humans through ascribing authority to sound, rather than words or objects. As such, these relationships are not a matter of belief or assumption, but rather of immediate sensory experience (Engelke 2007). Sound and voice become, therefore, discrete modes of recognising and identifying an Other and contribute to a better understanding of the materiality of spirits (Engelke 2007; Espirito-Santo 2015; Brabec de Mori 2015). More than that, the efficacy of the shamanic voice and the sounds it produces is crucial in considering the ritual as legitimate and efficient, particularly in the context of post-Soviet socioeconomic transformations and commodification of shamanic practice as well as the ways in which authenticity of shamanic practice is defined and validated in Kyzyl today. In this way, curses in Tuva offer an important view on sound and, specifically, sounds in shamanism, as imbricated in the intricacies of colonial transition and its long-term implications.

As we have seen so far, everyday life in Tuva is deeply permeated by the significance of sounds and music making. Its central role in Tuvan cosmology continues to attract various anthropological inquiries. The importance of sound in the context of landscape is particularly clear in the study of the throat singing practice *khöömei* as I have extensively discussed in Chapter 4. Yet, sounds in Tuva do not pertain only to the sphere of artistic performance and representation. For example, Harrison (2004) analyses the agentive role of sound in hunting practices,

116   *Voiced into being*

in particular when Tuvan hunters seek to control prey. The songs performed on such occasions include specific ideophones that are meant to trigger a desired mental state or behaviour in an animal. In the ethnographic study of Tuvan shamanism, Van Deusen (2004) illuminates how music and sound making constitute key components of ritual practices. In her account, drumming, shamanic singing and words used by shamans during rituals are imbued with power to communicate with spirits and provide healing.

Given the fact that in Tuva music is deeply entwined with the ambient environmental sounds, and in order to clarify my argument, it is essential to engage with the intricacies of conceptual differences between Tuvan sound and music. In the past, scholars (see Feld 1990, 2015; Seeger 1987) sought to shorten the distance between sound and music by, for example, exploring the importance of local terminologies and meanings. In many conversations with my Tuvan friends, music making and sound making were often discussed interchangeably without drawing any specific distinctions. This intertwining can be well illustrated in, for example, the aforementioned throat singing. As discussed in Chapter 4, in *khöömei*, the key characteristic in defining sound and music facets is timbre. Rather than through the organisation of discrete, multiple sounds (as in classical music based on the 12-note system), *khöömei* emerges from a steady coordination and subordination of the fundamental sound (drone) and its partials (overtones). In short, it is music produced through the ability to extract and manipulate the timbral qualities of *one* rather than *many* sounds, blurring therefore the line between where sound ends and music begins. The overlap between sound and music can also be seen as fundamental for Tuvans' communication with spirits, animals and the environment, which is experienced through a combination of calls, cries, throat singing, ideophones and non-linguistic vocalisations (see also Levin 2006: chap.5). Similar sonic interweaving, as I will show, takes place during shamanic rituals. One of the most important parts of these rituals is occupied, for example, by chants with their unique-to-the-event structure and form. If we consider music as 'an intention to produce something like music (or structured similarly to what *we* call music)' (Seeger 1987: xiv, original emphasis), then shamanic chants can be considered as a vivid example of such intentionality. However, in my analysis I am less concerned with music as a distinct category of the sonic and more focused on the potent qualities of human sounds and voice. More than that, I believe that in the Tuvan ethnographic context a rigid conceptual differentiation between music and sound may conceal more rather than it reveals. Therefore, in line with recent theoretical propositions in sound studies (Steingo & Sykes 2019), my analysis follows a 'conjunctural approach' to sound (ibid.: 7), which seeks to bring together different fields, such as musical, linguistic and paralinguistic. In other words, by sound I am referring to an array of sonic phenomena, encompassing musical sounds (shamanic singing), but also sounds within words, signals, such as shouts and other non-linguistic vocalisations, brought together in and through the shaman's voice. In this way, I intend to show that Tuvan shamans use their voices to navigate the potent qualities of various sounds in order to voice into being

Voiced into being 117

concrete sonic ontologies within which shamans, spirits and clients become distinct *sonic beings*.

Sound in transition

In order to fully explore the role of sound in Tuvan shamanism, it is important to consider it within the context of transition from the Soviet to post-Soviet eras and the wider experience of colonialism in general. During colonisation, shamanic sounds were often connected with the colonial representations of shamanism as 'primitive' or 'incomprehensible' (see Steedly 1993). Soviet ethnography also tended to exoticise shamans while ascribing any form of shamanic practice to cultural facets of ethnic groups in their pre-revolutionary state (see Levin & Potapov 1964; Vitebsky & Alekseyev 2015). In the same way, different forms of shamanic sonic performances in Tuva were primarily mentioned as part of wider ethnographic projects focused on documenting pre-Soviet ethnic groups and their origins (see Diakonowa 1970). During the Soviet times, shamans were widely perceived as medical charlatans and religious deceivers (Balzer 2003: 243). As mentioned in the Introduction, in Tuva, shamanic practice was extremely risky and undertaken on a significantly smaller scale. Very few shamans would agree to perform, offering only divination practices (normally conducted through the use of objects, such as stones or animal bones) and some healing rituals (performed, for example, through food offerings and feeding the fire). A rare occurrence constituted private feasts to which only selected friends were invited. During these secret ceremonies, spirits were provided with food offerings while delivering, through shamans, answers to some of the guests' questions. The use of drums and chanting, however, was strictly forbidden. Given the central role of sound in Tuvan shamanism and its clear absence in the Soviet period, this raises questions concerning the efficacy and validation of shamanic work in the Soviet era. As I have mentioned earlier, shamanic practice under the Soviet regime was extremely limited and many essential rituals (such as rituals associated with good fortune, extensive healing practices, cursing, death and clan rituals) simply did not take place. The shamans who continued, in secrecy, to maintain interaction with spirits and offer certain practices, usually came from a long line of powerful shamans (like my friend Hovalygmaa) that were well known to people. This, combined with the already highly challenging living conditions and the danger surrounding any involvement in shamanism, left little room for questioning the shamanic powers at the time. However, the situation radically changed with the collapse of the Soviet Union. With the disintegration of the Soviet regime, sound became one of the main domains through which proliferating shamanic practices and their efficacy started to be compared and validated. After the Soviet dissolution, many Tuvans were faced with dramatic and abrupt changes, often leading to unemployment, poverty and crime. In this environment, turning to shamans was commonly considered as the last possible resort. As people's demand for shamanic help increased, so did the numbers of shamans available. This in turn, triggered a significant wave of uncertainty and suspicion around shamanic practice more

118   *Voiced into being*

broadly (I shall return to this point in Chapter 6). Shamans started to be considered as greedy business people focused more on making a profit than helping their clients (see also Lindquist 2008; Pimenova 2013). In this uncertain environment, sound and shamanic voice have become important factors in contesting and reconfirming the true intentions of the shaman. In short, the ideas about sound as directly linked with experiencing the spirits' material presence (a point which I explore later) have become intimately intertwined with the politics of legitimation, actively generating and reflecting what being a 'real shaman' (*jozulug hamnar*) means in the context of post-socialist uncertainty.

Death curse

Let us return now to Ajdyn's story. Ajdyn was a middle-aged man, tall and athletic, working in Kyzyl as a taxi driver. He lived near the banks of the Yenisei River along with his five children, his wife and his mother. I first met him at a different cursing ritual that concerned his cousins, two brothers Sajan and Bajlak (I have discussed this encounter in Chapter 4). During that ritual, the events took an unpredictable turn and while helping the brothers the shaman detected a powerful death curse inflicted on Ajdyn by his ex-wife's family. Later on, I discovered that Ajdyn was a suspect in a murder case that involved a relative of his ex-spouse. Five days after we visited Sajan's and Bajlak's flat, the shaman and I arrived at Ajdyn's home in order to conduct a curse deflection ritual. Ajdyn picked us up from the shaman's house in the early afternoon. He was wearing a grey tracksuit and remained completely silent on the way to his flat, which strongly contrasted with the shaman's incessant flow of words describing her recent encounter with new clients in Krasnoyarsk. We parked the car next to one of the numerous blocks of flats and Ajdyn carefully took the shaman's drum. We followed him to the staircase that led to black heavy metal doors, behind which a one-bedroom apartment was hidden, with a small kitchen and even smaller bathroom. Children were jumping and playing around; his mother sat at the kitchen table and studied me very carefully; Ajdyn's wife chatted with the children while preparing food. As usual we commenced our visit with a meal and a long discussion, which concentrated this time on another story about a wedding curse and a petty criminal who had married one of Ajdyn's relatives against the family's will.[1] After the food, I was asked to sit in the corner for the duration of the ritual, away from the family gathered on the sofa, whilst the shaman prepared her costume and the drum. Everyone was told to cover their heads with hats, except for Ajdyn who sat at the far right of the couch and tightly held a special knife (*orzee*) offered by the shaman which was used only in the presence of death curses. When everyone was ready the shaman hid in the corner, away from our sight. Hovalygmaa began her work with a long, piercing howl which marked the commencement of most of her rituals. What took place afterwards, however, left me shivering for the rest of the day and was still reverberating in my head and in my dreams many days later. With no warning, the shaman's howl abruptly changed into a loud scream, a sort of petrifying cry that randomly rose and fell only to transform into a nasty, mean laugh, resembling

Voiced into being 119

the cry of a crow, intermixed with quiet howling. Next, the shaman engaged in a 15-minute vocal performance which included a mixture of soothing humming and squeaking laughter combined with hissing, whistling and roaring, accompanied by the sounds of the drum. At times, her voice was sharp and piercing only to abruptly transform into a long delicate cry as if nursing a child to sleep. The shaman finished the first part of the ritual by hitting the floor twice with a wooden stick. 'They are here, do not look at me and cover your head with your hands or they will steal your *sünezin*' ('soul'), she announced, a common warning in the presence of spirits. She ran around the flat with *eeren* ('shamanic token') shaking the little bells attached to it and moving her arms as if she was sweeping the room. In the second stage of the ritual the shaman, while continuing to drum, began to sing the shamanic chant, allowing her voice to rise and fall and shift swiftly from heavy and deep crescendos to softer and seemingly faster passages. She stopped every ten or so minutes, each time instructing the client and his family what they should concentrate their thoughts on and reminding them to carefully listen to her voice. Below I provide fragments of the narrative the shaman sang during this stage of the ritual.

> **Azyglarym spirits, chetkelerim spirits clean up my child ohoo,**
> *Azyglarym uchtii dashtyi aryglangar chetkelerim ooj,*
> **Kargysh-chatka curse take them away dwellers of the lower sky ohoo,**
> *Kargysh-chatka yradyngar burgannarym ooj,*
> **Aza chetker spirits move them away send them away my gods from the upper sky, ohoo.**
> *Aza-bukpu, aza-chetker yradyngar burgannarym ooj,*
> **I am asking for mercy and turning with my head upwards to you my gods from the upper sky**
> *Örsheel dileesh örütejleen,*
> **Send away misfortune, aza spirits make them not come clean up the dirty child**
> *Aza-bukpu, halap-choruk keldirbenger azjy-tölge aryglangar*
> **Separate, push away all the obstacles, make tornadoes for the children**
> *Haj-la halan, haj-la bachyt chok-la bolza öleng cherden chajladyngar, hovuzjuktung kazylgayn*
> **Melt away 3 misfortunes Push away 4 bad lucks Cut off 5 misfortunes my gods from the upper sky, ohooo**
> *üsh-le halap estip, dört-le hajny chajladyngar, höj-le halap üzükte-le, Burgannarym ooj!*

The chant lasted for about 20 minutes. Throughout the entire ritual I was discreetly looking at Ajdyn and his family trying to follow some of their reactions. Two of the children and the women were sitting still, their hands pressed to their chests, carefully following the shaman's moves. The third child found particular amusement in the shaman's voice and moved around whilst discreetly dancing to the sounds produced by Hovalygmaa. The most intriguing reactions came, however,

120   *Voiced into being*

from Ajdyn. His athletic figure suddenly shrunk and his handsome face with strong features somehow softened, transforming his posture and expression into that of a terrified child, rather than a full-grown man. Moreover, Ajdyn jumped every time the shaman's voice changed into squeaking laughter or involved sudden shifts in tempo. On two occasions, I noticed that when the shaman produced piercing cries Ajdyn grabbed his knife and held it tightly to his chest, occasionally letting out a loud sigh. Towards the end of the ritual, he discreetly wiped tears from his face. After the ritual finished, he seemed to relax his body on the sofa as if regaining his manhood. When we left Ajdyn's flat, the shaman was exhausted and could barely walk down the stairs. 'I did my best, it was really hard', she told me. 'Did it work?', I asked her. 'Yes. But I will be ill for many days now', she concluded sadly. Ajdyn's story draws attention to a number of 'sounded' elements that interweaved producing the curse deflecting event. The ritual commenced with a variety of sounds pointing to different emotive states, such as hums, howls and cries. These were gradually intertwined with sounds generated through the utterance of words during the chant. The ritual was also accompanied by the sound of the drum and the sounds produced by the shaman's token. What, then, constituted the power to deflect the death curse? In order to answer this, let me return once again to Ajdyn's story in greater detail.

The power of shamanic voice

As implied by Hovalygmaa, in Tuva the ability to produce sounds in a particular way imbues shamans with specific power, which allows them to conjure the spirits, ask for help, negotiate or get rid of them. In this process, the shaman's voice and its accurate modulation are essential for the efficacy of shamanic work, both in relation to spirits as well as to the clients and the audience. These sounds are powerful and potent in a sense that they constitute actions rather than a mere form of representation. Ajdyn's story offers a good illustration of this point. As Hovalygmaa explained it to me, she was told by the spirits what sounds to make and how to adjust her voice and tempo in order to successfully remove Ajdyn's curse. The spirit directly responsible for cursing was responsive to a particular intonation and specific modulation of the voice. Thus, the shaman first produced distinct sounds, such as howls or high-pitched short screams that were meant to irritate the spirit and catch its attention. Then, she included more soothing sounds, such as humming, in order to convince the spirit to leave the victim. She also asked gods and other spirits for help, which took place during the chant. In order to do so, she had to modulate her voice in the way that was expected of her. For example, she first sang softly and reverted to higher tones in order to please the spirits while suddenly shifting to stronger and low-pitch sounds when seeking spirits' and gods' immediate support and protection for the victim. The spirit responsible for the curse finally left, an event marked by Ajdyn shedding a tear. As the shaman explained, it was the spirit crying while being forced to abandon the body and the house. If the sounds were not well-performed the spirit could have attacked Ajdyn again. Inaccurate performance could have led

Voiced into being 121

to the death or illness of the shaman, which is why Hovalygmaa did not stop the ritual despite gradually suffering from exhaustion. Sloppy performance, or too short a one, could have further aggravated the gods and other spirits. Similar appears to apply in the rare instances when people decide to curse one another without support from the shamans (as I mentioned in Chapter 1). This type of cursing is conducted through muttering harmful words complemented by spitting or throwing sand. While these can be concrete words, they also need to be pronounced with specific intonation and rhythm. For example, in order for such a curse to acquire power, it has to be repeated in a steady, uninterrupted manner seven times. The words have to be clearly pronounced in a decisive voice. While such cursing is already considered highly dangerous (as it occurs without shamans), further mistakes or improper pronunciation of words may involve additional danger and harm. The mastery of sounds and their powers remains therefore with shamans.

In Tuva the ability to produce sounds in a particular way imbues the shamans with power, which allows them to both conjure the spirits and simultaneously maintain a necessary distance. Thus, they stabilise the unsettlement created by the drum through (re)arranging a cosmic setting within which humans and non-humans can 'coexist at acceptable levels of ambiguity' (Taylor 1996: 207). In this process, the shaman's voice and its accurate modulation are essential for the efficacy of the shamanic work, both in relation to spirits as well as to the clients and the audience. Consequently, in order to remove or inflict curses the shaman has to properly generate a variety of sounds, such as screams or humming, to make the spirits (responsible for curses) either leave the victims or attack them. The importance of accurate performance as a means of achieving particular effects, such as the alleviation of suffering, conveys also beyond the Tuvan context. Piedade, for example, shows how among the Wauja of the Upper Xingu in Brazil 'a sacred flute performance involves an effort to achieve perfection in execution of the musical motifs and in the development of the form in order to guarantee the beauty and acuity needed to maintain cosmic balance' (2013: 317). Similarly, among the Yaminahua shamans, shamanic songs do not have invariant narrative (although some of them, mainly songs constructed from myths, may have a fixed combination of metaphors and images) (Townsley 1993: 458). Performance of a song is in fact contingent on the shaman's skill, their visionary experience and intentions. Moreover, songs are not perceived as an individual project and are said to be partially created by the Yoshi spirit, who gives or shows the songs to the shamans. Songs are meant to produce concrete visionary experiences in the shamans themselves and facilitate communication with spirits, which is an integral part of this visionary experience. Hovalygmaa's emphasis on the powerful role of sounds was shared with me by other shamans working in Kyzyl. It was common for them to stress that the importance and efficacy of the ritual depend on how they produce different sounds and use their voices, rather than on what the chant is about. In short, the ability to make sounds in particular desired ways imbues shamans with power to stabilise turbulence triggered by the presence of a curse. It is sound that allows cosmic configurations to be established afresh by removing

122   *Voiced into being*

the spirit responsible for cursing and providing protection against the person who requested the curse. In this way, through sounds, a novel, fragile, sociocosmic setting is produced.

As I noticed in Ajdyn's ritual, and in many others that I afterwards witnessed, the drama of curse, and the negotiations it entails, is recognised not only by the shaman but also by the client, who responds to changes in the different registers of the shaman's voice by moving, making a particular facial expression or changing posture, actively participating in the process of (re)shuffling sociocosmic interactions. For example, in the conversation after the ritual, Ajdyn tended to disregard the importance of words from the chant which he fully understood. As he stressed, it was the shaman's voice that made him feel as if physically lighter. While responding to abrupt shifts in intonation and pitch, he gradually experienced a relief from the curse. Moreover, because the shaman sang very well and produced a lot of sounds, he quickly became aware of the presence of the spirits in the room and could notice them for a very brief moment, which frightened him (I shall return to this point later). Thus, as he explained, he grabbed the knife tightly and jumped a few times as the shaman uttered piercing sounds, such as loud screams and gurgling laughter. While sharing his observations with me, he never referred to the story the shaman described in her song. In a similar manner, his relatives present during the ritual talked primarily about the shaman's voice and the different sounds that the shaman made, rarely referring, or attributing any clear significance, to the words used in the chant.

This recursive feedback allows an interesting spin on the manner in which sound has been conceptualised in anthropology to be introduced here, in particular, in the context of shamanic chants and singing. In Ajdyn's story, the flow of the ritual proceedings is not contingent on the power of words and language, but on the manipulation of a variety of sounds uttered by the shaman (including sounds within words as well as those outside of conventional speech). Therefore, sounds cannot be merely considered as 'a side aspect in the utterance of speech' (Severi 2015: 246). Instead of functioning as vehicles of meaning, they become the activators of communication among different actors involved in the ritual, the communication primarily directed towards non-humans. The occurrences are not punctuated by alternations in the narrative, that is, a move from one scene (disaster) to another (asking gods for help). Spirits and clients respond to the changes in the shaman's voice, the sudden strengthening of it or alterations in the intonation and tempo. The core of the ritual depends, therefore, on how the words and a chant are performed rather than on what they are about, what they resemble or indicate. Key to the ritual are the sounds considered as actions through which the shaman undertakes a duel with the spirit responsible for cursing and asks other spirits for help in alleviating Ajdyn's suffering. Consequently, rather than approaching interactions between spirits, shamans and audience solely through the means of words, the case of Tuvan shamanism highlights the importance of other codes employed in navigating relationships, that is, sounds.

Within this system, as I am going to illustrate, sounds do not simply establish and control communication. As mentioned earlier, the high quality of the

Voiced into being   123

shaman's vocal performance allowed Ajdyn to catch a glimpse of the spirit. Using her voice, the shaman arranged an incomplete, sensory encounter, which confirmed the strength of her skills. Thus, the potency of sound revealed important mechanics through which two lines of relationships are directly experienced and validated. The first one concerns humans and non-humans whereas the second relates to the client and the shaman. Let us explore this point in more detail.

Encountering the spirit

In Tuva, as in other ethnographic contexts in Siberia (Broz 2007; Humphrey 2007), the ability to interact and see non-humans is a skill that equally pertains to recognised practitioners, such as shamans, as well as to laymen. For my Tuvan friends, these encounters, specifically in the ritual context, are defined and experienced through sound. Therefore, rather than using words or objects, it is through voicing spirits into being that Tuvan shamans stage fragmentary confrontations between humans and non-humans. In order to explain what I mean by this, I refer to Severi's concept of transmutation through singing (2014) and Brabec de Mori's idea of materialising spirits through sounds (2015).

In his discussion on transmutating beings, Carlo Severi (2014) analyses the concept of transmutation as a cultural form of translation that involves the exploration of a set of multiple relations between different forms of cognition. Thus, Severi expands the definition of translation from linguistics to other forms of translation, such as intersemiotic transmutation (2014: 41). This process is based on synesthetic fusion, which implies that what is seen can be constantly translated into what is heard and *vice versa* (2014: 47, original emphasis). In this way, through singing, an acoustic image is generated which in turn 'produces indexical presence where musical ways are being mobilized in order to define complex non-human beings' (2014: 59). In short, as Severi argues, particular ways of singing produce a certain melodic contour or motif, which in turn indicates an image that stands for a certain spirit acting in the current situation. Most importantly, as Severi delineates further, 'transmutation is not limited to the description of the appearance of the beings it represents' (2014: 59). Instead, 'music and visual iconographies aim to construct images of concepts and relationships, rather than imitations of appearances'. As the shaman addresses the 'invisible' spirit through singing, the relationship between the musical motif and the being is strengthened and, rather than imitating the spirit, it becomes the spirit. In this way, Severi shows how a particular kind of ontology can be actualised by musical ways in order to recognise complex non-human beings. While drawing on Severi's analysis, Brabec de Mori in his work on Peruvian Amazon healers (2015) discusses how spirits are materialised through means of the shaman's voice. He shows how the quality of the singer's voice can take on the agency allowing the 'sonic being' present in the ritual (2015: 35) to be identified. In this way, the spirit's physicality becomes substantiated through the singer's voice, meaning that the voice of the shaman constitutes the spirit's body.

124   *Voiced into being*

In Ajdyn's example, there is a clear connection between the shamanic voice and the discontinuous ways of sensing and seeing 'the other' as experienced by clients. Ajdyn's vision of sound and its role is characteristic of ongoing references to the shaman's voice as key to the experience of the spirits' presence. As he emphasised, he noticed the silhouette of the spirit responsible for his curse, because the shaman sang well. Ajdyn also reinforced the role of the shaman's screams and laughter as confirmations of the spirit's arrival, which made him grab the knife and remain vigilant. In this way, he was exposed to a sonic duel where the spirit was not represented or imitated but endowed with a particular presence articulated through the combination of specific sounds as well as shifts in tempo, pitch and intonational contour. The screams, howls and humming combined with alternations in the shaman's voice marked the momentary and incomplete material existence of the non-human as experienced by Ajdyn through catching sight of it. The ritual did not constitute a symbolic performance, but a dense dramatic event with sounds not only controlling relationships but also bringing them into direct sensory confrontations. While performing the chant and uttering sounds, Hovalygmaa, instead of mirroring a given cosmic landscape and its acoustic features, was voicing into being particular spirits. The cosmos was as if actualised and actively realigned, with the client being fully involved in the process. Thus, Hovalygmaa's voice instantiated a kind of agency that allowed her to establish links between humans and non-humans. Ajdyn's encounter did not constitute an isolated occurrence. Many of my Tuvan friends talked about how in the ritual context the presence of spirits can be witnessed through different senses, such as smell, touch or hearing. These always fragmentary, because experienced swiftly and never through all of the senses, encounters have been described to me as being hit by a cold wind, noticing a sudden murmur and, as in Ajdyn's case, catching a partial image of the spirit. What and how much can be seen always remained contingent on the potency of the shamanic vocal performance.

Encounters with spirits materialise through different sensory experiences, such as touch, smell or vision triggered through the means of sound point to another important aspect of sonic efficacies in the context of Tuvan shamanic practices. What happens during the cursing rituals illuminates dialogical features not only in relation to human/non-human interactions, but also in the context of dialogue among senses themselves. In other words, the ways senses work and the experiences they produce and shape cannot be understood in isolation. It is a kind of sensory synesthesia (as also mentioned by Severi), simultaneous joint perceptions which occur when, for example, a visual experience results from an impulse triggered by listening to specific sounds, or recognising familiar tastes (Feld 1990; Seremetakis 1996). In Tuva sounds do emerge as central to the efficacy of shamanic rituals, and the sounds produced by the shamanic voice allow for the fragmentary encounters with spirits. Nonetheless, as I have shown, sounds are intimately connected with other sensory modalities, creating thus a dynamic sensory totality (Silverstein 2019: 242) where through studying sound we come to comprehend also the visual and the haptic.

On authenticity

The question of inefficiency or even ritual failure rarely occurred in my conversations with shamans. Occasionally, they would mention that rituals might not work (rather than fail) mainly due to the clients' inappropriate engagement in the proceedings, such as inattentive listening and an overall lack of focus. On rare occasions, curses, such as alcoholism (*aragalaashkyn*), might be too advanced to deflect. From the perspective of the client, however, the success of the ritual is fully contingent on the spectrum of shamanic skills and, in recent times, their authenticity. Therefore, experiencing the presence of spirits is a crucial part of the ritual, as it confirms that the shaman is powerful enough to facilitate such experiences and that the curse will be removed. It is very common among Tuvans to say that a 'good shaman' (*eki hamnar*) is the one that can 'show' (*körgyzer*) people something. In other words, if the shaman is strong then the spirits will make themselves noticeable to the audience. Interestingly, the realm of the spirits is rarely available for scrutiny and it is not obvious whether spirits live in ways that mirror those of humans. Consequently, sudden confrontations with spirits, occurring sometimes in everyday practices or intense dreams, often trigger a lot of fear among Tuvans and require immediate intervention from shamans. Nevertheless, this seems to be quite different in the context of rituals, where the chance to see a spirit is equally feared and desired while it also constitutes solid proof of efficacy of the shaman's skills. Particularly in the post-Soviet context, as I have mentioned earlier, many of my friends tend to connect the sensory experiences of an Other with the authenticity of the shaman's work. Indeed, people often firmly maintain that the ability to bring 'spiritual' presence into direct physical experience is what strengthens the shaman's position within the community and confirms that their work is genuine. In other words, the shaman who can show the spirit is immediately considered not only as a strong shaman, but also as a shaman that can be trusted. The role of sound, rather than words or objects, therefore, is particularly instructive here of what validates relationships not only with non-humans but also with shamans. In order to illustrate this better, let me briefly turn to Engelke's (2007) account of the Christian faith in Africa. Engelke shows how for the members of the Friday Masowe Church in Zimbabwe material things, and in particular scripture, in fact constitute an obstacle to faith (2007: 3). Instead, it is voice which is key in validating beliefs as live and direct, whereas the Bible is never seen as '*a priori* evidence of truth' (2007: 19). In Tuva, in a similar manner, sound emitted through the shaman's voice is key: the presence of the spirit has to be sensually experienced. As in the context of the Friday Masowe Church and experiencing God, encountering spirits and the role of these encounters in cursing rituals cannot be acknowledged symbolically as they are not a question of a belief or an assumption. Instead, they have to be direct and immediate and this can only be facilitated by sound. In this way, 'spiritual' immediacy in Tuva constitutes a sounded quality.

The centrality of sensory experiences to the ritual lays out potential alternatives to think about sound not as opposed to the visual (Steingo & Sykes 2019),

126 *Voiced into being*

but as deeply intertwined with other senses: those of image, smell and touch. It also offers an innovative view on shamanic practice itself as explored through the often marginalised angle of sound and its mechanics. Considering curse dynamics and the sounded qualities of shamanic work in Tuva complicates further what we define as communication. What are described as seemingly randomly uttered sounds or a musical performance could be, in fact, a carefully designed sonic action which reveals complex sociocosmic dynamics that entail humans and non-humans alike. Focusing on the centrality of sound to experience social relationships in the post-Soviet context is also a way of exploring the role of sound in political, historical and economic shifts. The ability to facilitate the clients' communication with non-humans constitutes an important element of the shaman's reputation and proof of being an authentic shaman. In the uncertain context of life in Kyzyl today, sound and voice become key criteria via which a 'real' shaman can be revealed, offering analytical avenues to consider the politics of sound and the broader relationship between (post) colonialism and sonic ontologies. Hence, in the post-Soviet ritual setting, the central role of sound has reoriented the way shamanic sounds were perceived in the wider context of colonialism. In addition, it illustrates how crucial they are today for shamanic powers to be recognised as genuine and instructive, rather than exotic and backward. Beyond the specific context of shamanism, perceptions of sound as transformative, rather than mimetic, open pathways to reconsider sound in religious practices in general and, in particular, stressing a differential role of sounds in identifying non-humans and conceptualising relationships with them in religious practice. This, in turn, offers a further contribution to how the materiality and presence of spirits is conceptualised and discussed in anthropological studies. In other words, sound becomes key in coming to terms with how a subject defines his/her environment and experiences the matrix of interactions within it. Taken together, the dramatic cursing events in Tuva compel us to think about sound as powerful and unsettling. It is through sound that we are invited to come to terms with the kind of perceptions and interpretations that are at work when the cosmic decides to momentarily reveal its turbulent fabric.

In this chapter, I have focused on the potent and transformative qualities of sounds generated by the shaman's voice. The mastery of sounds has been directly equated by my interlocutors with the ideas of authenticity, specifically in the context of shamanic practice in Kyzyl today. The issue of being an 'authentic' shaman generates a lot of tension within the shamanic landscape in the capital. The ways in which some shamans work today is often defined by Tuvans through the notions of conflicts, disturbance and uncertainty, and thus a kind of uncontrolled turbulence I have described in the context of cursing. Similar descriptions have been employed in relation to other challenges and problems that have been present in Kyzyl, such as different kinds of affliction (HIV, alcohol addiction), infrastructural and technological changes and environmental crisis. Some of them have been directly defined as curses. Given this, in the next chapter, while expanding the context of mechanics of cursing and reemphasising its presence in the arena of Kyzyl, I turn to how everyday existence in the city is talked about and

Voiced into being 127

experienced in a way that curses are described and felt. As a way of concluding this book, I shall suggest, therefore, that certain aspects of life in Kyzyl today are like a curse.

Note

1 Every ritual that I participated in would always commence with an informal chat in the kitchen and sharing food.

Bibliography

Balzer, M. M. 1997. *Shamanic Worlds: Rituals and Lore of Siberia and Central Asia.* Armonk, New York-London: North Castle Books.

Balzer, M. M. 2003. Sacred Genders in Siberia. In G. Harvey (ed.), *Shamanism: A Reader,* 242–261. London: Routledge.

Basso, B. E. 1985. *A Musical View of the Universe.* Philadelphia: University of Pennsylvania Press.

Brabec de Mori, B. 2015. Sonic Substances and Silent Sounds: An Auditory Anthropology of Ritual Songs. *Tipiti: Journal of the Society for the Anthropology of Lowland South America* no. 13: 25–42.

Broz, L. 2007. Pastoral Perspectivism. A View from Altai. *Inner Asia* no. 9: 291–310.

Course, M. 2009. Why Mapuche Sing. *Journal of the Royal Anthropological Institute* (N.S) no. 15: 295–313.

Delaplace, G. 2014. Establishing Mutual Misunderstanding: A Buryat Shamanic Ritual in Ulaanbaatar. *Journal of the Royal Anthropological Institute* (N.S.) no. 20: 617–634.

Déléage, P. 2009. *Le chant de l'anaconda. L'apprentissage du chamanisme chez les Sharanahua (Amazonie occidentale).* Nanterre: Société d'ethnologie.

Diakonowa, W. P. 1970. *Pogrebelnyj obrjad Tuvincew kak Istorichesko-Ethnograficheskij Istochnik* [The Mortuary Ritual Among Tuvans as a Historical and Ethnographic Source]. Leningrad.

Empson, R. & Delaplace, G. 2007. The Little Human and The Daughter-in-law: Invisibles as Seen Through the Eyes of Different Kinds of People. *Inner Asia* no. 9: 197–214.

Engelke, M. 2007. *A Problem of Presence: Beyond Scripture in an African Church.* Berkley, California, London: University of California Press.

Espirito Santo, D. 2015. Liquid Sight, Things-like Words, and the Precipitation of Knowledge Substances in Cuban Espiritismo. *Journal of the Royal Anthropological Institute* no. 21: 579–596.

Feist, J. 2013. "Sound symbolism" in English. *Journal of Pragmatics* no. 45: 104–118.

Feld, S. 1990. Aesthetics and Synesthesia in Kaluli Ceremonial Dance. *UCULA Journal of Dance Ethnology* no. 14: 1–17.

Feld, S. 2012 [1982]. *Sound and Sentiment. Birds, Weeping, Poetics, and Song in Kaluli Expression.* Durham, N. C.: Duke University Press.

Feld, S. 2015. Acoustemology. In D. Novak & M. Sakakeeny (eds), *Keywords in Sound,* 12–21. Durham, N. C.: Duke University Press.

Gow, P. 1996. River People: Shamanism and History in Western Amazonia. In C. Humphrey & N. Thomas (eds), *Shamanism, History, and the State*, 90–114. Ann Arbor: University of Michigan Press.

Grant, B. 1995. *In the Soviet House of Culture: A Century of Perestroikas.* Princeton, N.J.: Princeton University Press.

128 *Voiced into being*

Harrison, D. 2004. South Siberian Sound Symbolism. In E. Vajda (ed.), *Languages and Prehistory of Central Siberia*, 199–214. Amsterdam: John Benjamins.

High, C. 2018. Bodies That Speak: Languages of Differentiation and Becoming in Amazonia. *Language and Communication* no. 63: 65–75.

Hodgkinson, T. 2005/2006. Musicians, Carvers, Shamans. *The Cambridge Journal of Anthropology* no. 25: 1–16.

Hoppal, N. & Sipos, J. 2010. *Shaman Songs*. Budapest: International Society for Shamanic Research.

Humphrey, C. 2007. Inside and Outside the Mirror: Mongolian Shamans' Mirrors as Instruments of Perspectivism. *Inner Asia* no. 9: 173–195.

Humphrey, C. & Onon, U. 1996. *Shamans and Elders*. Oxford: Clarendon Press.

Hugh-Jones, S. 1996. Shamans, Prophets, Priests and Pastors. In C. Humphrey & N. Thomas (eds), *Shamanism, History, and the State*, 90–114. Ann Arbor: University of Michigan Press.

Levin, T. 2006. *Where Rivers and Mountains Sing*. Indianapolis: Indiana University.

Levin, T. & Edgerton, M. 1999. The Throat Singers of Tuva. *Scientific American* no.281 (3): 80–87.

Levin, M. G. & Potapov, L. P. (eds). 1964. *The Peoples of Siberia*. Chicago: University of Chicago Press.

Lévi-Strauss, C. 1963. *Structural Anthropology*. Harmondsworth: Penguin.

Lindquist, G. 2008. Loyalty and Command. Shamans, Lamas, and Spirits in a Siberian Ritual. *Social Analysis* no. 52: 111–126.

Nuckolls, B. J. 2010. *Lessons Form a Quechua Strongwoman*. Tucson: University of Arizona Press.

Olsen, A. D. 1996. *Music of the Warao of Venezuela: Song People of the Rain Forest*. The United States of America: University Press of Florida.

Pedersen, A. M. 2011. *Not Quite Shamans*. Ithaca; London: Cornell University Press.

Piedade, A. T. C. 2013. Flutes, Songs and Dreams: Cycles of Creation and Musical Performance among the Wauja of the Upper Xingu (Brazil). *Ethnomusicology Forum* no. 22: 306–322.

Pimenova, K. 2013. The "Vertical of Shamanic Power": The Use of Political Discourse in post-Soviet Shamanism. *Laboratorium* no. 5: 118–140.

Riboli, D. & Torri, D. (eds). 2016. *Shamanism and Violence. Power, Repression and Suffering in Indigenous Religious Conflicts*. London; New York: Routledge.

Seeger, A. 1987. *Why Suya Sing: A Musical Anthropology of an Amazonian People*. Cambridge: Cambridge University Press.

Seremetakis, C. N. 1996. *The Senses Still: Perception and Memory as Material Culture in Modernity*. Chicago and London: The University of Chicago Press.

Severi, C. 2014. Transmutating Beings. A Proposal for an Anthropology of Thought. *Hau: Journal of Ethnographic Theory* no. 4: 41–71.

Severi, C. 2015. *The Chimera Principle: An Anthropology of Memory and Imagination*. Chicago: Hau Books.

Silverstein, S. 2019. Disorienting Sounds: A Sensory Ethnography of Syrian Dance Music. In G. Steingo & J. Sykes (eds), *Remapping Sound Studies*, 241–260. Durham, N.C.: Duke University Press.

Steedly, M. M. 1993. *Hanging Without a Rope*. Princeton: Princeton University Press.

Steingo, G. & Sykes, J. (eds). 2019. *Remapping Sound Studies*. Durham & London: Duke University Press.

Stépanoff, C. 2015. Transsingularities: The Cognitive Foundations of Shamanism in Northern Asia. *Social Anthropology* no. 23: 169–185.

Stoller, P. 1984. Sound in Songhay Cultural Experience. *American Ethnologist* no. 11: 559–570.

Tambiah, J. S. 1968. The Magical Power of Words. *Man* New Series, no. 3: 175–208.

Taylor, A. C. 1996. The Soul's Body and Its States: An Amazonian Perspective on the Nature of Being Human. *Journal of the Royal Anthropological Institute* (N.S.) 2: 201–215.

Townsley, G. 1993. Song Paths: The Ways and Means of Yaminahua Shamanic Knowledge. *L'Homme* no. 33: 449–68.

Vainshtein, S. 1981. *Nomads of South Siberia*. Cambridge: Cambridge University Press.

Van Deusen, K. 1997. Power of Words and Music in Tuvan Shamanism. *Shamanism* no. 10: 9–13.

Van Deusen, K. 2004. *Singing Story, Healing Drum. Shamans and Storytellers of Turkic Siberia*. Montreal: McGill Queen's University Press.

Vitebsky, P. & Alekseyev, A. 2015. Siberia. *Annual Review of Anthropology* no. 44: 439–455.

Witherspoon, G. 1977. *Language and Art in the Navajo Universe*. Ann Arbor: University of Michigan Press.

6 Beyond curses

In the midst of turbulent Kyzyl

It was the beginning of May and the whole city was preparing for the Victory Day celebrations.[1] Every day, amid the loud orders of the Russian military, the youth of Tuva practised parading along the streets of Kyzyl while the local choir, composed mainly of Tuvan men, rehearsed Soviet songs on a small stage situated at the heart of the central square. One afternoon, I was returning home from my Tuvan language lessons and I decided to cross the square to see how the preparations were coming along. The first thing I noticed was the air filled with brown clouds while a sandstorm characterised by numerous small tornadoes was looming on the horizon. As the square began to be consumed by wind and grains of sand, I watched a group of maybe 12-year-old girls practising their dance routine on stage. They were singing a 2014 world hit, 'Waka Waka' ('This Time for Africa'), a song performed by the Colombian pop star Shakira. In the midst of the approaching storm, they kept on imitating the singer's moves from the video clip and following the music. I was deeply struck by this almost surreal scene: a group of young Tuvans practising a Colombian pop star's hit about Africa at an event meant to commemorate the victory of the Soviet Union over the Nazis, performed in the middle of the steppe, in a sandstorm in Kyzyl, on the southern border of Siberia.

What is particularly compelling about this image is that in yet another way it brings together sound and turbulence while exemplifying the mosaic like forms of life in the capital of Tuva, where curses are an integral part. In this book, I have looked at sound and turbulence and the ways in which they come together in cursing rituals. I have discussed how the sounds of shamanic drums produce one kind of semi-controlled turbulence while the shamans' clients become subjected to another kind of uncontrolled and dangerous turbulence produced by curses. I have also explored how shamanic voice and the sounds it delivers become a powerful tool capable of controlling cursing practices and the dynamics within ritual proceedings. What happens though if we step outside the ritual arena? As a way of concluding this book, I would like to move beyond the immediate context of curses as embedded in shamanic rituals and consider some of the challenges faced by Kyzylians today, such as growing tensions between shamanic societies and shamans who work individually, alcohol addiction, extensive reliance on technology and the environmental crisis. While reflecting the complexity and the eclectic

DOI: 10.4324/9781003245391-9

Beyond curses 131

character of everyday life in Kyzyl (like the one I have just described in relation to the Victory Day celebrations), these challenges in yet another way combine shamans and sounds, while pointing to the kind of uncontrolled turbulence I have discussed in relation to the experience of curses.

This book has shown how instances of cursing arise from conflicts among humans and reflect wider tensions, which include humans and spirits alike, while producing at the same time a distinct sociocosmic drama. Being cursed is described as a form of intrusion, when spirits responsible for curse infliction disturb the victims and 'mess' with them. This, in turn, generates the experience of turbulence exemplified in confusion, as well as erratic and unpredictable behaviour. The same ideas of conflict, disturbance and uncertainty used to describe these experiences have been employed by Tuvan friends to talk about, among other things, a growing distrust towards shamans, losing the ability to hear certain sounds and being confronted with environmental changes, such us industrial and infrastructural development. As one Tuvan friend pointed out, facing these challenges is like a curse. Therefore, by bringing together the diverse topics that I have discussed in this book, I would like to consider here what Bubandt (2014) calls 'experiential symbiosis' where occult practices and certain global issues, such as the environmental crisis 'although embedded in a different epistemological logic, experientially may exist and function in a form of symbiosis' (2014: 241). In other words, I suggest that some of the aforementioned issues faced by Tuvans are experienced and talked about in the same way that curses are described and felt. At the same time, these issues open avenues to consider wider questions of disturbance and uncertainty associated with the present and the future of indigenous communities in Siberia in general.

Shaman show

The ethnography presented in this book shows how Tuvan shamans constitute central personas in the process of (un)folding sociocosmic interactions, which entails humans and non-humans alike and which is exemplified in curses. Beyond the immediate context of shamanic rituals, Tuvan shamans have also become, in particular, politically and socially involved actors whose roles have ranged from promoting indigenous cultures in regional and international arenas to addressing immediate problems faced by Tuvans on a daily basis in the form of counselling (I will return to this point later). Particularly instructive in this process has been the collapse of the Soviet regime. There has been a great amount of anthropological work dedicated to exploring the transition from socialist to post-socialist realms and the way this shift has reshaped understandings of shamanism (see, for example, Balzer 2005, 2008; Shimamura 2004; Vitebsky 2003). Tuvan shamanic practice is, inevitably, situated within the implications of this transition. Nonetheless, dynamics among shamans and the organisational side of their practices point to wider questions of authenticity and trust, and the ways in which Tuvans think about their present and their future today – 30 years after the end of the Soviet Union.

132 *Beyond curses*

Throughout this book, numerous stories and narratives occasionally circled back or subtly echoed the troubling times immediately after the Soviet disintegration, when Tuvans were facing numerous economic, political and social challenges, similar to those other indigenous groups in Siberia were going through. As has been seen, living conditions in Tuva, especially at the beginning of the 1990s, were characterised by pervasive unemployment as well as widespread crime and violence. As a result, there has also been a strong trend towards the revitalisation of pre-Soviet practices, mainly through the establishment of shamanic societies instigated by the Tuvan intelligentsia along with the local government (see also Lindquist 2005; Pimienova 2013; Zorbas 2013, 2021). In this way, Tuvan shamans have been equipped with a new political role as the leaders of the so-called revivalism and the emblems of 'tradition' or ethnicity. However, when speaking to Tuvans, the perception of shamanic practice as a political tool and a symbol of identity, although successful in the academic and international arenas, within the sphere of everyday life constitutes an unusual arrangement and a subversion of the conceptualisations of shamanic practice as it is usually understood. This is particularly visible in the conflict and tensions between shamans associated with shamanic societies and shamans operating individually.

Shamanic practice among Tuvans is embedded in a particular skill of seeing and hearing what usually cannot be seen or heard (*bürülbaazyn*). As such, it is a technique of knowing rather than a system of knowledge, thus, attesting to the fluid and mobile characteristics of life in Tuva in general. Given the fact that spirits are said to constitute an integral element of everyday existence among Tuvans, shamanic practice is described within a rhetoric of mundane practicality, such as housekeeping, rather than being associated with the 'supernatural' milieu. However, shamans working for societies offer a very different kind of shamanic experience. After the end of the Soviet regime, eight shamanic societies were established in Kyzyl. These organisations were run by Mongush Borakhovich Kenin-Lopsan, the President for Life of all shamans and an academically trained and highly respected Tuvan expert on shamanism. The group of societies brought together shamans from all over Tuva. Despite having concrete political aims, from the Tuvans' perspective the establishment of the societies primarily had pragmatic implications. This is how one of the shamans who, at the time, supported Kenin-Lopsan described this process to me:

> Creating societies was a political move. Kenin-Lopsan and I fought a lot. In Soviet times the shamans practised in secrecy. We knew who had a real gift and who was a charlatan. After the nineties youngsters would come with us, follow us, study. You can't learn shamanism from the book, that neo-shamanism, that's silly. You know, at the end of the Soviet Union there was complete chaos here: alcoholism, crime and poverty. People needed help and they had to be reminded of our traditions. Do you know why Kenin-Lopsan named himself a president? Because 'president', that means something, it is a powerful word.

Beyond curses 133

Indeed, as presented in many stories from that time, disease, unemployment and a persistent lack of food had a significant influence on living conditions in Kyzyl. As a result, the capital transformed into a place where the shamans' help was consistently required. Not long after, other 'religious' organisations, in particular the Orthodox Church, became suspicious of what they described as 'illegal medicine' offered by shamans trying to evade taxation. A practical need for official recognition of the shamanic societies was expressed and, in this way, eight shamanic societies were established in Kyzyl. The process of becoming a member of a society included lengthy training and was usually finalised with a test based on a practical examination in healing (see also Levin 2006, Stelmaszyk 2021). In this form, the members of a given society were assessing the prospective shaman's real powers and skills. Each new shaman would specialise in only one practice, for instance, divination with cards or treatment of headaches. Very often, the tests were performed on Kenin-Lopsan himself. The future shamans were asked, for example, to diagnose the causes of the President's high blood pressure or persistent headaches. In other cases, they were told to conduct divination rituals, including readings of the future and the past of the President. Some of these tests resulted in unexpectedly discovered secrets the content of which, with time, would become the subject of many humorous anecdotes circulating around Kyzyl. After the exam had concluded, Kenin-Lopsan would decide whether the student had passed and could become a shaman.[2] After that, the newly appointed shaman would receive a certificate, which stated what practices and treatments he or she could specialise in.

With time, shamanic societies, which were officially recognised as religious organisations, began to receive financial support from the government, as well as other forms of support becoming available for the shamans, such as assistance in obtaining a house lease or tax exemptions (VAT, income tax, property taxes) as well as means of transport (cars to visit their clients in rural areas) (Pimienova 2013: 127–129). The associated shamans were further guaranteed a minimum wage and would obtain regular salaries. As time passed, the links between the state and the shamanic societies weakened and soon enough they were forced to become self-sufficient. In addition to this, many shamans decided to leave the societies, which had started demanding a high percentage of their income in exchange for affiliation and access to clients. Not long after, those who chose to remain began to be accused of quackery and greediness focusing on personal benefit. Kyzylians started to be highly suspicious of the shamans working for the societies, and the relationships with them were characterised by fears of deep frustration and uncertainty. Many would whisper that affiliated shamans had been offering 'shaman-shows' (Rus. *shamanshow*) while seeking to keep prospective clients by telling them lies, for instance, convincing them that the client suffered from curses. Indeed, in the wake of Soviet disintegration, the initial concentration and 'resurgence' of shamanic practitioners in the capital underwent, with time, an unexpected disruption. The development of shamanic societies and the proliferation of 'fake' (*shyn eves hamnar*) shamans in Kyzyl has created conflicts and divisions within the scene of shamanic practice. This, in turn, has perpetuated the

134 *Beyond curses*

feelings of uncertainty and doubt among Kyzylians. Today, there are only three societies in Tuva which continue to offer services. *Dungur* ('Drum'), the oldest one, is situated in the centre of Kyzyl, whilst *Tos Deer* ('Nine skies') and *Adyg-Eeren* ('Bear spirit') are on the outskirts of the city. The process of becoming a member of a society no longer requires tests and training. Instead, it relies simply on verbal confirmation of the future shaman's skills, which only increases the feelings of overall uncertainty concerning shamanic practice.

When I first arrived in Kyzyl, my main aim was to visit one of these shamanic societies. Much to my surprise, numerous requests for any kind of access or help were met with general resentment and a consistent refusal on the grounds of general distrust towards those associated with the shamanic societies. In the end, one of the lecturers from the University of Kyzyl agreed to take me on a brief trip to one of the societies. Nevertheless, she was not sure where it was and we were forced to spend a couple of hours wandering around the streets looking for what I expected to be at least a small villa. We finally arrived at a small wooden house with a big sign indicating that we had reached our destination (see Figure 6.1).

As we entered a small waiting room, there was no trace of a lavish reception desk or the extravagant furniture and decorations I had been told were common in the past. We were asked to go into another room where the chairperson of a spiritual religious organisation, as her business card stated, was occupied with her mobile phone while a little girl was running around her legs. She did not look at us, and we had to wait for a while before she finally greeted us. My friend provided a long introduction, describing who I was and why I was in Tuva. The woman asked me about my date of birth and who my parents were. She defined

Figure 6.1 Shamanic society

Beyond curses 135

my 'aura', gave me her business card and warned me to be vigilant of the shamans' tricky behaviour. We thanked her profusely and moved back to the living room, where I noticed a comprehensive price list, including divination, healing and cleansing rituals, as well as a little cash box guarded by three women sitting around a small table. I was allowed to have a look into a third room where three shamans dressed in fur coats sat at their tables awaiting their clients. The room revealed quite an unusual setting. One of the shamans was blind and kept wobbling. A woman opposite him was wearing sunglasses and had a number of stones in front of her, indicating she was a specialist in reading the future. The man in the back was occupied with carving his shamanic instruments and quietly laughing. The shamans were not willing to speak to me, but gave me their business cards, asking me to phone them in order to make an appointment. We thanked them and moved towards the exit. No one looked at us. My friend asked me if I had seen enough and delicately implied she would not be willing to return.

What in particular triggers my friends' apprehensiveness and apparent disregard for shamanic societies? Apart from the widespread suspicion of greediness, Tuvans are particularly discouraged by the shamans' tendency to exhibit unusual moves, such as a sudden loss of consciousness or rolling eyes, thus reinforcing the idea of 'shaman-show'. While exploring the intricacies of shamanic practice, I have discussed how shamanic efficacy relies heavily on sound, and classic elements of trance-like experiences, such as speaking in tongues or presenting unusual physical moves, are generally absent. Shamans from the societies put particular stress on the performative and technical effectiveness of the shaman's work, including spectacular instances of trance and mediumship that have little to do with the usual conceptualisations of shamanic practice as artistry. The shifts in the characteristics of shamanic practice and in particular the new political and business-oriented agendas advertised by shamanic societies illustrate the process by which the economic situation in Kyzyl emancipated shamanic practice from its contingency on creative interactions with spirits embedded in the efficacy of sounds. Through a strong emphasis on its exhibition value, shamanism offered by societies has become commodified and thus designed for reproducibility whilst disturbing Tuvans' understanding of what shamanic practice is, or should be, about.

Another aspect of shamanic societies that seems particularly disturbing to Tuvans is the fact that there is a fixed price list for each ritual: 'Good shamans never advertise themselves and they will never tell you how much money you have to pay', I was told by one of Hovalygmaa's clients. Many of my Tuvan friends complained about a lack of privacy too: 'There are four tables and fours shamans in one room, there is no intimacy, no possibility to talk about what is important', explained Marina, a Buryat who works at the state university. She admitted that she would visit the societies out of curiosity: 'I went just to see what it was like. They sent me to my shamans in Buryatia and rushed me out, it was not pleasant and left me really confused and anxious'. Another woman, Olga, who runs a small tour guide business for tourists from Europe and North America in Kyzyl, described why she was unwilling to take her customers to the societies:

136 *Beyond curses*

You have no idea what you can expect from them. They demand insane amounts of money like ten thousand rubles for a show (approximately one hundred pounds, the highest price for the most complicated death ritual). They are rude and greedy. I have three reliable shamans to whom I always go with our clients. They can tell you something real about shamanism, not this commercial stuff. Otherwise, you can never tell if what they say is true. Very often they just invent all sorts of curses and rituals in order to make sure that you are going to come back and they can make more money.

Interestingly, as Hovalygmaa herself admitted, the shamans in Kyzyl enjoy the fame they have been receiving since the 1990s.

All researchers and tourists want to meet us and shamans sometimes take advantage of it. If we do not like someone we would just make up stories, tell you things that are entirely not true and then laugh at you behind your back. How are you going to tell what is real or not?

she smiled at me. 'Be careful, shamans often say things out of tiredness or boredom, sometimes fear'. Alexandr, a local musician, also warned me:

These days they are well educated and familiar with multiple academic texts on shamanism rather than learning from their ancestors or other shamans. They come up with their own theories on what shamanism is and what they are actually doing. They are messing with people and we do not always trust them.

As mentioned earlier, the shamanic societies no longer conduct any tests in order to verify the authenticity of shamanic powers. Affiliation with a society is often based on a verbal assertion that a person has some shamanic skills. Shamanic practice on many occasions becomes a last resort for desperate Tuvans who find themselves in serious economic and financial situations and approach shamanic societies as a possible source of employment. I had an opportunity to discuss this process with one of the local journalists who studied numerous cases of homeless people taken in by the societies. She explained:

They come in and say somebody in the family was a shaman, they have a calling or they have dreams. In exchange, they get one meal a day and a place to sleep. They do not have to wander around in winter. I know this because I interview them all the time.

In a similar fashion, some people become self-declared shamans simply to make a living. My landlady never really liked shamans and was highly suspicious of their practices. She would always tell me I should drop my research and focus on something that was not an illusion and a lie. This is how she justified her suggestion:

You know these days anyone can become a shaman. Let me tell you a story. I have a friend who is shamanising. Once, I sat down with her and said:

Beyond curses 137

'Masha, tell me honestly, can you see things?' And Masha told me the truth: 'Honestly, Arzaana, I am no shaman. But what am I going to do? My husband left me, I lost my job and I have kids to feed. This is a sure thing these days, I really need the money'.

Such declarations stand in direct conflict with what shamanic practice means to Tuvans and only perpetuate already well-established feelings of uncertainty and distrust associated with shamanic societies.

In opposition to this, there is a network of individually operating shamans, like my friend Hovalygmaa, whose knowledge and practices constituted the heart of this book. These individual shamans do not advertise their work, and they can only be found through trusted friends or neighbours. Their relationships with shamans from the societies are rather tense and often conflictual. Unlike shamans from the societies they do not have business cards and do not seek to advertise their work. This is usually the first indication that the shaman is not an impostor or does not have a business-focused agenda. Money is another factor playing a key role in the assessment of the shaman's good intentions. As was discussed earlier, the role of the shaman includes the perpetual navigation of fluctuating energies which generate and fuel sociocosmic interactions between humans and spirits. This process involves constant elements of reciprocity, and shamans are always expected to receive something, usually financial remuneration, for their work. Nonetheless, a genuine and trustworthy shaman is never expected to ask for a specific amount of money. On a number of occasions, in particular involving foreign clients, I witnessed how the shamans felt unease when directly confronted with questions about how much money they wanted to be paid or whether a given amount was enough. They tended to turn their heads or walk away without providing any answers, leaving irritated clients behind them.[3]

Apart from relative social isolation and the absence of a fixed price list, independent shamans are often characterised by their already well-established reputation and usually, if they have successfully helped a member of a family or a friend, their support will be recommended further. This does not mean, however, that they are always fully trusted. As I have discussed in Chapters 4 and 5, sounds play an important role in verifying shamanic powers and validating the authenticity of their skills. The real shaman is the one who through the means of sounds facilitates intermittent encounters with non-humans which can be also experienced through other senses, such as touch and smell. Interestingly though, Tuvans have also developed an array of smaller 'tests' to which they like to subject individual shamans outside the ritual context. These are not only tests used in order to reconfirm shamanic powers but also to verify how efficient and effective they are. Some of these methods involve testing the shaman's visionary skills through checking if shamans can see through objects and read people's minds. In these cases, clients often tease shamans by asking them, for instance, to describe how many people are sitting behind the walls of the given building. One of the most popular tests involves demanding the shaman to say something that is intimately related to the client's life and that, apart from them, only the dead could know.

138 *Beyond curses*

Given the deep fear of the dead held by many Tuvans, correct answers usually constitute a very powerful confirmation of shamanic skills and guarantee further recommendations. Moreover, it is very common to conduct a wider comparison of the efficacy of the shamans' work through something similar to a diagnostic test. In these cases, one client decides to visit a number of shamans asking exactly the same question to each. Afterwards, the answers are compared. Their consistent overlapping constitutes a good indication of authentic shamanic skills. The shamans themselves admit that they have to undergo one of the most significant tests: the overcoming of their own ego. If the shaman becomes engrossed by fame and a desire to increase financial income, then within the groups of independent shamans they are disregarded and often ostracised.

Openly displaying financial profit and striving towards fame and recognition trigger tensions and disagreements between individual shamans and shamans affiliated with societies. The distrust displayed by Tuvans towards the more business-oriented practices provided by the shamanic societies also results in a broader distrust towards shamanic work, including independent shamanic practice, as a whole. Furthermore, the 'unauthentic' exercise of shamanic rituals conducted by the societies equally distorts and disturbs perceptions of how shamans should normally operate. This pervaded by the context of distrust and suspicion of relations between shamanic societies, individual shamans and Tuvans in general is one of the examples of 'turbulence' which my friends experience outside of the ritual arena. Another example, which continues to bring together shamans and turbulence beyond the realms of shamanic ceremonies, is the numerous afflictions, such as depression, alcohol addiction and HIV, that affect people, often leaving them either confused or ostracised and thus turning to shamans as the last resort.

Curses of civilisation

Ongoing increase in alcohol addiction was one of the most common issues mentioned by my interlocutors in relation to problematic aspects of life in Kyzyl today. This and similar problems prevailing in many other parts of post-Soviet Siberia (Grant 1995; Pedersen 2011) have been described in Tuva as a form of epidemic which could not be controlled by state institutions and, thus, has become central to shamanic practice (Zorbas 2013, 2021). The ongoing unemployment, poverty as well as unhappy marriages continue to lead to widespread instances of alcohol addiction, which results in further growing violence and suicide among Tuvans. This problem concerns both men and women, although it predominantly affects men with women becoming the main providers and supporters of their family (see Mongush 2006). Regular consumption of alcohol in Tuva was introduced with the beginning of the Soviet Union. Before the Soviets, only male members of the community and those over 40 would drink *araka*, vodka made out of sheep's milk. During numerous rituals I have participated in, alcohol was described to me as a force that overtakes people and which they cannot resist. I was usually provided with vivid descriptions of people who, while suffering from alcohol addiction, were in fact led by the spirits responsible for inflicting the curse. These spirits were said to encourage people to drink, creating an urge that was beyond one's control. There is an interesting link here between the physical experiences of excessive drinking and the ways in which curses can affect the human body and personhood.

As has already been seen, the ethnographic context of Tuva encourages the notion of personhood to be approached as a wider cosmic project, a distinct cosmocentric structure that involves a set of relations with spirits and the cosmos as a whole. Illuminating the connections between the production of human personhood and cursing, curses introduce disturbance to the victims while moving them from a condition of relatively continual balance to turbulence, a process that becomes materialised through diverse bodily (de)formations. Consequently, the body, rather than a given and static isolated entity, becomes a field of action allowing for the acquisition and production of particular kinds of (cursed) personhood and particular kinds of turbulent sociocosmic dynamics. This uncontrolled turbulence which affects the body that I have described in the context of cursed personhood resembles the bodily reactions in the experiences of heavy intoxication. Both of these conditions usually imply the onset of sudden, erratic behaviour. Both can be seen as the influence of an external force. In cases of alcohol intoxication the amount consumed can be recognised by a number of physical symptoms, such as the smell of the person's breath or baggy eyes. As was seen in Chapter 3, similar signs are sought by shamans when looking for the potential presence of curses. Perhaps, this is why some Tuvan friends would refer to alcohol addiction as a novel curse or a 'curse of civilization' (Rus. *civilizationnaja porcha*). In fact, the early onset of a drinking problem can be removed with the help of a shaman through the curse deflection ritual. More than that, some clients enjoy using a possible weakness for drinking as one of the afflictions they can direct towards their enemies with the help of the shaman. Interestingly, alcohol abuse may also involve the spirits, which can become drunk and aggressive if fed during outdoor ceremonies with vodka rather than tea with milk (the former was a common practice in Soviet times). While heavy drinking usually bears lethal consequences (for example, showing a hangover or being intoxicated at the ritual may result in death), alcohol may also have some beneficial use during shamanic rituals. Occasionally, vodka is carried by shamans as an additional tool aiding the removal of curses, for example, because it can contain harmful energy collected from the client's body as mentioned in Chapter 2.

The striking difference between the experiences of being cursed and suffering from alcohol addiction is the way in which these are generally viewed by the community. While some forms of curses, such as illness or bad luck, may trigger sympathy, people suffering from alcohol addiction are usually ostracised and left to their own suffering. Perpetually drunk and often homeless Tuvans are rarely offered help as their condition is considered too advanced and shameful to the rest of the community. Another kind of disturbance which tends to be referred to as a curse of civilisation is HIV. People affected by HIV often seek help from shamans, while struggling to fully comprehend the causes and implications of their affliction. For example, Hovalygmaa would regularly receive visits from confused clients who, when finding out about their HIV status, demanded curse

140 *Beyond curses*

deflection rituals. In such cases, she would refer them back to medical doctors while suggesting that certain things cannot be fully confronted by shamans.[4]

Witnessing or suffering from alcohol addiction, the presence of unknown dangers such as the HIV virus and other struggles often connected with these, such us unemployment, can lead to the person suffering from experiences of depression or anxiety. In Kyzyl, there is a growing awareness of different mental health issues, such as depression – another example of what some friends would call *civilizationnaja porcha*. It is shamanic figures who tend to play an important role in supporting their community when it comes to psychological distress. Shamans are often seen by people as the closest to the community – they are the ones who visit clients in their flats and collect stories of people's struggles and suffering. Most importantly, their observations are often taken into consideration by the local authorities and institutions while considering different ways of improving living conditions in the capital. One example is the much-celebrated Father's Day in Kyzyl. It is not only meant to boost men's confidence and self-esteem but also to improve the overall image of the family as strong, stable and healthy. In support of this, some shamans proposed offering a bowl with tea and milk first to a man at the end of each purification ritual (before this, a bowl with tea and milk would be given to a person in the closest vicinity to the shaman). As I had the opportunity to see for myself, this change became a permanent element of the ceremonies. All of these actions, in turn, are meant to prevent ongoing divorces and instances of adultery which often lead to the aforementioned drinking problems, suicides and depression. Another intriguing example constitutes workshops offered by shamans, which focus on diverse ways in which, for example, women can become more confident and less prone to psychological distress. As shaman Hovalygmaa described, during these workshops female shamans can use their make-up skills and costumes in order to instil more power in their audience and convince women to loudly voice, just like shamans, their problems, fears and concerns. In this way, shamans become locally involved activists and social workers for whom counselling and spreading emotional support is as important as facing curses.

The narratives of disturbance and uncertainty that accompany issues such as alcohol addiction and distrust towards shamans point to a kind of experiential symbiosis between curses and everyday life, which allows shamans and turbulence to be considered beyond the immediate context of the ritual. However, this book has been not only about shamanic practice, turbulence and cursing events but also about sound. As mentioned earlier in this conclusion, the powerful use of sounds and the ability to loudly voice things transpires, for example, in the workshops offered by shamans or becomes heavily exasperated during the so-called 'shaman shows' for the purpose of financial profit and tourist entertainment. What happens, though, when sounds are no longer heard?

Technological developments

The second part of this book has focused on a discussion on the potent role of sounds in Tuva and their importance to shamanic work. Sound performances constitute the centre of shamanic proceedings and become particularly dramatic in the context of cursing rituals. In my discussion, I have looked at sounds as imbued with transformative and communicative potency. Focusing on a variety of instrumental (drums) and human sounds and expressive techniques employed by the shamans, I have proposed that it is through sound that diverse relationships are constituted, experienced and validated in the cursing rituals. Given the growing interest in the theorising of sound and music, I believe that the ethnographic context of Tuva becomes an important contribution to considerations of shamans, spirits and clients as sonic beings. It also allows us to inquire into what sound does and what can become known through and with sound (Feld 2015). In the cursing events that I have described, the shaman Hovalygmaa exercises the art of conjuring the spirits while confronting and reconfiguring sociocosmic dynamics, and thus voicing into being a particular moment of an intrinsically fragile cosmos. Her drum creates what I have called semi-controlled turbulence and unsettles and opens up a given cosmic configuration, allowing the shaman to undertake negotiations with spirits within it. She is further expected to allow the audience to physically encounter the presence of spirits through their senses. Sounds are also, central to an array of Tuvan practices beyond shamanic rituals, such as throat singing, travelling and interactions with the environment. However, what happens when this deeply sounding surrounding which is vital for spirits, shamans, humans, animals and plants becomes changed or damaged through processes like climate change, resource exploitation or infrastructural development? Do the ways of hearing and listening transform? Can sounds be silenced?

The past 30 years have brought a widespread use of the internet, social media and mobile phones to Kyzyl. While these technological tools have been widely embraced by most of the community, their increasing importance has alternated the ways Tuvans interact with spirits and the environment through the senses, including sounds. When I discussed the role of social media in Kyzyl at the Tuvan University, Elena, one of the lecturers, began our conversation by saying: 'We can't hear spirits any more'. As she implied, reliance on the internet and mobile services has, to a certain extent, muted Tuvans' ability to listen to their sounded surroundings and thus interact with spirits in the usual ways. In order to illustrate her point, she referred to the troubling differences between generations:

> Our children are lost in the taiga. The development of technological media 'cools' youths' interests in our ways of living. When confronted with trips to the taiga or the steppe younger generations are lost, confused. They don't know how to interact with the forest, how to behave. They cannot hear or listen.

Elena also discussed how in the past her relatives, who lived in the remote areas of Tuva, could easily read through the sounds of the environment and employ what she called their intuitive skills in order to, for example, predict the arrival of

142 *Beyond curses*

unexpected guests. As she suggested, continual use of cell phones and the internet has slowly silenced these abilities, making people rely more on diverse technological devices rather than their sensorial skills.

On the other hand, the internet, mobile phones and social media play a rather different role among shamans for whom, as we have seen, sounds constitute one of the essential means of work. Instead of adversely affecting their ability to engage with sounds, technological devices seem to greatly facilitate administrative and organisational aspects of shamanic work. The possibility to remain connected on a wider scale has become one of the indispensable elements of shamanic practice today, both among individual shamans and shamans from the societies, thus bringing together human and technological media, in particular social media, in an explicit fashion. Mobile phones have become for shamans a portable list of regular clients and allow them to organise their diary more effectively. It is not unusual for shamans to have Facebook pages and Instagram profiles which permit them to establish contacts with wider networks of clients while also exposing certain elements of their own private life. While some of my interlocutors would question lack of face-to-face interaction, considered by many Tuvans as an important aspect of a ritual, some shamans, among them Hovalygmaa, do not find it problematic to conduct certain ceremonies (including cursing rituals) via Skype in order to help people living outside of Tuva. As she explained, the internet allows her to expand her practice and reach further. She only needs to see the image of the room and the client's face in order to be able to use her voice, summon the spirits and undertake adequate negotiations. There is no request for any payment; however, voluntary donations are usually made afterwards via bank transfers. Thus, the widespread reliance on technology, such as phones, tablets and social media, seems, according to some of my interlocutors, to restrain their intuitive skills and distinct ways of interacting with their surroundings based on the extensive use of senses and, in particular, sounds. However, it also facilitates networks of communication between clients and shamans and allows them to move their ritual practices beyond the physical borders of Tuva.

Apart from the growing reliance on certain technologies, another element which triggers some form of disturbance that affects Tuvans' ability to interact with the environment through senses such as sound is infrastructural development. A particularly burning topic constitutes in this case the question of building a railway track from China to Moscow through Kyzyl. As emerged from many of the discussions I held with my interlocutors, the train has become a kind of a symbol of the uncertain future for Tuvans. The possibility of growing industrialisation which comes with diverse infrastructural projects, like high-speed trains, deeply worries many Tuvans and threatens the stability of their community because of what these changes seem to entail. This became evident after I met Tania, one of the students from the University of Kyzyl. One day, Tania and I were walking down the hill near the Yenisei River while discussing her projects, dedicated to spreading the importance and meaning of different rituals conducted in pre-Soviet times among the young generation of Tuvans. Tania explained how she felt confused during a variety of ceremonies, such as *shagaa* (the Tuvan New Year which

Beyond curses 143

usually takes place in February, depending on the Buddhist monks' astrological calculations), which for her was an intriguing yet meaningless combination of actions and sounds. Like many other Tuvan friends, she complained about the conceptualisation of different rituals solely through the prism of academic debates and theoretical ideals, associated with wider political and ethnic processes in Siberia. 'We need some understanding, but among normal people, not at the level of academia or the government', she insisted. She concluded,

> Look, we had two huge leaps. The first, at the beginning of the Soviet Union. The second we are experiencing right now. We are too slow, we have a different understanding of time and space. Soon enough, we are going to be in reservation camps, while the trains pass by with great speed and we are left confused.

The fact that major infrastructural projects are a direct threat to the environment and to the practices of indigenous communities has been clear for a long time. In Tuva, as Tania stressed, continuing industrialisation and urbanisation silences the sounded environment that constitutes an integral part of Tuvan life, whereby the possibilities to hear and interact with non-humans, such as spirits and animals, become interrupted or muted.

Taking all the above together, Kyzyl today has become a platform upon which the diverse elements of everyday life combine and re-combine, producing diverse tensions. Different challenges and processes, such as novel forms of affliction, distrust towards shamanic societies and environmental changes are comprehended by friends and interlocutors through the ideas of disturbances and uncertainty that together produce a kind of uncontrolled turbulence that we have witnessed in the context of curses. In this way, the fabric of everyday life in Kyzyl and the dynamics within it are experienced and talked about in the same way that curses are described and felt. The phenomenon of curses allows us, therefore, to better understand the intricacies of life in Kyzyl at the present. What about the future?

(Un)certain futures

On one occasion, I participated in an intense and difficult ritual conducted in the middle of the deep steppe. I sat in the isolated, small wooden hut where 15 members of the clan were gathered awaiting the ritual. The shaman was trying to prolong the life of a very sick 70-year-old man suffering from post-surgical inflammation.[5] The ritual had a number of dramatic twists, and it was not until the very late evening that the shaman decided it was time to return to Kyzyl. When we got into the car, she pulled a smartphone out of her pocket. 'There is no reception here and I spent a whole day without Facebook', she said clearly irritated in Russian and looked at me, truly concerned. I burst out laughing and asked if she realised that she was a powerful shaman whose skills and strengths could traverse seas and mountains and who just admitted her dependency on social media and the internet. 'I am a shaman of the twenty first century and it is not my Facebook

144 *Beyond curses*

profile that you should be concerned about', she explained with a smile, and we both laughed as the car slowly drove towards the distant capital.

Indeed, whenever giving a lecture or a presentation on Tuvan shamanic practice I mention the use of social media and Skype as possible ways to inflict or deflect curses, my audience usually welcomes it with excitement and a kind of surprise. Despite quickly growing attention to decolonialism, an image of a shaman with a drum performing mysterious rituals while updating their Instagram profile will come across for many as an intriguing occurrence. As I continue my anthropological work in Siberia, I have recently discussed this point with a Nanai shaman, Leonid, who lives in Far East Russia in the Khabarovsk region, where the Nanai, the Eveny and the Olchi reside. He finds many of the stereotypical images, such as that of a shaman with a drum, that get randomly snatched from indigenous cosmologies (for different political, economic and personal aims) as highly damaging and obscuring what really seems to matter today (this also dovetails with Hovalygmaa's response to my comment regarding her Facebook activity). This is how Leonid expresses his concerns:

> Listen, I don't need to go and drum to find out what weather we are going to have tomorrow. I can Google it. We have different, more pressing issues at stake at the moment. Now, it is time for everyone, not only the Nanai, but also ethnographers, artists, people who have different religions to come together.

Leonid's comment does not show disregard for shamanic practice. Quite the opposite, it actually suggests that in the wake of global issues, such as climate change and environmental crisis (in Siberia visible through, for example, melting permafrost and taiga fires), it is crucial to look at indigenous cosmologies and what they propose more attentively.

Numerous recent anthropological works have highlighted and explored the need for such attentiveness in the wake of the environmental crises (Bodenhorn & Ulturgasheva 2022; Escobar 2020; O'Reily 2020). Within these studies, there are loud calls for new methods, research designs and theoretical frameworks to allow for diverse cosmologies, such as indigenous, scientific and political to interweave while driving international debates on topics, such as climate change. One of these frameworks is the concept of pluriverse which draws attention to 'the practice of a world of many worlds' (Blaser & de la Cadena 2018: 4). Particularly instructive here is the recent work of Escobar (2020) on pluriversal politics. In short, Escobar calls for a new research design, a design which offers a new vision of pluriversal bioregion occupied by multiple worlds. As he writes:

> Design is no longer for experts alone; we all design our own existence, and this applies with even more relevance to communities that are defending their own ways of life (…) The first step would be to create a team and a space for collaborative design with multiple actors, including at least the following: territorial-ethnic organizations, traditional authorities, and communitarian councils; groups of women and young people along the rivers and in the

Beyond curses 145

cities; academics, intellectuals, and artists; NGOs; the media; and the state. The first job for this group would entail creating a different imaginary of the region than that of the prevalent narrative based on megaprojects, growth, consumerism, trade, 'productivity', development, and so on.

(Escobar 2020: 130)

Echoing Escobar's proposal, other theoretical models on pluriverse encourage exploring 'heterogenous worldings coming together as a political ecology of practices, negotiating their difficult being together in heterogeneity' (De la Cadena & Blaser 2018: 4). Can the concept of pluriverse allow for parsing both theoretical and ethnographic questions around the uncertain futures of indigenous peoples in Siberia? I believe that Hovalygmaa's and Leonid's comments speak to this analytical and methodological model. The way forward is, therefore, to engage with ethnographic compositions which trace 'ecologies of practices' (De la Cadena & Blaser 2018: 4) while exploring the entanglements of worlds and cosmovisions, including indigenous, scientific, political, economic and so on. We can then begin to understand the issue of permeability and mechanisms which encourage or discourage certain practices and thoughts to be more permeable than others (see also Bodenhorn 2012). As the environment changes, so do indigenous cosmologies. Hopefully, the ethnography presented in this book has been strong enough to excite readers not only about the mystery of shamanic worlds and curses but also about the complexity of the context in which shamanic practice takes place today. Perhaps, while looking closer at an array of stories discussed here we can begin to wonder what kind of negotiations take place between different cosmovisions (as concepts of pluriverse encourage us to do) and what is actually negotiated into being. Turning our heads towards (un)certain futures, we can ask whether theoretical models of co-design are doomed to fail or perhaps we can begin to trace certain pockets of 'hope', or 'permeability', while addressing more seriously the calls for more inclusive models of strengthening indigenous worlds.

The final encounter

I spent the last night of my fieldwork in the basement of the Tuvan Cultural Centre with some foreigners who had arrived in Kyzyl in order to improve their throat singing skills. While falling asleep, I listened to them practising, the sound of which constantly intertwined with some distant Tuvan voices. These were the concluding sounds that accompanied the end of my year's adventure. At five in the morning, I walked to the bus station, crossing the empty streets of the city. As the bus drove through the steppe, I noticed the hill where Hovalygmaa and her family had their *ovaa*. We had visited this place only a few weeks earlier. I discreetly waved to it, saying in this way a kind of symbolic goodbye to the city and friends who live in it. As we reached the Sayan mountains, I turned my head and saw how the vast open space with the famous road leading to Kyzyl was disappearing behind me. Soon after, we were driving smoothly through Khakassia, where I met my Russian friends. A day later, I reached Moscow and, before I

146 *Beyond curses*

knew it, I was at Heathrow airport. While waiting for my flight to Edinburgh, I watched an Italian woman arguing angrily with her partner, about something she clearly struggled to find in her bag. The woman was waving her hands uncontrollably and constantly raising her voice while the man tried to calm her down with an apologetic tone and polite smiles. All of a sudden, curses and Kyzyl no longer seemed that distant.

Notes

1 Victory Day commemorates the Soviet Union victory over the Nazi Germany in the Second World War.
2 On the rare occasions of a student failing, they would usually repeat their training.
3 As it was explained to me, the financial offering depends on the amount of time spent on a consultation as well as the gravity of the problem discussed and the client's financial situation.
4 In Kyzyl, there are networks of cooperation between different practitioners, such as medical doctors, shamans and Buddhist lamas. I have discussed this in full length here (Stelmaszyk 2018).
5 Life expectancy in Tuva is said to be rarely higher than 60 years old. Consequently, as my interlocutors explained, the shamans do not undertake any ritual proceedings concerning people over that age. As they say, if one lives up to 60 years old it implies their life has been filled and should not be unnecessarily prolonged. Nevertheless, in cases of family members and close friends the shamans might make exceptions.

Bibliography

Balzer, M. M. 2005. Whose Steeple is Higher? Religious Competition in Siberia. *Religion, State and Society* no. 33 (1): 57–69.

Balzer, M. M. 2008. Beyond Belief? Social, Political and Shamanic Power in Siberia. *Social Analysis* no. 52 (1): 95–110.

Blaser, M. & de la Cadena, M. (eds). 2018. *A World of Many Worlds*. Durham and London: Duke University Press.

Bodenhorn, B. 2012. Meeting Minds; Encountering Worlds: Sciences and Other Expertises on the North Slope of Alaska. In M. Konrad (ed.), *Collaborators Collaborating*, 225–244. New York; Oxford: Berghahn Press.

Bodenhorn, B. & Ulturgasheva, O. (eds). 2022. *Risky Futures: Climate, Geopolitics and Local Realities in the Uncertain Circumpolar North*. Oxford, New York: Berghahn Books.

Bubandt, N. 2014. *The Empty Seashell. Witchcraft and Doubt on an Indonesian Island*. Ithaca and London: Cornell University Press.

Escobar, A. 2020. *Pluriversal Politics. The Real and the Possible*. Durham and London: Duke University Press.

Feld, S. 2015. Acoustemology. In D. Novak and M. Sakakeeny (eds), *Keywords in Sound*, 12–21. London: Duke University Press.

Grant, B. 1995. *In the Soviet House of Culture: A Century of Perestroikas*. Princeton, N.J.: Princeton University Press.

Levin, T. 2006. *Where Rivers and Mountains sing*. Indianapolis: Indiana University.

Lindquist, G. 2005. Healers, Leaders and Entrepreneurs: Shamanic Revival in Southern Siberia. Culture and Religion. *An Interdisciplinary Journal* no. 6 (2): 263–285.

Mongush, M. 2006. Modern Tuvan Identity. *Inner Asia* no. 8: 275–296.

O' Reily, J. et al. 2020. Climate Change: Expanding Anthropological Possibilities. *Annual Review of Anthropology* no. 49: 13–29.

Pedersen, A. M. 2011. *Not Quite Shamans*. Ithaca; London: Cornell University Press.

Pimienova, K. 2013. The "Vertical of Shamanic Power": The Use of Political Discourse in post-Soviet Shamanism. *Laboratorium* no. 5 (1): 118–140.

Shimamura, I. 2004. The Movement for Reconstructing Identity through Shamanism: A Case Study of the Aga-Buryats in Post-socialist Mongolia. *Inner Asia* no. 6 (2): 197–214.

Stelmaszyk, M. 2018. Turbulent beings. Curses and systems of healing cooperation in post-Soviet Tuva. *Curare, Journal of Medical Anthropology.* no. 41 (1+2): 51–62.

Stelmaszyk, M. 2021. Voiced into being: The power of sound and the phenomenon of cursing in Kyzyl, Tuva. *Journal of the Royal Anthropological Institute.* no. 27 (1): 90–107.

Vitebsky, P. 2003. From Cosmology to Environmentalism: Shamanism as Local Knowledge in a Global Setting. In G. Harvey (ed.), *Shamanism: A Reader*, 276–298. London: Routledge.

Zorbas, K. 2013. Shirokogoroff's "Psychomental Complex" as a Context for Analyzing Shamanic Mediations in Medicine and Law (Tuva, Siberia). *Shaman* no. 26 (1–2): 81–102.

Zorbas, K. 2021. *Shamanic Dialogues with the Invisible Dark in Tuva, Siberia: The Cursed Lives*. Cambridge: Cambridge Scholar Publishing.

Index

agency 13–14, 59, 123–4: of becoming a person 75; of inflicting misfortune 31; immediate 31; of the shaman's voice 109

alcohol addiction 4, 126, 130, 138–40

alcoholism 20, 33, 82, 125, *see* curses of civilization

Amazonia 65, 73; reversibility 74; *see* perspectivism

ambiguity 28, 58–62, 108–9; *see also* evil; shaman; shamanic practice; uncertainty

amoral familism 41

animism 75; Amerindian 76, Southeast Asian 76

Arhem, K. 65, 72–4, 76

Balzer, M. M. 4, 50, 114, 117, 131

Bird-David, N. 72, 78–9

body 31–2, 61, 71; shaman's 57, 63–4; cursed 72–8, 82–5, 139; *see* curse; shaman

Brabec de Mori, B. 114–15

Broz, L. 35, 73, 76, 123

Bubandt, N. 18, 131

Buddhism 9, 50, 55, 76

Buddhist: ceremonies 8, 60; deities 59; karmic system 34; lama 33; mantra 2; monks 55, 143

Buyandelgeriyn, M. 4, 12, 18, 51

clan 8, 30, 36, 146; curses 5, 31, 80; ritual 39, 45, 117; structure 71

classical music 99, 106–7, 116; *see also* throat singing

climate change 141, 144

colonialism 117, 126

Comaroff, J. and Comaroff, L. J. 12

confession: traditional 9, 50–1, 55, *see also* religion

corporeality 71, 74, 78; *see also* body

cosmic: chain 79; configurations 6, 102, 109, 121; dynamics 13, 19; patterns 108; and political 62; relationships 38, 81; and turbulence 6, 102, 105

cosmocentric: personhood 72, 79, 81, 139

cosmology: animistic 72–6, 79; in Inner Asia 31; multi-layered 52; transitional 108; Tuvan 51, 54, 58, 60, 86, 108, 115

cultural revivalism 55

curse 1–6, 19, 27–30; beyond 130–1; of civilization 138–40; clan 30–1; and economic ties 43–4; and family ties 40–3; in Inner Asia 11–14; and misfortune 34–6; and personhood 82–6; and politics 44; *see also* body; drum; ritual; shamanic practice; sound; turbulence

cursing: the mechanics of 29, 31–3; battles 38–9, 44, 46; a tripartite mechanism 50; *see also* infliction; deflection; ritual; sound

deflection: and ambiguity 108–9; curse 3, 4, 6, 11, 14, 18, 84; and protection 60; and a ritual context 19, 33, 42, 45; 104, 115, 139

Desjarlais, R. 78–80

divination 50–1, 135; mechanisms 64; practices 4, 71, 117; *see* ritual

drumming 36, 60, 94, 102–3; and singing 5, 16, 63–4, 96, 116; and space 107; and voice 66

drums 4, 6, 13; shamanic 14, 20, 85, 105–9, and sounds of 57, 93–4, 96, the role of 101–7; *see also* ritual; turbulence

150   Index

echo 79–80, 96; *see* Desjarlais;
Ulturgasheva
Eliade, M. 18, 54, 57, 59, 64, 102
Empson, R. 12–13, 35
environment 16–17, 19, 28, 141; and
abrupt change 117–18; nomadic 39;
political 45–6; and senses 141–3; and
throat singing 98, 116
environmental crisis 18, 20, 126,
130–1, 144
Errington, S. 77
Escobar, A. 144–5
evil 31, 60–2, 104
ethnographic: enquiry 3, 14, 113, 116;
sensitivity 15; and sounds 64
ethnographic context 17, 20, 53, 55, 63,
99; of Kyzyl 29, 46; of Siberia 123; of
Tuva 58–9, 72, 76, 79, 85, 109, 139;
ethnography: in this book 15, 18, 131, 145;
sensory 15; Soviet 117
experiential symbiosis 131, 140 *see*
Bubandt

Fausto, C. 59
Feld, S. 5, 15, 114, 116, 124, 141
fieldwork 11, 28, 70, 98, 145;
anthropological 2
fortune 34–7, 60, 74–6, 80, 102, 117

Geshiere, P. 12, 18, 41
good luck 19, 34–6; 58, 60, 84, 103
gossip 3, 13–14, 30, 32, 40–1, 93
gossiping 29–32, 41, 82

Hamayon, N. R. 6, 18, 35, 62, 65
High, C. 12–13, 59, 114
HIV 20, 126, 138–40
homeostasis 72, 78, 82
Humphrey, C. 7, 13, 29, 31, 39, 44, 63, 76,
115, 123

image 16, 82, 115, 123, 126, 144;
knowledge 54, 65; physical 74; throat
singing 99, 101 *see* personhood
indigenous: communities 3–4, 9, 12, 50,
131, 143; cosmologies 144–5; groups
132; languages 65
infliction: curse 3, 66, 83, 95, 105, 131;
form of 132, 09; process of 37, 50;
purpose of 108; and a ritual context
11, 27, 51, 60; and sociocosmic
arrangements 14
Inner Asia 7, 12–14, 38, 51, 63

khöömei: theory of 96–101; tradition of 2,
16; *see* sound; throat singing
knowledge 11, 15; and throat singing 97,
99; and shaman's work 5, 54–5, 58, 132;
and visions 64
kolkhoz 8, 43

language: and performance 114, 122; and
turbulence 30, 96–7
Latour, B. 81, 85
Lavrillier, A. 53, 74
Levin, T. and Edgerton, E. M. 16, 99
Levin, T. and Süzükei, V. 16, 95–7

magical business: 4, 11, 27
materiality: and body 85; of curses 72, 82;
of the soul 73–4; of spirits 115, 126;
see also sound; voice
mental health 140
misfortune 5, 19, 31, 34–6, 50, 53; and
personhood 78
music 53, 65, 85, 114; between sound
and 17, 116; classical 99–100, 106–7;
making 16, 115; and throat singing
94–106; Tuvan 11

occult economies 12–13, 29; *see* Comaroff;
Geshiere
ontological: ambivalence 4; breakdown
108; border 95; dimensions of
being a human 72–6; potency 115;
propensities 15
ontology: sonic 6; of bad speech 13;
of sound 14, 123; of misfortune 34;
Tuvan 19, 34, 71, 76, 96, 98; *see*
Swancutt

Pedersen, A. M. 4, 11–12, 31, 33, 51, 63,
73, 108
Pedersen, A. M. and Willerslev, R. 54–5,
73–4, 108
personhood: cursed 18–19, 71–6, 80, 82–6,
94, 109; human 78–81, 95, 139; in
Tuva 71, 77; *see also* body; deflection;
infliction; turbulence
perspectivism: Amerindian 76;
appropriation of 65; notions of 73, 79;
premise of 74
Pimienova, K. 8–9, 51, 71, 132–3
pluriverse 144–5
pollution 36, 55, 64, 74, 80
post-Soviet 4, 29: era 4, 117; Kyzyl 19, 39,
41, 43; realm 8; sensibilities 29; times

Index 151

39; transformations 115; turmoil 51; *see also* ritual
post-socialist: transformation 4
pre-Soviet 29–30, 38, 41; ethnics groups 117; practices 132; times 41–2, 45, 50, 93, 143; Tuva 19, 39, 43, 44

Rappaport, A. R. 105–6
reincarnation 74, 76
relations: between different forms of 123; economic 8, 43–4; family 39–42; intersubjective field of 72; political and administrative 44–6; social 14–15; with spirits 65, 75, 79, 113
religion 8, 55, 105–6; *see also* Buddhism; confession
research design 144–5
ritual: clan 36–7; cleansing 3, 34, 37, 55–6, 62, 71, 84; death 60–1; divination 19, 133; post-Soviet 126; *see* drum; shamanic ritual; sound; turbulent

Seeger, A. 114, 116
senses 16–17, 124, 126, 137
Severi, C. 114, 122–4
shadow 73, 79–80
shaman 3–6, 19; an artisan of curses 62–6; and authenticity 51, 66; becoming a 56–8; diagnosing 33, 35; *see also* curse; drum; shamanic practice; sound; turbulence
shaman show 131–8
shamanic: chant 16, 30, 60, 116; initiation 57; instruments 4, 6, 18–19, 57, 64, 135; societies 2, 4, 20, 66, 130–8; trance 6, 63–6
shamanic practice 18–20, 49–51; and authenticity 115, 131–8; and curses 3–12, 138–44; as housekeeping 55–6; an intrinsic ambiguity 58–62, 108; institutionalisation of 50; and sound 17, 95, 117–18, 126; *see also* drum; turbulence
shamanic ritual 8, 15, 17–20, 36, 85, 131, 141; and costume 16, 63, 97; and sounded performance 113–15, 124–6
shamanism 1–2, 4–9, 18; dark 58–9; in Inner Asia 13; in Mongolia 12; as a religion 55; as a system of beliefs 53; Tuvan 16, 49–50, 116–17, 122; in Southeast Asia 65
Siberia 19, 43, 53, 63, 74, 123, 131; and crisis 144–5; ethnic processes in 140

sociality 29, 34, 36, 78, 81, 108; dangerous 3
sociocentric 79; *see* personhood
sociocosmic: drama 33–4, 66, 131; dynamics 81, 126, 139, 141; interactions 35, 85, 122, 137; political scene 3; politics 13; relations 107
sonic: actions 14; beings 6, 62, 64; memory 95; performance 117; phenomena 17, 85, 116
soul 5, 85, 119; and being human 72–4, 78; and dreams 57
sound 6, 14–18; power of 64–6, 114–17; the theory of 93–6, 98–101, in transition 117–18
Soviet: dissolution 39; era 28; times 4, 33
Sovietisation 4, 8, 43
sovkhoz 8, 43
spirits 5, 15, 29, 31–4, 51–5, 61–6; *see also* body; curse; personhood; shamanic practice; sound; turbulence
Steingo, G. and Sykes, J. 15, 17–18, 116, 125
Stepanoff, Ch. 51, 56, 74
Süzükei, V. 16, 94–5, 98–100
Swancutt, K. 4, 13, 31, 33, 34, 35, 59

Tausig, M. 107
taxonomy: of curses 19; of shamans 57–8, 60–1
technological: changes 18, 126; development 108, 140–3
technology 15, 20, 53, 130, 142
tests 133, 134, 136–8
throat singing 2, 16, 20, 94–102, 107, 109, 116
timbre 96–8, 100, 107, 116
tone 97; of voice 51
Townsley, G. 16, 54, 64–5, 108, 114, 121
transition 38, 106–8, 115, 117, 131
turbulence 5, 17–18, 30, 96–8; controlled 101, 109; uncontrolled 82, 127, 131, 139, 143; semi-controlled 6, 20, 130, 141; *see* throat singing
turbulent: cosmos 108; interactions 3; movement 105–6; person 18–19, 85; ritual 107; space 86, 95, 103, 105; spirits 20, 96

Ulturgasheva, O. 72–3, 79–80, 85, 144
uncertainty 12, 117, 126, 131, 133–4; and ambivalence 4; as centre of 14; cosmological 85; and economy 44, 46; elements of 107–8; and future 143–5

152   *Index*

Vainshtein, S. 7–8; 39, 43
Viveiros de Castro, E. 65,
   73–4, 76
voice 98, 101, 103; and authenticity
   125–7; and encountering spirits 123–5;
   the power of 119–23; in shamanic

performance 114–17; shaman's 6, 13,
   16, 63–6

Willerslev, R. 18, 53–5, 64, 73–4, 108
witchcraft 12, 59; and the Azande 35;
   see also occult economies